PATHOLOGIES *of* REASON

New Directions in Critical Theory

Amy Allen, General Editor

New Directions in Critical Theory

Amy Allen, General Editor

New Directions in Critical Theory presents outstanding classic and contemporary texts in the tradition of critical social theory, broadly construed. The series aims to renew and advance the program of critical social theory, with a particular focus on theorizing contemporary struggles around gender, race, sexuality, class, and globalization and their complex interconnections.

Narrating Evil: A Postmetaphysical Theory of Reflective Judgment, María Pía Lara

The Politics of Our Selves: Power, Autonomy, and Gender in Contemporary Critical Theory, Amy Allen

Democracy and the Political Unconscious, Noëlle McAfee

The Force of the Example: Explorations in the Paradigm of Judgment, Alessandro Ferrara

Horrorism: Naming Contemporary Violence, Adriana Cavarero

Scales of Justice: Reimagining Political Space in a Globalizing World, Nancy Fraser

PATHOLOGIES *of* REASON

⊰ On the Legacy of Critical Theory ⊱

Axel Honneth

Translated by James Ingram and others

Columbia University Press   New York

Columbia University Press
Publishers Since 1893
New York   Chichester, West Sussex

Pathologien der Vernuft. Geschichte und Gegenwart der Kritischen Theorie © 2007
Suhrkamp Verlag, Frankfurt am Main
Copyright © 2009 Columbia University Press
Paperback edition, 2023

Library of Congress Cataloging-in-Publication Data
Honneth, Axel, 1949–
   [Pathologies der Vernunft. English]
   Pathologies of reason: on the legacy of critical theory / Axel Honneth;
translated by James Ingram and others.
      p. c.m.
   Includes bibliograpical references (p.   ).
   ISBN 978-0-231-14626-5 (cloth) — ISBN 978-0-231-14627-2 (pbk.) —
ISBN 978-0-231-51837-6 (e-book)
   1. Critical theory—History.   2. Social sciences—Research—History.
I. Title.
   HM585.H65   2009
   301.01—dc22

                                                      2008044202

CONTENTS

FIVE

Performing Justice: Adorno's Introduction
to *Negative Dialectics*
71

SIX

Saving the Sacred with a Philosophy of History:
On Benjamin's "Critique of Violence"
88

SEVEN

Appropriating Freedom: Freud's Conception
of Individual Self-Relation
126

EIGHT

"Anxiety and Politics": The Strengths and Weaknesses
of Franz Neumann's Diagnosis of a Social Pathology
146

NINE

Democracy and Inner Freedom: Alexander Mitscherlich's
Contribution to Critical Social Theory
157

TEN

Dissonances of Communicative Reason:
Albrecht Wellmer and Critical Theory
165

*Appendix: Idiosyncrasy as a Tool of Knowledge:
Social Criticism in the Age of the Normalized Intellectual*   179

Notes   193

Bibliography   215

PREFACE

In this volume, I have collected essays that, although apparently disparate, emphasize the timeliness of Critical Theory. There may seem to be little call for this today. A series of excellent studies on the history of the Frankfurt School, along with monographs on its individual representatives over the past decades, have clarified the multiformity of the approaches we attribute to this theoretical tradition that arose in the 1920s. Indeed, the real difficulty may well consist in identifying the unity of a single Critical Theory in the multiplicity of its theoretical forms. The solution I have found for this problem in my own investigations is contained in the title of the present volume. Through all their disparateness of method and object, the various authors of the Frankfurt School are united in the idea that the living conditions of modern capitalist societies produce social practices, attitudes, or personality structures that result in a pathological deformation of our capacities for reason. It is this theme that establishes the unity of Critical Theory in the plurality of its voices. As heterogeneous as the works bound to it may be, they always aim at exploring the social causes of a pathology of human rationality.

But the theme of regarding the living conditions of our societies as causes of a possible deformation of reason also indicates where I see the timeliness of Critical Theory. Today, primarily under the pressures of aimless professionalization, there is a threat that the bond between philosophy and social analysis will be conclusively broken. With this, a central heritage of German Idealism—namely, the chance to understand rationality as dependent on social-historical processes—begins to disappear as a possibility of thought. In this situation, Critical Theory, as obsolete as some of its approaches may be, represents a salutary challenge. Further developing it would mean, while including theoretical renewals, exploring once again for the present whether the specific constitution of our social practices and institutions damages the human capacity for reason. In the second essay collected here, I have tried to sketch what individual tasks today would be connected to such a reactualization of Critical Theory. This will also make it clear why I think it makes sense to include contributions on Kant's philosophy of history and Freud's concept of freedom in this volume.

Along with Gunhild Mewes, whose help with the technical preparation of the manuscript was irreplaceable, I want to thank Eva Gilmer and Bernd Stiegler from Suhrkamp Verlag, who have from the beginning provided me with friendly advice on the planning of this volume.

Frankfurt am Main, February 2007

Chapter 1, translated by Robert Sinnerbrink and Jean-Philippe Deranty, appeared in *Critical Horizons: A Journal of Philosophy and Social Theory* 8, no. 1 (August 2007): 1–17; chapter 2, translated by James Hebbeler, appeared as Axel Honneth, "A Social Pathology of Reason," in *The Cambridge Companion to Critical Theory*, ed. Fred Rush (New York: Cambridge University Press, 2004); chapter 4, translated by James Ingram, appeared in *Constellations* 12, no. 1 (March 2005): 50–64; chapter 7 was originally translated by Andrew Inkpin; chapter 8, translated by Chad Kautzer, appeared in *Constellations* 10, no. 2 (June 2003): 247–55; chapter 10, translated by Reidar K. Maliks, appeared in *Constellations* 14, no. 3 (September 2007): 305–14. The translations have been more or less revised for the present volume.

PATHOLOGIES *of* REASON

ONE

THE IRREDUCIBILITY OF PROGRESS

Kant's Account of the Relationship
Between Morality and History

At the very start of the second section of his essay "The Contest of the Faculties," at the center of which stands the now famous idea of "signs in history," Kant mocks a certain category of the prophetic narrating of history. His ridicule is directed at all those prophets, politicians, and intellectuals who in the past presumed to be able to predict a decline of morals or a political-cultural decadence. Such soothsayings, Kant says with unconcealed irony, are nothing other than self-fulfilling prophecies. Indeed, the authors of such prophecies, through their own misdeeds, have themselves essentially contributed to history, having taken precisely the negative direction of development that they believed they could anticipate.[1] The proximity to Walter Benjamin that appears to flash up through such remarks is not accidental, nor is it trivial in relation to Kant's work. On the lowest level of his philosophy of history, precisely where it concerns the affective meaningfulness of factual events and occurrences, Kant as much as the author of the "Theses on the Philosophy of History" was convinced that everything social derives from an "origin" that "the historical interpreter cannot contemplate without horror."[2]

Like Benjamin, Kant sees historical development up to the present as largely a product of the intentions and deeds of the victors. Under their "unjust coercion,"[3] the horrors and "crimes against human nature"[4] pile up into veritable mountains, such that all the sensitive historical observer can perceive in this historically unordered material is one singular "sighing" of humanity. But Kant did not wish to remain satisfied—and here, too, there is a kinship with Benjamin—with merely chronicling such a victors' history. At least in the last thirty years of his life, Kant was much more preoccupied with the question of whether or not the signs of a "turn for the better"[5] could be elicited from the vale of tears that is the historical process. Indeed, Kant's philosophy of history was born out of the impulse to correct the uncompensated wrongs of the past by representing such wrongs as the "spur to activity . . . towards the better."[6] Even before fulfilling any of its systematic tasks in the architectonics of his work, Kant's philosophy of history represents the ambitious attempt to brush history against the grain in order to tear it away from the hands of the supposed victors.[7]

Admittedly, the path that Kant opens up in order to achieve this goal is completely different from that of Benjamin. While the author of the Arcades project wanted to solve this problem by attempting to resume an interrupted communication with the countless victims of the past through the construction of magical memory-images,[8] the Königsberg philosopher approaches the task with entirely different methodological resources. Kant was neither familiar with the perspective of a writing of history from below nor really able to foresee the ideological dangers of an unreflective optimism concerning historical progress. Instead, Kant had before him as an opponent a form of the philosophy of history that unintentionally shares the condescending view of the victors. Such a historical view has no confidence that the common people have any aptitude for moral improvement, and hence this view sees everything negativistically, as being dragged into a continuous process of decline. Kant's attempt at a construction of historical progress is opposed to such a negative-triumphalist or, as he puts it, "terroristic conception" of history, within which the guilt of the dominant for the "piling up of atrocities" is inevitably denied.[9]

In what follows, I am interested in the question as to what kind of theoretical meaning this historical-philosophical hypothesis of progress can have that would still be relevant for our present context. To provide an answer to this question, I must, of course, avert attention from the affective sediment of the Kantian philosophy of history and bring into view its systematic grounding in the architectonics of Kant's work. I wish to proceed by (1) reconstructing Kant's different justifications for the assumption of historical progress and (2) explaining his presentation of this process of historical progress itself. In the course of this, I shall distinguish in both parts of my presentation between the system-conforming and the system-bursting or, so to speak, unorthodox, versions of historical progress. This is in order, finally, to be able to show at the end that only a combination of both system-bursting versions of progress can prompt us to confer a systematic meaning on the Kantian philosophy of history once again. At the same time, a new light will be cast, I hope, on the relationship between the Kantian and the Hegelian philosophy of history.

Kant is known to have had two, if not three, explanations for why we should have the right methodologically to comprehend human history, taken as a whole, as a purpose-directed process of progress. It is not rare to find even in one and the same text two of these justificatory approaches immediately next to one another; indeed, the impression is not entirely unjustified that Kant hesitated between these different alternatives right up to the end of his life.[10] Among the competing frameworks, the one that without doubt possesses the most prominence today is the one that a series of interpreters have quite rightly designated as "theoretical" or "cognitive"[11] because its point of departure is a theoretical interest of our reason. Accordingly, we have at our disposal a thoroughly legitimate need to unify our view of the world, which is torn between law-governed nature and freedom. We reconstruct the unordered happenings of the past according to the heuristic theme of an intention of nature, and we do this so that it appears to us as though it were a process of political and moral progress. Kant had in fact developed this argument, in its basic features, in his essay "Idea for a Universal History with a Cosmopolitan Purpose" (1784). But it is only in section 83 of his *Critique of Judgment* (1790) that we find the formulations that must have halfway satisfied Kant methodologically. If we leave out of consideration the differences between the two writings, taken together they present us with the most suitable textual foundation to illustrate Kant's first justificatory model for the hypothesis of progress.

The starting point of this construction consists in the thesis that our reason cannot be satisfied with leaving a gulf that continues to persist between the realm of the laws of nature and the sphere of moral freedom. Rather, we possess a purely cognitive interest in giving unity to the law-governed world of appearances, a unity that is later transposed into a continuum with the principles of our practical self-determination. This need for an integration of both worlds complies with our capacity for reflective judgment. In contrast to determinative inferences or judgments, reflective judgment does not derive particulars from universal principles; rather, it can supply a universal for a plurality of particular appearances.[12] The category of "purposiveness" is the conceptual principle that stands at the disposal of reflective judgment, in the same aprioristic way the moral law does for practical reason and causality does for theoretical reason. If we now apply this thought of "purposiveness," conceived through reflective judgment, to the field of human history, as Kant does in *Critique of Judgment*, section 83, we get a methodological justification of history: history's "senseless course"[13] can be understood counterfactually, so to speak, as the result of a purpose-directed intention, one that nature pursues with us human beings throughout all of our deplorable confusion.

From this point, it is only another small step to the hypothesis of progress, in which Kant's philosophy of history culminates. To the question of which purpose it could, in fact, be, that nature, heuristically taken as a subject, has assumed with respect to human history, Kant answers in agreement with his system that this cannot be human happiness. Rather, it can only be our aptitude "in general for setting [ourselves] purposes,"[14] hence our practical freedom. Accordingly, we are permitted to use the heuristic theme of an intention of nature for the retrospective reflection on our own history, in order to think the multitude of lamentable, seemingly chaotic events as an ordered unity. Such a unity is what the model of a directed process of improvement of our aptitude for the positing of purposes would allow us to see. The concept encompassing all the enabling conditions of such practical freedom is what Kant calls "culture,"[15] the development of which breaks down, according to him, into the competing strands of the civilizing of our nature as need-driven beings and the improvement of our cultural and intellectual "skills." This picture of a progress in human culture intended by nature, however, is only rounded out if Kant's supplementary remark is taken into account: namely, that both the disciplining of need and the extension of mental aptitudes could only really succeed under the conditions of a civil constitutional state—indeed, a cosmopolitan arrangement ensuring peace.[16]

Now it is evident that Kant was never really satisfied with this first justificatory model of his hypothesis of progress. For the very fact that he added the phrase "With a Cosmopolitan Purpose" to the title of his essay "Idea of a Universal History" indicates that he also attempted to provide his construction with a practical moral justification.[17] An alternative of this sort can be found everywhere in Kant's writings that he allows the counterfactual assumption of a purpose-directed effectiveness of nature in human history to be grounded in a practical, not a theoretical, interest of our reason. The primary writings to mention in this context are "On the Common Saying: 'This May Be True in Theory but It Does Not Apply in Practice'" (1793) and "Perpetual Peace" (1795), both composed after the completion of the *Critique of Judgment*. Kant argues here in a genuinely different manner than in the framework of his first justificatory model inasmuch as he maintains that the hypothesis of historical progress is an undertaking that is indispensable as a condition of making possible and realizing the moral law. For compliance with the categorical imperative demands that we regard the realizability of the moral ought as something that itself could already be effective in the historical past. Once again, it is necessary to abstract here from the differences between the two relevant essays in order to identify very briefly the core of the Kantian argument.

This time the starting point of Kant's reflections is not found in the viewpoint of an observer who has missed a cognitive association between nature and freedom. Rather, it is found in the perspective of an agent who knows himself or herself to be bound to the moral law. Everything Kant says in the following is therefore valid only under the restricting condition that the moral standpoint has already been taken up. For subjects with such an orientation, we must be able to say that they must regard the realizability of the moral ought as something possible if they do not want to fail in their task from the start. Indeed, already in the *Critique of Practical Reason* it was said that moral duty must be presupposed as possible, for "it would be practically impossible to strive for the object of a concept that would be, at bottom, empty and without object."[18] Now, Kant executes the decisive step in his argumentation with the thesis that this presupposition of the attainability of the morally good possesses both an intersubjective and a temporal dimension, because such a presupposition must be applied to all moral agents in the past, present, and future. We who share the moral standpoint must represent for ourselves not only our cooperating contemporaries but also the well-intentioned members of past and future generations as subjects who are convinced of the realizability of the good. With such an act of universalization, which Kant manifestly held to be unavoidable, however, the moral agent is placed in a position where he or she can no longer avoid assuming a tendency in human history toward the better. For already with the idea that the intentions of like-minded peers in the past could not have remained entirely fruitless, there unavoidably follows for Kant the idea of an increasing yield of moral deeds from generation to generation. Hence Kant believes that he can say of the subject who knows himself to be bound to the moral standpoint that such a subject must be able to represent history, in the interests of the realizability of the good, in no other way than as a movement toward the better that is never entirely "broken off."[19]

Kant himself, however, appears to trust this second construction so little that, as with the previous one, he does not let it get by entirely without the operation that the epistemic doubter performs by means of his reflective power of judgment in the face of the gulf between freedom and necessity. The certainty of progress that the moral actor develops because he grants the same strength of will to all of his predecessors that he has to grant to himself is not sufficient, according to Kant, to equip him with an adequate measure of certainty. Hence in the end, Kant also prescribes to such an actor a proportioned use of his power of judgment in order to reassure himself against doubts that may arise about the purposiveness of nature, which "visibly exhibits [a] purposive plan"[20] arising from historical chaos. It is this retrospective reassurance regarding an intention of nature that in the last instance provides the moral actor with a feeling of guarantee that he is contributing, through his own efforts, to the advancement of a process toward the good. As the first model does for the cognitively concerned subject, Kant's second model gives the morally hesitating subject the task of heuristically securing for itself a progress of history willed by nature, a task whereby this subject "reflectively" constructs and adds to the chaotic multiplicity of historical events the plan of a purpose-directed unfolding of history.

The two justificatory models that we have become acquainted with thus far are each closely connected with theoretical premises that arise from Kant's three *Critiques*. In the first model, this internal connection comes to light in the idea of a progress generated by nature, which is presented as the construction that our reflective power of judgment uses to react to the cognitive dissonance between the law-governedness of nature and moral freedom. In the second model, a similar connection becomes apparent, but here Kant allows the moral agent to be ruled by a degree of doubt concerning the practical effectiveness of his actions, a move that appears necessary only under the assumption of a pure, unsullied obedience to the moral law, undisturbed by empirical inclinations. Since both constructions, as has been shown, are marked in different ways by the train of thought that Kant encountered with his two-world doctrine, it cannot be surprising that the two together, albeit for different reasons, take refuge in the concept of the power of judgment. In the first case, the hypothetical construction of an intention of nature that guarantees progress satisfies an interest of our theoretical reason; in the second case, it satisfies a need pertaining to our practical reason. The third model that emerges in broad outline in Kant's historical-philosophical writings appears to be relatively free of additions of this sort, for the extent to which the problematic presuppositions of the two-world doctrine play a role in this model remains restricted.

A first indication of this third model can already be found in the text "On the Common Saying," which in essence presented the basis for the second construction proposal I have just sketched. In an inconspicuous passage, Kant says there of Moses Mendelssohn—for Kant, the typical representative of a "terroristic" conception of history—that he, too, "must have reckoned" on a progress toward the better, "since he zealously endeavored to promote the enlightenment and welfare of the nation to which he belonged."[21] The argument Kant employs here is perhaps best described as "hermeneutic" but possibly also as "explicative": Kant attempts to make intelligible or to explicate which concept of history someone who understands their own writerly activity as a contribution to a process of enlightenment would necessarily have to commit themselves to. A subject with such a self-understanding, Kant wants to demonstrate, has no alternative than to understand the developmental process that precedes him as the gradual achievement of something better and, conversely, to construe the time that still lies before him as an opportunity for further improvement. For the normative standards according to which this subject measures the moral quality of his current circumstances in his practical engagements demand from him that he judge the conditions of the past as inferior and the potential circumstances of the future as superior. The remark a few lines later, in which Kant attempts once again to refute Mendelssohn's view of history, is also to be interpreted in the sense of this "transcendentally" necessary orientation of meaning:

That the outcry about man's continually increasing decadence [i.e., of the human race] arises for the very reason that we can see further ahead because we have reached a higher level of morality. We thus pass more severe judgments on what we are, comparing it with what we ought to be, so that our self-reproach increases in proportion to the number of stages of morality we have advanced through during the whole of known history.[22]

The building blocks of the explicative or hermeneutic justificatory model that can be glimpsed through these lines are conspicuous in both of Kant's historical-philosophical contributions; these are the only ones that contain no reference to an "intention of nature." Indeed, they make use of the thought—not utterly implausible, even today—of a natural disposition of human beings toward freedom. Yet at no point do they mention the idea of a purposiveness willed by nature, the idea that played such an important role in the writings we have dealt with up to this point. The first of these texts, the essay "An Answer to the Question: 'What Is Enlightenment?'" (1784), appeared six years before the *Critique of Judgment*; the second text, "Contest of the Faculties" (1798), was published eight years after the publication of the third *Critique*. Hence it might be the case that both contributions were composed with a sufficient distance from that key work that they were not intellectually ruled by its proposal of the notion of an "intention of nature."

The entirely distinct character of the new model, as opposed to the approaches sketched previously, already becomes clear in the fact that Kant now appears to have a completely different circle of addressees in mind. He no longer turns to the observer of world history animated by cognitive doubts but also no longer to the historically unlocated, so to speak, situationless, moral subject. Rather, Kant turns toward an enlightened public, who in one way or another are participants in a political and moral process of transformation. What also changes with this altered form of address is the role of Kant as author, as he attempts to demonstrate the irreducibility of the concept of historical progress. He speaks as a disinterested but nonetheless understanding and sympathetic observer who wants to show those who participate in the historical process of transformation which implicit presuppositions they would have to be able to observe in their own remarks and actions if they were to take up the role of spectators of themselves. In both texts, the historical reference point that allows the readership to be addressed as practical participants is roughly the same, even if, of course, some differences subsist because of the time lag between them. In the earlier essay, it is the political consolidation of enlightenment, conceived of as a lengthy process during the reign of Frederick II; in the historical-philosophical second section of "Contest of the Faculties," it is the decisive historical break in mentality brought about by the French Revolution.

Kant now wants to show that those individuals who affirmatively (indeed, enthusiastically) sympathize with these events—justified as they are on the grounds of practical reason—have thereby implicitly committed themselves through such affirmation to understanding the course of human history, which initially seemed chaotic, as a practical-moral process of progress. The standpoint of their historical consciousness shifts in the moment of affirmation because now they must unify all historically prior occurrences and circumstances in light of the most recent developments into a directed process in which the moral achievements of the present mark a successful intermediary stage. The identification with the idea of universal civil and human rights—as they attained expression with the political reforms of Frederick II or with the constitutional project of the French Republic—suddenly gives our representation of the course of human history a relatively reliable sense of direction. For on the basis of standards we have thereby assumed, we are virtually compelled to see in slavery, in despotic regimes—indeed, in every form of the restriction of legal autonomy in general—the victorious stages of a progressive process that points to a future that is to be further morally shaped with our involvement. Thus, the teleological schema that Kant could previously explain only by means of the trick of an intention of nature now becomes the narrative organizational principle of historical self-reassurance in the politically driven process of enlightenment.

To be sure, even this third justificatory model is further subordinated to the premises of the *Critique of Practical Reason*. For otherwise Kant could not justify why the affirmation of the reforming and revolutionary events, for their part, could claim moral legitimacy. But compared with the previously elaborated explanatory approaches, the principles of the moral law play a fundamentally altered role. This is because they are no longer treated solely as timeless and placeless imperatives; rather, they are viewed at the same time as the source of institutional transformations. Now they also possess, it could perhaps be said, an element of empirical or historical reality.[23] In his third model—as though with this first step he were already moving toward Hegel—Kant, with the greatest cautiousness, situated practical reason historically. It is this moderate de-transcedentalization that enables him to conceptualize the hypothesis of progress as the product of a perspectival shift of the historical subject himself or herself. With this step, it could perhaps be said, Kant approaches Hegel's idea of a historical realization of reason, but without at the same time assuming Hegel's conclusion that there is an objective teleology of the historical process. Kant is protected from reaching that point by the "hermeneutic" thought that the chaotic multiplicity of history must appear as a directed process of progress only to those individuals who must historically situate themselves in their present context in the interests of political and moral improvement. In the next step, I examine whether any clues supporting this third justificatory model can also be found in the conceptual determinations Kant used to characterize the process of historical progress.

While in his writings on the philosophy of history as a whole Kant paid relatively little attention to grounding the hypothesis of progress, he devoted much more energy and care to the question of how the concrete unfolding of this hypothesis of progress could appropriately be determined. In some passages, it even looks as though this task of a morally inspired reinterpretation of history fascinated him to such an extent that, against the grain of his temperament, he gave free rein to his imagination. Such a speculative loss of inhibition comes to light especially in those writings where Kant undertakes, in agreement with his construct of a natural intention, to uncover the secret plan that is supposed to have been operating behind the historical actions and atrocities of the human species.

In such contexts, Kant uses all his power of imagination simply to suggest to us that we recognize even in the most repugnant and objectionable facts of our history the secret intention by which nature has intended our moral progress.

In the writings on the philosophy of history, however, this descriptive model is challenged precisely as much as the two other types of foundation that rely on the idea of an "intention of nature." In fact, in the two essays that avoid making reference to this heuristic construction of our faculty of judgment, a totally different tendency can be discerned, according to which the historical path leading to a better future is described not according to the model of a natural teleology but, rather, as the product of a human learning process. In the rare remarks that Kant dedicated to the alternative model just sketched, he pursues his attempt to "de-transcendentalize" practical reason by situating it historically. This unofficial vantage point, however, which is to a certain extent system-bursting, remains obviously overshadowed by the explicit attempt to reconstruct human history as though it were underpinned by the teleological plan of an intention of nature.

Kant strictly follows the basic idea underlying his first two justificatory models when, throughout large parts of his writings on the philosophy of history, he pursues the aim of discovering a natural teleology within the confusion of the species' history. In this, he allows himself to be guided by the hypothesis that the means used by nature to educate the human species must have been the mechanism of social conflict. Even if Kant, in marked contrast to Hegel, never showed any signs of an inclination toward social theory, he nevertheless proves in the corresponding passages of his work to be an author with a significant measure of sociological imagination. Depending on the context, however, two separate versions of the assumption can be found in his writings, according to which the medium intended by nature for the perfecting of the human being must have been social antagonism.

The first version, which can be found above all in the essay "Idea for a Universal History," starts from the premise of an "unsocial sociability of the human being,"[24] which means that we simultaneously possess a deep-seated desire for social belonging and an equally basic tendency toward individuation.[25] As Kant continues, with explicit reliance on Rousseau, it is supposed to follow from this dual nature that human subjects continuously strive for new achievements that would distinguish them from others, and they do so solely in order to find, in their "enviously competitive vanity,"[26] recognition from the social community. But once humanity sets out on this road of the struggle for distinction, boundaries can no longer be set, according to Kant, for the spiritual development of the species, because the urge to achieve—due to a lack of opportunities—is finally forced to extend even to the increase in our capacity to make ethical judgments. The historical progress in the human being's way of thinking, as we can summarize this first version, is the result of a social struggle for recognition that was forced on us by nature when it endowed us with an "unsocial sociability."[27] However, Kant's reflections rely so heavily on Rousseau's critique of civilization—according to which selfishness and vanity are the driving motives behind an intensifying struggle for distinction—that they have little in common with Hegel's concept of a morally motivated conflict.

In the second version we can discern in Kant's model of social conflict, it is war that takes over the role that was played by the struggle for distinction in the first version. The relevant texts here, in particular, are the writings on "Conjectures on the Beginning of Human History" and "Perpetual Peace." In both essays, Kant transfers the function responsible for the increase in cultural achievements, which he previously held is owed to the vanity of human beings, to our heightened sense of honor, a sense that, according to him, is kept continuously alert by the constant threat of war.[28] Like the desire to distinguish oneself, the need for the community to prove itself in war also incites ever-new cultural achievements, which lead to the "reciprocal promotion" of social well-being and, indeed, even increase the level of the country's freedom.[29] Kant clearly encounters difficulties, however, when he tries to draw out the positive implications of such assumptions concerning the internal "blessings" of war—that is, benefits that war is supposed to have exerted over human morality. For perhaps he might still justifiably demonstrate why the constant threat of war has pushed people historically to be motivated and prepared to make peace, but he certainly can no longer show that this, therefore, must have also been linked with an increased understanding of the universal, or of the universally valid, moral law. Such explanatory difficulties might well be why this second version of the model of conflict plays overall only an extremely marginal role in Kant's work. For as long as he entertains the trick of an intention of nature, it is without a doubt the second version that dominates, according to which the struggle for distinction intended by nature forces us to progress in the moralization of our mores and modes of conduct.

Kant's writings on the philosophy of history also sketch another alternative to this approach, one that completely renounces the construction of a natural teleology. Admittedly, the new descriptive model does not quite manage to succeed without the mechanism of social conflict, but it does give it a completely different twist than in the framework that suggests a natural providence. Kant toys with the possibility of such an alternative in all the passages where he considers nature only as the origin of a specific human capacity of the human being and not as the original cause of a plan that concerns us. This is the case in both of the essays already mentioned, as it is in the hermeneutic and the explicative models discussed previously. The starting point of the concept of progress this entails consists in the conviction that not only "unsocial sociability" but also the faculty of free intelligence belongs to the natural capacities of the human being—that is, intelligence bound only to reasons. Nature has endowed us, in contrast to animals, with an "inclination and vocation to think freely."[30] On the ontogenetic level, as Kant shows in his "Pedagogy,"[31] this faculty of intelligence makes a certain learning process inevitable, because every child, under minimally favorable conditions of socialization, is required to appropriate for himself or herself reasons that are stored up in his or her cultural environment. The child's reason [*Vernunft*] is formed through the internalization of the social reserve of knowledge that is amassed in the society in which the child grows to maturity with the help of his or her parents or other primary caregivers. If, however, all societies dispose over a certain store of rational knowledge, then one can with good reason infer from this that a certain aptitude for learning can be supposed to exist at the level of the history of the species. For every generation will not merely repeat the process of knowledge acquisition the previous generation has gone through; rather, it will be able to enrich the heritage it takes up, so that overall, in the chain of successive generations, the scope of knowledge is extended in a cumulative manner. Once such a mechanism of learning spanning the generations is presupposed, human history, taken as a whole, could therefore be understood as a cognitive process of progress: indeed, as the unfolding of moral rationalization.

Now, in sketching an alternative descriptive model that does not rely on a natural teleology, Kant is by no means naive enough to ground historical progress on such an ideal picture of collective learning. Rather, since his pretheoretical intuition about human history is, in fact, as I said at the outset, an extremely dark one, it is only logical that he should have included counterforces in his model that threaten to block or interrupt the always-possible anthropological process of the cumulative enhancement of reason. In the two texts that are relevant here, Kant identifies two such complications that must be included in the image of the learning process in order to make it more complete.

First, Kant takes into account the habitual constitution of human nature, which can lead to a situation in which the existing aptitude for intelligence is prevented from coming to fruition in the changing of the generations, thus making a cumulative transfer of knowledge impossible. According to the well-known formulations of his essay "What Is Enlightenment?," intellectual "laziness" and "cowardice" are the main reasons that "such a large number of [human beings], even when nature has long emancipated them from alien guidance . . . nevertheless gladly remain immature for life."[32] The unfolding of the learning process of the species is historically dependent on structures of character and mentality that mark the members of a given society. The human being's aptitude for intelligence can therefore demonstrate cumulative effects only when it encounters a social culture that allows the corresponding virtues and modes of behavior to prosper. To this extent, Kant must basically place under the cognitive learning process another, habitual process of education that historically ensures that the types of sensitivity and models of behavior necessary for the realization of our intellectual aptitude are also provided.[33] In this context, though, he equally seems to consider the socializing effects of the public use of reason, through which subjects are encouraged in an ever-greater measure to use their understanding autonomously. In contrast to Hegel, who hardly ever emphasizes the political and public conditions of our thinking, Kant is deeply convinced that the human beings' capacities for reflection grow the more the individual is put under the pressure of public justification.

Second, Kant takes into account that the obstacle to learning also stands in close relationship with the tendency of human beings to limit themselves—out of the urge to conform or a lack of courage—to conventional thinking. According to this account, the hierarchical structure of all previous societies allows the dominant to maintain their subordinates in a social state that negates all chance of an undistorted, free use of their own faculty of intelligence. The "victors," to cite Benjamin once more, have at their disposal cultural instruments of power that prevent the lower social classes from advancing along the cognitive learning process. As though in a text by Bertolt Brecht, Kant writes, again in his essay on Enlightenment: "Having first infatuated their domestic animals, and carefully prevented the docile creatures from taking a single step without the leading-strings to which they were tied, they next show them the danger which threatens them if they try to walk unaided."[34] Throughout the course of human history, intimidation, the threat of violence, and state censorship have been the instruments the powerful have used to prevent the dominated from learning that could have morally undermined their own domination. To this extent, Kant is sociologically realistic enough to see through the blockages that, as a result of the unequal distribution of cultural power, oppose the learning process spanning the generations. This is why the historical realization of reason, which unfolds in the form of a heightening of the faculty of intelligence and rationality, is not a continuous but, rather, a deeply discontinuous process.

At this level, though, Kant also seems to count on an antidote capable of putting back into motion and renewing the learning process that had been halted or interrupted by the instruments of power. If we generalize by a few degrees his idea of the "signs of history," which Kant presents in the second part of his essay "The Contest of the Faculties," the aforementioned idea now states that moral attainments with universalistic validity necessarily leave traces in social memory. This is because events of such magnitude, which affectively touch on the "interests of humanity,"[35] can no longer fall into oblivion with respect to the species' learning capacity. The result is that, like stages or degrees, they mark a progress in the process of a future emancipation of humanity that is irreducible. In memory of these moral "bolts" [*Sperrriegel*] securing the past, says Kant, there will always be people in human history who, "when favorable circumstances present themselves, . . . rise up and make renewed attempts of the same kind as before."[36] Kant's very strong emphasis here on the threshold function of specific events in historical evolution probably has much to do with his focus on the public conditions of the human use of reason. For such occurrences, which signal political-moral progress, establish a level of justification for the entire public that can be disregarded, in the future, only at the cost of public exposure.

To be sure, a satisfactory model of historical progress cannot be constructed from these fragments of an alternative explanatory model in Kant's writings. However, his few remarks perhaps allow us plausibly to claim that Kant, in the unofficial part of his philosophy of history, counts on a process toward the better, one that takes the shape of learning process that is repeatedly violently interrupted but that can never be fully halted. The idea of such a conflict-ridden learning process admittedly only suits the foundation of historical progress that Kant offered in his hermeneutic and explicative model. For the civilizational and moral improvements on the basis of which the idea of human capacity of learning is developed can in no way be thought of, even hypothetically, as the results of a natural intention. Rather, they can only be thought as the work of the united efforts of human subjects. Kant therefore assumes, just like Hegel, a teleology of directed progress, but he does not deliver it over to the anonymous process of an unfolding of spirit. Instead, he takes this teleology as a construction that subjects acting in the sense of enlightenment must achieve in order to gain a clear consciousness of the historical place of their own projects. The combination of these two system-bursting elements thus leads to the consequence that the thought of a learning process spanning generations must be understood as a construction that necessarily shapes the historical self-understanding of the supporters of the Enlightenment. All those who actively side with the moral achievements of the Enlightenment are thus forced to see the history preceding them as a conflict-ridden learning process, which, as heirs of this process, they have to continue in their own time. In all probability, such a hermeneutic reduction of the idea of progress represents the only possibility for making Kant's philosophy of history fruitful for the present.

Translated by Robert Sinnerbrink and Jean-Philippe Deranty

TWO

A SOCIAL PATHOLOGY OF REASON

On the Intellectual Legacy of Critical Theory

With the turn of the new century, Critical Theory appears to have become an intellectual artifact. This superficial dividing point alone seems to greatly increase the intellectual gap separating us from the theoretical beginnings of the Frankfurt School. Just as the names of authors who were for its founders still vividly alive suddenly sound as if they come from far away, so, too, the theoretical challenges from which the members of the school had won their insights threaten to fall into oblivion. Today a younger generation carries on the work of social criticism without having much more than a nostalgic memory of the heroic years of Western Marxism. Indeed, the last time the writings of Herbert Marcuse and Max Horkheimer were read as contemporary works already lies over thirty years in the past. There is an atmosphere of the outdated and antiquated, of the irretrievably lost, which surrounds the grand historical and philosophical ideas of Critical Theory, ideas for which there no longer seems to be any kind of resonance within the experience of the accelerating present. The great chasm that separates us from our predecessors must be comparable to that which separated the first generation of the telephone and movie theater from the last representatives of German Idealism. The same irritated astonishment with which Walter Benjamin or Siegfried Kracauer may have looked at the photo of the late Friedrich Schelling must today overcome a young student who, on her computer, stumbles across a photo of the young Horkheimer, posing in a bourgeois Wilhelmine interior.

However much the traces of lost experiences are reflected in the physiognomy of now-forgotten faces, so much greater are the presuppositions of the past age reflected in its intellectual premises and constructions. Critical Theory, whose intellectual horizon was decisively formed in the appropriation of European intellectual history from Hegel to Freud, still relies on the possibility of viewing history with reason as its guiding thread. But there may be no other aspect of Critical Theory more foreign to today's generation, which has grown up conscious of cultural plurality and of the end of "grand narratives," than social criticism founded on this sort of philosophy of history. The idea of a historically effective reason, which all the representatives of the Frankfurt School from Horkheimer to Jürgen Habermas firmly endorsed, will be incomprehensible if one can no longer recognize the unity of a single rationality in the diversity of established convictions. And the more far-reaching idea that the progress of reason is blocked or interrupted by the capitalistic organization of society will only trigger astonishment, since capitalism can no longer be seen as a unified system of social reason. Though thirty-five years ago, starting from the idea of an "emancipatory interest," Habermas once again tried to ground the idea of emancipation from control and oppression in the history of the species, today he concedes that "such a form of argumentation belongs 'unambiguously' to the past."[1]

The political changes of the past several decades have not been without influence on the status of social criticism. Consciousness of a plurality of cultures and the experience of a variety of different social emancipation movements have significantly lowered expectations of what criticism ought to be and should be capable of. Generally speaking, there is prevalent today a liberal conception of justice that uses criteria for the normative identification of social injustice without the desire to further explicate the institutional framework of injustice by embedding it within a particular type of society. Where such a procedure is felt to be insufficient, appeals are made to models of social criticism that are constructed in the spirit of Michel Foucault's genealogical method or in the style of Michael Walzer's critical hermeneutics.[2] In all these cases, however, criticism is understood as nothing more than a reflective form of rationality that is supposed to be anchored in the historical process itself.

Critical Theory, in contrast—and in a way that may be unique to it—insists on a mediation of theory and history in a concept of socially effective rationality. That is, the historical past should be understood from a practical point of view: as a process of development whose pathological deformation by capitalism may be overcome only by initiating a process of enlightenment among those involved. It is this working model of the intertwining of theory and history that grounds the unity of Critical Theory, despite its variety of voices. Whether in its positive form with the early Horkheimer, Marcuse, or Habermas or in its negative form with Theodor Adorno or Benjamin, one finds the same idea forming the background of each of the different projects—namely, that social relationships distort the historical process of development in a way that one can only practically remedy. Designating the legacy of Critical Theory for the new century would necessarily involve recovering from the idea of a social pathology of reason an explosive charge that can still be touched off today. Against the tendency to reduce social criticism to a project of normative, situational, or local opinion, one must clarify the context in which social criticism stands side by side with the demands of a historically evolved reason.

In what follows, I take a first step in that direction. First, I detail the ethical core contained in Critical Theory's idea of a socially deficient rationality. Second, I outline how capitalism can be understood as a cause of such a deformation of social rationality. Third and last, I establish the connection of practice to the goal of overcoming the social suffering caused by deficient rationality. Each of these three stages involves finding a new language that can make clear in present terms what Critical Theory intended in the past. Still, I often have to content myself here merely with suggesting lines of thought that would have to be pursued to bring the arguments of earlier Critical Theory up to date.

Even if it may be difficult to discover a systematic unity in the many forms of Critical Theory, taking the notion of the negativity of social theory as our point of departure will serve us well in establishing a first point of common interest.[3] Not only the members of the inner circle but also those on the periphery of the Institute for Social Research perceive the societal situation on which they want to have an effect as being in a state of social negativity.[4] Moreover, there is wide-spread agreement that the concept of negativity should not be restricted in a narrow way to offences committed against principles of social justice but, rather, should be extended more broadly to violations of the conditions for a good or successful life.[5] All of the expressions that the members of the circle use to characterize the given state of society arise from a social-theoretical vocabulary grounded in the basic distinction between "pathological" and "intact, non-pathological" relations. Horkheimer first speaks of the "irrational organization" of society; Adorno speaks later of the "administered world"; Marcuse uses such concepts as "one-dimensional society" and "repressive tolerance"; and Habermas, finally, uses the formula of the "colonization of the social life-world."[6]

Such formulations always normatively presuppose an "intact" state of social relations in which all the members are provided an opportunity for successful self-actualization. But what is specifically meant by this terminology is not sufficiently explained by merely pointing out the fact that it contrasts with the language of social injustice in moral philosophy. Rather, the distinctiveness of the expressions only becomes manifest when the obscure connection taken to exist between the social pathology and defective rationality comes to light. All the authors mentioned above assume that the cause of the negative state of society is to be found in a deficit in social rationality. They maintain an internal connection between pathological relationships and the condition of social rationality, which explains their interest in the historical process of the actualization of reason. Any attempt to make the tradition of Critical Theory fruitful for the present must thus begin with the task of bringing this conceptual connection up to date, one grounded in an ethical idea whose roots are in the philosophy of Hegel.

The thesis that social pathologies are to be understood as a result of deficient rationality is ultimately indebted to Hegel's political philosophy. He begins his *Philosophy of Right* with the supposition that a vast number of trends toward a loss of meaning manifested themselves in his time, tendencies that could be explained only by the insufficient appropriation of an "objectively" already possible reason.[7] The assumption behind Hegel's diagnosis of his own time lies in a comprehensive conception of reason in which he establishes a connection between historical progress and ethics. Reason unfolds in the historical process by re-creating universal "ethical" institutions at each new stage; by taking these institutions into account, individuals are able to design their lives according to socially acknowledged aims and thus to experience life as meaningful. Whoever does not let such objective ends of reason influence his or her life will suffer from the consequences of "indeterminacy" and will develop symptoms of disorientation. If one transports this ethical insight into the framework of the social processes of an entire society, Hegel's diagnosis of his time basic to his *Philosophy of Right* emerges in outline form. Hegel saw the outbreak of dominant systems of thought and ideologies in his own society that, by preventing subjects from perceiving an ethical life that was already established, gave rise to widespread symptoms of the loss of meaning. In light of this diagnosis, Hegel was convinced that social pathologies were to be understood as the result of the inability of society to properly express the rational potential already inherent in its institutions, practices, and everyday routines.

When this view is detached from the particular context in which it is embedded in Hegel, it amounts to the general thesis that each successful form of society is possible only through the maintenance of its most highly developed standard of rationality. According to Hegel, this claimed connection is justified on the basis of the ethical premise that it is only each instance of the rational universal that can provide the members of society with the orientation according to which they can meaningfully direct their lives. And this fundamental conviction must still be at work, when, despite their different approaches, critical theorists all claim that it is a lack of social rationality that causes the pathology of capitalist society. Without this ethical assumption, already found implicitly in Hegel, one cannot justify establishing such a connection. The members of society must agree that leading a successful, undistorted life together is only possible if they all orient themselves according to principles or institutions that they can understand as rational ends for self-actualization. Any deviation from the ideal outlined here must lead to a social pathology insofar as subjects are recognizably suffering from a loss of universal, communal ends.

Nevertheless, this ethical core of the initial hypothesis, common to the various projects of Critical Theory, remains for the most part overlaid by anthropological premises. The rational universal that is supposed to vouchsafe an "intact" form of social life is understood as the potential for an invariant mode of human activity. Horkheimer's thought contains such an element in his conception of work, according to which the human mastery of nature is directed "immanently" toward the goal of a social condition in which individual contributions transparently and mutually complement one another.[8] One might then say with Marx that the emergence of social pathology depends on the fact that the actual organization of society falls short of the standards of rationality that are already embodied in the forces of production. In the case of Marcuse, the authority of a rational universal is shifted increasingly in his later writings to the sphere of aesthetic practice, which appears as the medium of social integration in which subjects can satisfy their social needs in noncoerced cooperation.[9] Here, then, the social pathology sets in at that moment in which the organization of society begins to suppress the rational potential that is at home in the power of the imagination anchored in the lifeworld. Finally, Habermas secures the Hegelian idea of a rational universal by means of the concept of communicative agreement, whose idealizing presuppositions are supposed to meet the concern that the potential of discursive rationality regains universal acceptance at every new stage of social development. We can speak therefore of a social pathology as soon as the symbolic reproduction of society is no longer subjected to those standards of rationality which are inherent in the most highly developed form of linguistic understanding.[10]

In all these approaches to Critical Theory, the same Hegelian idea—namely, that a rational universal is always required for the possibility of fulfilled self-actualization within society—is continually incorporated, only in different characterizations of the original human practice of action. Just as with Horkheimer's concept of human work or with Marcuse's idea of an aesthetic life, Habermas's concept of communicative understanding above all serves the aim of fixing the form of reason whose developed shape provides the medium for both a rational and a satisfying integration of society. It is with reference to such an authority of rational practice that critical theorists can analyze society according to a theory of reason qua diagnosis of social pathologies. Deviations from the ideal that would be achieved with the social actualization of the rational universal can be described as social pathologies since they must accompany a regrettable loss of prospects for intersubjective self-actualization.

In the path of intellectual development from Horkheimer to Habermas the idea of a universal rationality changed, of course, not only in regard to its content but also in regard to its methodological form. While Horkheimer combines with his concept of work the notion of a rational potential that is to serve subjects directly as an aim of cooperative self-actualization in a "community of free human beings,"[11] Habermas understands the idea of communicative understanding no longer as a rational aim but only as the rational form of a successful mode of socialization. In Habermas, the idea that only a fully realized rationality guarantees a successful community of the members of society is radically proceduralized insofar as the rationality that gives rise to action oriented toward understanding is now supposed to ensure only the conditions for, and no longer the fulfillment of, autonomous self-actualization.[12] Yet this formulation cannot obscure the fact that an ethical idea hides beneath anthropological ways of speaking about an original mode of human action. The concept of communicative action, whose rationality imposes on human beings an invariant constraint, still indirectly contains the idea of a successful social life that one finds directly in Horkheimer's concept of work and Marcuse's concept of aesthetic practice.

The representatives of Critical Theory hold with Hegel the conviction that the self-actualization of the individual is only successful when it is interwoven in its aims—by means of generally accepted principles or ends—with the self-actualization of all the other members of society. Indeed, one might even claim that the idea of a rational universal contains the concept of a common good, which the members of a society must have rationally agreed on in order to be able to relate their individual freedoms to one another cooperatively. The different models of practice that Horkheimer, Marcuse, and Habermas offer, then, are all only representatives of that one thought, according to which the socialization of human beings can only be successful under conditions of cooperative freedom. However the particulars of the anthropological ideas may be sorted out, they ultimately stand for an ethical idea that places the utmost value on a form of common practice in which subjects can achieve cooperative self-actualization.[13]

Even those writings that appear to have been farthest from Critical Theory's fundamental ethical ideas reflect this first premise. In *Minima Moralia*, for example, Adorno vehemently denies any possibility of a universal moral theory by arguing that the "damages" of social life have already led to such fragmentation of individual conduct that orientation in terms of comprehensive principles is no longer possible. Instead, his "reflections" are supposed to show only in aphoristic, isolated cases which ethical and intellectual virtues remain that might resist instrumental demands by stubbornly insisting on nonpurposive activity. But the standards by which Adorno measures the harm done to the form of societal interaction betray his retention of the ideal of a cooperative self-actualization in which the freedom of the individual makes possible that of the other. In various places in the text, he explains even the historical genesis of social damage by direct reference to the loss of "good universal."[14] Moreover, Adorno takes as basic a concept of practice that, following Hegel's example, ties ethical principles to the presupposition of rationality. Only where common modes of action are established that individuals can accept as rational goals of self-actualization can there be a question of a successful form of socialization. The fact that Adorno at the same time has in mind above all the model of "nonpurposive" or "disinterested" communication—for which he takes unselfish, unalloyed giving or love as his paradigmatic examples[15]—follows from the quasi-aesthetic premise he shares with Marcuse: the forms of mutual action that are best suited to self-actualization are those in which human nature achieves noncoerced expression by fulfilling sensuous needs through interplay with the other.

The idea of the rational universal of cooperative self-actualization that all the members of the Frankfurt School fundamentally share is as critical of liberalism as it is of any intellectual tradition today that one might call "communitarian." While a certain approximation to liberal doctrines is reflected in the young Habermas because of the increasing weight he gives to the legal autonomy of individuals, he does not go as far as to say that there are no differences between the social-ontological premises of liberalism and those of Critical Theory. Instead, he continues to hold the conviction (as did Marcuse, Horkheimer, and Adorno) that the actualization of individual freedom is tied to the assumption of a common practice that is more than just the result of the coordination of individual interests. All the concepts of rational practice that find application in Critical Theory are tailored according to their intended use to actions whose implementation requires a higher degree of intersubjective agreement than liberalism allows. To be able to cooperate on an equal basis, to interact aesthetically, and to reach agreements in a noncoerced manner, a shared conviction is required that each of these activities is of an importance that justifies, if necessary, the neglect of individual interests. To this extent, Critical Theory presupposes a normative ideal of society that is incompatible with the individualistic premises of the liberal tradition. Orientation in terms of the idea of cooperative self-actualization includes, instead, the notion that, as long as subjects are not able to achieve a successful social life, they have not recognized the common core of convictions regarding values that lie behind their respective individual interests. The idea of a "community of free human beings" that Horkheimer formulates in his essay "Traditional and Critical Theory"[16] also forms the normative leitmotif of Critical Theory, where the concept of community is strictly avoided because of its ideological misuse.

Were one to press this line of thought further, one could easily get the impression that the normative concern of Critical Theory coincides with that of "communitarianism."[17] But just as it differs from liberalism in its orientation toward a "universal" of self-actualization, one can distinguish Critical Theory from communitarianism in terms of the link between this universal and reason. No critical theorist has ever abandoned the Hegelian idea that cooperative practice, along with the values attendant to it, must possess a rational character. Indeed, it is precisely the point of Critical Theory to see individual self-actualization as tied to the assumption that there is a common practice, one that can only be the result of an actualization of reason. Far from understanding the tie to comprehensive values as an end in itself, the critical theorist views the establishing of a cooperative context as fulfilling the function of increasing social rationality. Otherwise, there would be no way to imagine why the identified forms of practice in each case should always be the result of a social rationalization and no way to understand why the negative state of the present must always be an expression of deficient rationality. In contrast to communitarianism, Critical Theory subjects universality—which should, at the same time, be both embodied by and realized through social cooperation—to the standards of rational justification. While there may be various conceptions of reason in Critical Theory from Horkheimer to Habermas, they all ultimately come down to the same idea—namely, that the turn to a liberating practice of cooperation should not result from affective bonds or feelings of membership or agreement but from rational insight.

The tradition of Critical Theory thus differs from both liberalism and communitarianism by virtue of a particular kind of ethical perfectionism. To be sure, unlike the liberal tradition, Critical Theory holds that the normative aim of society should consist in reciprocally making self-actualization possible. At the same time, it understands its recommendation of this aim to be the well-grounded result of a certain analysis of the human process of development. As is the case with Hegel, it seems that the boundaries between description, on the one hand, and prescription and normative grounding, on the other, are blurred here as well. The explanation of the circumstances that have blocked or skewed the process of the actualization of reason should have in and of itself the rational force to convince subjects to create a social practice of cooperation. The perfection of society that all the members of Critical Theory have in mind must be, according to their common view, the result of enlightenment through analysis. The explanatory interpretation that they offer to this end, however, is no longer written in the language of Hegel's philosophy of spirit. To the contrary, there is a general consensus that a definitive "sociologizing" of the categorial frame of reference is a precondition for such an analysis. The second defining feature of Critical Theory then, consists in the attempt to explain the pathological deformation of reason sociologically. It deserves a place in the legacy of Critical Theory for today in the same way as should hold for the idea of cooperative self-actualization.

There is a growing tendency today to carry out social criticism in a form that does without sociological explanation. This development arises from the fact that, for the most part, it is considered sufficient to expose certain injustices in society on the basis of well-founded values or norms. The question of why those affected do not themselves problematize or attack such moral evils is no longer seen to fall within the purview of social criticism as such. The division that has been thereby established is deeply shaken, however, as soon as a causal connection is produced between the existence of social injustices and the absence of any public reaction. Social injustice would then be seen as possessing, among other things, the property of causing directly and on its own the silence or apathy that is expressed by the absence of public reaction.

A supposition of this kind serves as the basis for most of the approaches of Critical Theory. However strongly influenced by Marx they may be in their particulars, almost all of the approaches to

Critical Theory share a central premise of his analysis of capitalism concerning this one point: the social circumstances that constitute the pathology of capitalist societies have the peculiar structural feature of disguising precisely those states of affairs that would otherwise provide particularly urgent grounds for public criticism. Just as one can find the assumption sketched here in Marx's account of "fetishism" or in his theory of "reification,"[18] it is present in Critical Theory in concepts like "false consciousness," "one-dimensionality," and "positivism."[19] Such concepts are means to characterize a system of convictions and practices that has the paradoxical quality of distracting one's attention from the very social conditions that structurally produce that system. For the kind of social criticism that Critical Theory practices, this observation leads to a broadening of the tasks that must be carried out. In contrast to the approaches that have achieved dominance today, Critical Theory must couple the critique of social injustice with an explanation of the processes that obscure that injustice. For only when one can convince the addressees by means of such an explanatory analysis that they can be deceived about the real character of their social conditions can the wrongfulness of those conditions be publicly demonstrated with some prospect of their being accepted. Because a relationship of cause and effect is assumed to obtain between social injustice and the absence of any negative reaction to it, normative criticism in Critical Theory has to be complemented by an element of historical explanation. A historical process of the deformation of reason must causally explain the failure of a rational universal, a failure that constitutes the social pathology of the present. This explanation must at the same time make intelligible the de-thematization of social injustice in public discussion.

Within Critical Theory there has always been agreement that the historical process of a deformation of reason can only be explained within a sociological framework. Although the ethical intuition behind the whole undertaking ultimately sustains itself on the Hegelian idea of a rational universal, its proponents are at the same time so much the heirs of classical sociological thinkers that they are no longer able to draw on the Idealist concept of reason when explaining deviations from that universality. Instead, the processes of deformation that have contributed to a lack of social rationality—to the establishment of a "particular rationality"[20]—come to be analyzed within a categorial framework that emerges from Horkheimer to Habermas, in which there is a theoretical synthesis of Marx and Weber. Indeed, Marx had already stood the Hegelian concept of reason "right side up again" when he tied the expansion of justified knowledge to the completion of a social practice in virtue of which subjects might incrementally improve the conditions of their material reproduction. It would no longer be the internal compulsion of spirit but, rather, the external challenges of nature that would lead to a learning process consisting in a science of experience that justifies talk of the actualization of reason.

But for the critical theorists, Marx's anthropological epistemology was insufficient to give a truly sociological explanation of the historical process that Hegel had described in his philosophy as the self-unfolding of spirit. Only by taking up key concepts in Weber— whose early reception was often influenced by an unconventional Lukácsian reading[21]—is the picture made complete, at least insofar as the connection between any practice-bound learning process and social institutionalization is significantly clarified. In blending together Weber and Marx, the members of the Frankfurt School arrive at the shared conviction that the potential of human reason unfolds in a historical learning process in which rational solutions to problems are inextricably bound up with conflicts regarding the monopolization of knowledge. Subjects respond to the objective challenges repeatedly posed by nature and social organization at each new stage by constantly improving their knowledge of action, yet this knowledge is so deeply embedded in social conflicts over power and control that it achieves lasting form in institutions often only to the exclusion of certain other groups. For Critical Theory it thus remains beyond doubt that one must understand the Hegelian actualization of reason as conflictual—that is, as a multilayered learning process in which generalizable knowledge is only gradually won through improved solutions to problems and against the opposing groups in power.

Of course, in the history of Critical Theory this fundamental idea has also been subject to constant revision. Initially, Horkheimer only relates this conflictual learning process to the treatment of nature, making it difficult to imagine how rational improvements are also supposed to have taken place in the organization of social life.[22] Adorno widens the spectrum in the wake of Weber's sociology of music by recognizing rationalization in the arrangement of artistic material, which serves the goal of extending calculative sovereignty into aesthetic practice.[23] In the work of Marcuse one can find indications that would seem to justify the assumption of a collective learning process in the acquisition of internal nature, with corresponding setbacks resulting from power formations.[24] Habermas is the first to achieve a systematic breakdown of the various learning processes, an analysis he grounds on the variety of ways in which human beings relate to the world through their linguistic practice. He is convinced that we can expect human rational potential to develop along at least two paths: one directed toward an increase in knowledge of the objective world; the other toward a more just solution to interactive conflicts.[25]

But the gain in differentiation comes at the cost of no longer being able to consider historical growth in rationality together with those social conflicts which, following Weber's sociology of domination, were more clearly before the eyes of early Critical Theory. In Habermas's work we find a gulf between the dimension that, for instance, Bourdieu investigated in the cultural formation of monopolies,[26] and rational learning processes—a gulf whose presence is fundamentally inconsistent with the original concerns of the critical tradition. Nevertheless, because Critical Theory requires a post-Idealist version of the thesis that Hegel outlined in his conception of the actualization of reason, it cannot forego the degree of differentiation exemplified by the Habermasian conception of rationality. To be able to see the ways in which socially institutionalized knowledge has rationalized itself—that is, how it has exhibited an increasing degree of reflexivity in overcoming social problems—one must distinguish just as many aspects of rationality as there are socially perceivable challenges involved in the reproduction of societies, which depends on agreement.

In contrast to the Habermasian approach, which carries out such a differentiation on the basis of the structural particularities of human language, there may be a superior conception that ties the aspects of social rationalization (in an internal realist sense) more closely to the ability of socially established values to disclose problems. In that case, invariant values of linguistic communication would not reveal the direction in which the rationalization of social knowledge is to proceed. Rather, the historically produced values present in social spheres of meaning would play this role. Furthermore, the concept of reason with which Critical Theory attempts to grasp the increases in rationality in human history is subject to the pressure of incorporating foreign and new, particularly non-European, points of view. For this reason, it is not surprising that the concept of social rationality must also take on an ever-wider and more differentiated meaning to be able to take into account the multifaceted nature of learning processes. In any case, it is a post-Idealist version of the Hegelian notion of the actualization of reason that now provides the necessary background for the idea that may well form the innermost core of the entire Critical Theory tradition, from Horkheimer to Habermas. According to that tradition, the process of social rationalization through the social structure that is unique to capitalism has become interrupted or distorted in a way that makes pathologies that accompany the loss of a rational universal unavoidable.

One finds the key to this thesis, in which all the elements treated separately until now are brought together, in a concept of capitalism energized by a theory of rationality. It is not difficult to see that Critical Theory has achieved such a concept less through a reception of Marxist works than through the impetus provided by the early theory of Lukács. With *History and Class Consciousness*, it is first possible to glimpse in the institutional reality of modern capitalism an organizational form of society that is structurally tied to a certain, limited state of rationality. For Lukács, who was by his own admission significantly influenced by Weber and Georg Simmel, the characteristic feature of this form of rationality consists in the fact that its subjects are forced into a type of practice that makes them "spectators without influence" of events, divorced from their needs and intentions.[27] The mechanized division of labor and the exchange of goods call for a form of perception in which all other human beings appear to be unfeeling, thing-like entities, with the result that social interaction is bereft of any attention to those qualities that are valuable in themselves. If we were to describe the result of Lukács's analysis in a terminology closer to contemporary ideas, we might say that a certain form of practice achieves dominance in capitalism that compels indifference to those aspects of other human beings that are valuable. Instead of relating to one another with mutual recognition, subjects perceive themselves as objects that are recognized only according to the interests of each.[28] In any case, it is this diagnosis by Lukács that provides Critical Theory with a categorial framework within which it is possible to speak of an interruption or distortion of the process of the actualization of reason with the historical learning process taken as basic, the structural forces of society that Lukács reveals in modern capitalism present themselves as obstacles to the potential of rationality socially latent on the threshold of the modern age. The organizational form of social relations in capitalism prevents rational principles that, as far as our cognitive potential is concerned, are already at hand, from applying to practical life.

Of course, we must again qualify this explanatory scheme according to the various presuppositions regarding the manner and course of the historical process of rationalization that are at work in each case of Critical Theory. In Horkheimer, for example, one finds the thesis that the capitalist organization of production brings with it an opposition to individual interests that is hindered by the "application of the whole spiritual and physical means of dominating nature."[29] Horkheimer later broadens his reflections in concert with Adorno via the somewhat implausible hypothesis that there is an emotional rationality inherent in the form of interaction within nineteenth-century bourgeois families whose potential could not be brought into play because of increasing tension introduced by competition and monopolization.[30] The work of Adorno, in particular *Minima Moralia*, is full of such speculations that inevitably take the form of a diagnosis of the growing impossibility of a type of love which, in the family, was able to reconcile individual with general interests without coercion. The social privileging of rationally purposeful, utilitarian attitudes in capitalism prevents the development of a nonlegalistic form of rational universal that is in-herent in the structure of private relationships in the form of mutual affection and forgiveness.[31] Marcuse, roughly taking Schiller's *Letters on the Aesthetic Education of Mankind* as his guide, describes the pro-cess of increasing aesthetic sensibility as ending with modern capi-talism—a form of society which he, like Lukács (though also with an air of Heidegger), depicts as a complex of generalized knowledge at one's disposal.[32] Finally, in Habermas we find the idea that one can-not separate the potential of communicative rationality from capi-talist conditions because the imperative of economic exploitation penetrates even the sphere of the social lifeworld. Even though the family and the political public have long since emancipated them-selves from their traditional bases of legitimization, the principles of rational communication cannot gain acceptance in those settings because they are increasingly infiltrated by the mechanisms of sys-tematic management.[33]

However different these attempts at explanation may be, the basic scheme that underlies each of these criticisms of capitalism remains the same. Critical theorists, not unlike Lukács (though in a more sophisticated manner and without the excessive historical emphasis on the proletariat), perceive capitalism as a social form of organization in which practices and ways of thinking prevail that prevent the social utilization of a rationality already made possible by history. At the same time, this historical obstruction presents a moral or ethical challenge because it precludes the possibility of orienting oneself in terms of a rational universal, the impetus to which could only come from a fully realized rationality. Whether the concept of capitalism, grounded in a theory of rationality and underlying the interpretation of history outlined here, can once again be recovered today is certainly an open question. The possi-bilities for organizing the activity of a capitalist economy seem too multifarious, as well as too mixed up in other non-rationally pur-posive patterns of social activity, to reduce the attitudes of the ac-tors involved to a single pattern of instrumental rationality. Newer studies also suggest, however, that, in capitalist societies, those at-titudes or orientations most rewarded with social success are those whose fixation on individual advantages demands merely strategic associations with oneself and other subjects.[34] As a result, we cannot exclude the possibility of still interpreting capitalism as the institutional result of a cultural lifestyle or of a product of social imagination in which a certain type of restricted, "reifying" rationality is the dominant practice.[35]

But the commonalities within Critical Theory transcend this point. Its central representatives share not only the formal scheme of diagnosing capitalism as a set of social relations of blocked or distorted rationality but also the idea of the proper method of therapy. The forces that contribute to the overcoming of the social pathology are supposed to stem from precisely that reason whose actualization is impeded by the form of organization present in capitalist society. Just as was the case with the other elements of the theory, a classical figure of modern thought plays a formative role here; Freud has the same significance for the central content of Critical Theory as do Hegel, Marx, Weber, and Lukács. It is from his psychoanalytic theory that Critical Theory takes the thought that social pathologies must always express themselves in a type of suffering that keeps alive the interest in the emancipatory power of reason.

Today even the question of how one might practically overcome injustice no longer generally falls within the domain of social criticism. With the exception of approaches modeled on Foucault that take transformation of the individual's relation to herself as a condition of criticism,[36] the question concerning the relationship between theory and practice remains closed off from contemporary consideration. Explanation of the causes that may be responsible for obscuring social injustice are thought to belong just as little to the business of criticism as do perspectival characterizations of the conversion of knowledge into practice. One such perspective calls for a social-psychological theory of the subject that makes intelligible why individuals who themselves are conditioned by a particular way of thinking and practice should be further responsive to the rational content of the theory. It must explain whence the subjective forces can come that, despite all the delusion, one-dimensionality, and fragmentation, would still offer a chance for conversion of knowledge into practice. However heterogeneous the field of social criticism may be today, one feature is typical: there is hardly an approach that understands such a characterization to be part of its proper task. The question of the motivational state of the subjects that must be the focus of attention here is instead largely passed over because one no longer expects reflection on the conditions of conversion into practice to be a part of critique.

Nevertheless, from its beginnings, Critical Theory has been so greatly indebted to the tradition of left-Hegelianism that it considers the initiation of a critical practice that can contribute to the overcoming of social pathology to be an essential part of its task.[37] Even where skepticism regarding the possibility of practical enlightenment prevails among its authors,[38] the drama of the question of enlightenment arises out of the mere assumed necessity of an internal connection between theory and practice. Critical Theory, however, no longer understands the determination of this mediation as a task that one might undertake by philosophical reflection alone. Instead of appealing to a speculative philosophy of history, which for Marx and Lukács remained wholly self-evident, Critical Theory relies on the new instrument of empirical social research for information about the critical readiness of the public.[39] The result of this methodological reorientation, which constitutes a further distinctive feature of Critical Theory, is a sobering assessment of the state of consciousness of the proletariat. Contrary to what is assumed by the Marxist wing of left-Hegelianism, the working class does not automatically develop a revolutionary readiness to convert the critical content of theory into society-changing practice as a result of the consummation of the mechanized division of labor.[40] The idea that Critical Theory could provide the continuity between theory and practice by merely appealing to a certain predetermined addressee is thus abandoned. The considerations that are being employed in its place all come down to the expectation that the conversion into practice will be effected by precisely the rationality that the social pathology has distorted but not wholly dispossessed. In place of the proletariat, whose social situation had previously been considered the guarantor of responsiveness to the critical content of the theory, a submerged rational capacity must resurface for which all subjects in principle have the same motivational aptitude.

Admittedly, this kind of change of perspective requires an additional line of thought, for at first glance it is not at all clear why the motivation for critical practice should be expected from the same rationality that according to the theory is highly deformed. In other words, how can critical theorists trust that they will find a necessary degree of rational readiness for the conversion into practice if the socially practiced rationality turns out to be pathologically disrupted or distorted? The answer to this question falls within an area of Critical Theory that is established on a continuum between psychoanalysis and moral psychology. Its continual task is to uncover the motivational roots that sustain the readiness for moral cognition in individual subjects, despite any rational impairment.

Here it is helpful to distinguish between two steps of the argument, even if critical theorists have not always drawn a clear distinction between them. From the fact that a deficit in social rationality leads to symptoms of social pathology, one first infers that subjects suffer from the state of society. No individual can avoid seeing himself or herself as being impeded by the consequences of a deformation of reason (or being so described) because, with the loss of a rational universal, the chances of successful self-actualization, which depends on mutual cooperation, are also diminished. Critical Theory no doubt takes Freudian psychoanalysis as its methodological model for how it establishes a connection between defective rationality and individual suffering. Certainly, a similar connection is already found in Hegel's critique of Romanticism, which cannot have been without influence on the Frankfurt School, But the impetus to bring the category "suffering" into connection with the very pathologies of social rationality probably finds its origin in the Freudian idea that every neurotic illness arises from an impairment of the rational ego and must lead to individual cases of stress from suffering.[41]

The methodological application of this fundamental psychoanalytic idea to the field of social analysis is not just a theoretical move that Habermas has contributed to Critical Theory.[42] In his early essays, Horkheimer already describes social irrationality in concepts modeled on Freud's theory, insofar as they measure the degree of social pathology by the effect of forces foreign to the ego.[43] And everywhere Adorno speaks of individual or social suffering, one can hear overtones of the Freudian supposition that subjects have to suffer under the neurotic restriction of their genuinely rational capacities. Thus one reads in *Negative Dialectics* that every suffering possesses an "inward-turning form of reflection": "the moment of the flesh proclaims the knowledge that suffering ought not be, that things should be different."[44] The use of such a concept of suffering, which surfaces here as an instance of the experience of the interplay between spiritual and physical forces, has unfortunately remained until now largely unexplored within the reception of Critical Theory.[45] A more precise analysis would likely show that, as with Freud, suffering expresses the feeling of not being able to endure the "loss of ego [capacities]."[46]

From Horkheimer to Habermas, the idea that the pathology of social rationality leads to cases of impairment that frequently manifest themselves in the painful experience of the loss of rational capacities has guided Critical Theory. In the end, this idea comes down to the strong and frankly anthropological thesis that human subjects cannot be indifferent about the restriction of their rational capacities. Because their self-actualization is tied to the presupposition of cooperative rational activity, they cannot avoid suffering psychologically under its deformation. This insight, according to which there must be an internal connection between psychological intactness and undistorted rationality, is perhaps the strongest impetus Freud provides Critical Theory. Every investigation that nowadays points in the same general direction (though with improved methods) approaches its concerns from here.

But it is only by taking a second step, which Critical Theory does only rather implicitly, that one can extract from this thesis a means by which the severed relations to practice can be intellectually restored. And it is again Freud who provides the decisive suggestion: the stress from suffering presses toward a cure by means of exactly the same rational powers whose function the pathology impedes. An assumption about what in general is to count as a self-evident condition for admission into psychoanalytic treatment also accompanies this suggestion—namely, that the individual who subjectively suffers from a neurotic illness also wants to be free from that suffering. In Critical Theory, it is not always clear whether the stress from suffering that strives toward its cure pertains only to subjective experience or also to an "objective" event. While Adorno, who speaks of suffering as a "subjective impulse," seems to have the first alternative in mind, Horkheimer frequently uses formulations in which social suffering is treated as a magnitude of feeling capable of objective attribution. In the case of Habermas, there is sufficient evidence, particularly in his *Theory of Communicative Action*, to suggest the subjective way of speaking, whereas in Marcuse one can find both alternatives.[47]

In any case, Critical Theory presupposes that this subjectively experienced or objectively attributable suffering among the members of society must lead to that same desire for healing and liberation from social evils that the analyst must impute to his or her patients. Moreover, in each case, the interest in one's own recovery is supposed to be documented by the readiness to reactivate, against any resistance, those rational powers the individual or social pathology has deformed. All the thinkers belonging to the inner circle of Critical Theory expect in their addressees a latent interest in rational explanation or interpretation, since only winning back an integral rationality can satisfy the desire for a liberation from suffering. It is this risky assumption that permits a different connection of theory to practice than the Marxist tradition provides. The critical theorists share with their audience neither a space of common objectives nor one of political projects but, rather, a space of potentially common reasons that holds the pathological present open to the possibility of transformation through rational insight. Here, as well, one must consider the differences of opinion that prevail between the individual members of the Frankfurt School. One can best assess them by seeing which social-psychological or anthropological assumptions substantiate the thesis that individual responsiveness to rational arguments remains possible within any deformation of social life.

Turning to Horkheimer on this point, we find the idea that the memory of emotional security in early childhood sustains the interest in overcoming that form of rationality committed to a merely instrumental disposition. It remains unclear, however, how such a psychological drive is supposed to be directed at the same time toward attaining an "intact," undiminished rational power. If we assemble Adorno's scattered reflections on the topic, there is something to be said for seeing in the "mimetic sense" more than just an impulse to assimilate (to) the threatening object. Rather, one must also see suggested in it the inexhaustible remnant of a desire to grasp the other intellectually in a way that leaves the other his or her singular existence.[48] One can find such characterizations in Marcuse, as is well known, in a theory that involves erotic impulses of a life-drive whose aesthetic actualization requires a "conscious effort of free rationality."[49] It is frequently asked of this project, however, whether or not it sufficiently guarantees an expanded concept of social rationality.[50] Finally, Habermas had originally assumed in his version of an anthropology of knowledge of the human species an "emancipatory interest" that focuses on the experience of a discursive practice that is structurally present in a state of noncoercion and equality.[51] This early conception has since given way to a theory of discourse that no longer makes anthropological claims yet retains an assumption that the practice of argumentative discourse always allows the individual to be responsive to better reasons.[52]

All of these reflections present answers to the question of what experiences, practices, or needs allow an interest in full rational realization to continue to exist in human beings, despite the deformation or skewing of social rationality. Only as long as the theory can count on such a rational impulse for its grounding will it be able to relate itself reflexively to a potential practice in which the explanation it offers is implemented with a view to liberation from suffering. Critical Theory will only be able to continue in the form in which it has developed from Horkheimer to Habermas if it does not forsake the proof of such interests. Without a realistic concept of "emancipatory interest" that puts at its center the idea of an indestructible core of rational responsiveness on the part of subjects, this critical project will have no future.

With this last thought, the development of the motifs that constitute the core content of the legacy of Critical Theory has reached a matter-of-fact conclusion. The sequence of systematic ideas developed in this essay form a unity from which a single component cannot be omitted without consequences. As long as we do not abandon the aim of understanding Critical Theory as a form of reflection belonging to a historically effective reason, it will not be easy to give up the normative motif of a rational universal, the idea of a social pathology of reason, and the concept of an emancipatory interest. Yet it is also apparent that, of these three components of thought, none can still be maintained today in the theoretical form in which the members of the Frankfurt School originally developed it. All require conceptual reformulation and the mediation of the present state of our knowledge if they are still to fulfill the function that was once intended for them. That said, the field of tasks is outlined—tasks now left to the heirs of Critical Theory in the twenty-first century.

Translated by James Hebbeler

THREE

RECONSTRUCTIVE SOCIAL CRITICISM WITH A GENEALOGICAL PROVISO

On the Idea of "Critique" in the Frankfurt School

The common and widespread opposition of strong and weak criticism only represents a rather hopeless attempt to bring a discussion that has branched out in many directions under a simple denominator. For years, ever since the end of Marxism as an autonomous theory, the question of how it is possible to find an appropriate standpoint from which to critically interrogate liberal-democratic societies without borrowing from the philosophy of history has been discussed from the most diverse perspectives. On the one hand, a large part is played by material questions of social theory, which have essentially to do with the difficulty of pronouncing an alternative that is at once desirable and efficient outside the institutional framework of the highly developed societies of the West. On the other hand, philosophical questions that often seem to have almost methodological character also play an eminent role. At the center, then, stands the problem of describing and justifying a standpoint from which society and its institutional practices can be meaningfully theoretically criticized.

The impetus for this normative part of the debate has been a series of philosophical publications in which the hermeneutic turn of the analytical philosophy of language has given rise to a reexamination of the conventional models of social criticism. It suffices to recall such different authors as Richard Rorty and Michael Walzer in order to designate roughly the angle of attack this revision has taken. Despite all the obvious differences in their justificatory procedures, with both authors, there is roughly the same kind of basic argumentation. Any normative critique of an institutional order or a particular social practice, according to the premise on both sides, always already presupposes a certain affirmation of the prevailing moral culture in the society concerned. For without such identification with the preexisting value horizon, the critic would not even be in a position to identify as a social defect something that can also potentially be perceived as wrong by the other members of the society. In contrast, a form of social criticism that tries to bracket or transcend the accustomed local value horizon by appealing to external, universalistic moral principles necessarily takes too distanced a perspective to be understood by its addressees. It therefore always runs the risk of claiming an elitist specialized knowledge that can readily be abused for manipulative purposes. The conclusion to be taken from this line of thinking, accordingly, is that only a "weak," context-bound form of social criticism represents a politically and philosophically legitimate undertaking, whereas any "strong," context-transcending form of social criticism necessarily brings the risk of paternalism or even despotism.

Now, of course, it is obvious that this briefly reproduced argument poses a massive challenge for all those approaches that still try to appeal to the heritage of the Frankfurt School. Not only do these authors often themselves refer to the representatives of this tradition by trying to represent Marcuse's *One-Dimensional Man* or the *Dialectic of Enlightenment* as exemplary cases of a strong social criticism that no longer has a social place. What hits home even harder is the fact that many of the central writings of this school create the impression that it so distanced itself from the institutional order of the given society that its criticism has lost all normative reference points and thus must fall under suspicion of being a totalizing ideology. This would seem to imply nothing more strongly today, accordingly, than setting aside this obsolete model of social criticism as quickly as possible so that we no longer run the risk of claiming an elitist specialized knowledge. If in the following I nonetheless strive to defend the classical model of critique, which I still see partially at work with Habermas, I do so under provisos I would like to specify at the outset. First, I am seeking to reconstruct the ideal form of this kind of criticism, not its execution in individual writings by the Frankfurt circle. What interests me is the question of whether the central idea behind the whole project can still be defended today; its implementation is only of very subordinate importance for me. In a certain way, the second proviso is already connected to this: namely, that the following defense should by no means be understood as if it were also connected to a ratification of the material content of the social theory itself. Rather, I am among those who want to leave no doubt that the basic historical-philosophical and sociological assumptions of the Frankfurt School can no longer be defended.

In my reconstruction, I proceed first with a small but decisive modification of Walzer's schema of three types of social criticism. In this way, I show that, today, a comparison of different models of critique is only complete when the form of "genealogy" paradigmatically developed by Nietzsche is included (section I). Against this background, in a second step, I make it clear that their connection to the left-Hegelian tradition made it appear self-evident to the members of the Frankfurt School from the beginning to adopt an immanent, "interpretive," or, as I say, "reconstructive" mode of social criticism. Here, clearly, a differentiation of the ways of carrying out such a reconstruction beyond Walzer's is required so that we can characterize the specific intention of the representatives of Critical Theory (section II). But only the last step of my short remarks show where the real point of the model of social criticism that the Frankfurters at least in principle followed lies. Here, in working through the experience of National Socialism, a metacritical standpoint was built into the reconstructive program owing to the inclusion of Nietzsche's genealogy. The result of this fusion of Hegel and Nietzsche is the idea of a social criticism in which the immanent criticism of given conditions stands under the genealogical proviso that the norms or principles being claimed may long since have lost their original meaning (section III).

In his book *Interpretation and Social Criticism*, Michael Walzer undertakes a differentiation of models of social criticism that offers an ideal point of entry for the formulation of our question.[1] Walzer is convinced that the difference between the various approaches can be measured by how the procedure is procured with which the assertion of the underling norms or principles is attained. Where such a criterion is underlying, three distinct forms of social criticism can be raised, corresponding to the procedures of revelation, invention, and interpretation. In this context, the first type references all the social and critical approaches that appeal to an experience of religious or cognitive clarity in order to advance a hitherto socially closed realm of generally binding values. Here it is very obviously a kind of Platonism that provides the philosophical background for the ideals or principles in whose light social conditions are to be submitted to a grounded critique. While today intellectual tendencies may be emerging to reinvigorate a Platonism of this kind, in the following I do not further consider this type of social criticism because it does not seem to me sufficiently philosophically relevant.

Of much greater significance, in contrast, is the second model of social criticism that Walzer has designated "invention" after its underlying method of justification. By this, he means all the approaches that take their starting point from the outline of a generally valid procedure, the real or fictive carrying out of which is then to lead to justified norms. To use a less polemical name, in the following I call this procedure "construction" and treat it as today's most influential model of social criticism. Against this approach, Walzer raises as the last model in his sequence the procedure of "interpretation," which he, of course against the background of his own premises, has to explain as the royal road to social criticism. With this, he names nothing other than what was once called "immanent" criticism, even if the emphasis is now placed much more strongly on the hermeneutic dimension of the creative disclosure of existing cultural values or ideals. For reasons that will become clear in the steps of my argument, I do not call this critical procedure "interpretation" but "reconstruction," and, for now, as for Walzer, only the attempt to achieve the normative bases of social criticism by way of a reconstruction of moral norms that are anchored in the social practices of a given society is meant.

Thus, what results from these reflections on Walzer's proposal is a provisional distinction between two models of social criticism that today are relatively widespread and seem to possess a certain legitimacy. Predominant at the moment are doubtless those approaches that adopt construction as their means of justification. To name only the prominent contemporary example, reference can be made to John Rawls's early theory of justice, where a bundle of principles capable of general agreement are justified under the fictive conditions of an ideal original situation that can then be used to criticize the institutional order of a society.[2] This first critical model can be fundamentally distinguished from the second, that of reconstruction, in that for the latter only those principles or ideals that have already in some way gelled in a given society count as legitimate resources for social criticism. Here normative claims or ideals are to be reconstructed from within social reality itself; their transcending character allows the existing social order to be subjected to justified criticism. Even if Walzer concentrates on the hermeneutic dimension of interpretation when characterizing this approach, it should not be forgotten that Marxist ideology critique also belongs among its historical forerunners. Pushed by Hegel's critique of Kant, Marx too often operated with the idea that the bad reality of existing conditions must be measured against the demands that are simultaneously institutionally embodied as ideals. To this extent, this approach of reconstructive social criticism embraces a series of different versions whose differences will have to be elucidated.

Now, it nevertheless seems to me that this distinction between constructive and reconstructive procedures is not yet sufficiently exhaustive to include all models of social criticism encountered in contemporary social criticism. Here I do not have in mind speculative approaches that try to achieve a critique of social reality by opening up a radically new view of reality, a yet-unexhausted value horizon. Perhaps in such cases it is only a matter of further, profane versions of what Walzer calls "revelation." No, I think primarily of a social and critical procedure that can be retrieved from the writings of Michel Foucault, for example, where he almost positivistically shows the transformation of a normative ideal into a social practice of uprooted disciplining.[3] Here we do not find the critique of ideology's confrontation of idea and reality but, rather, the exposure of society as a social happening that has long been bereft of any normative justification through credible ideals. It seems to me to make sense to treat this procedure as a third model of social criticism and to call it "genealogy" with reference to Nietzsche. By this, I mean the attempt to criticize a social order by demonstrating historically the extent to which its defining ideas and norms already serve to legitimate a disciplinary or repressive practice.[4] Of course, this last formulation makes clear that this kind of procedure of genealogical exposure always requires an additional step to normatively justify why social discipline or political repression should represent a moral evil in the first place. In this sense, genealogy is in a certain sense a parasitical critical procedure, since it lives by presupposing a normative justification that it does not itself try to give.

If the conclusion is drawn from these introductory reflections, we thus attain a distinction between three models of social criticism. According to the procedure they primarily use, they can sequentially be designated with the concepts of "construction," "reconstruction," and "genealogy." With the constructive approach, as we have seen, it is a matter of using a procedure of justification capable of general agreement to attain normative principles in whose light the institutional order of a society can be criticized in a justified way. In reconstructive approaches, in contrast, the attempt is undertaken to uncover normative ideals of the institutions and practices of social reality itself that can be suitable for the criticism of the existing reality. And it can finally be said of the genealogical approaches that here social reality is to be criticized by demonstrating the necessary alternation of its normative ideals into practices that stabilize domination. Against the background of this systematic distinction, it now seems possible to me in the next step to take up the question of which idea of social criticism underlies the tradition of the Frank-furt School.

Even a quick look at what has been said so far seems to suffice to determine the type of social criticism the representatives of Critical Theory continuously followed. Their philosophical origins were still much too strongly rooted in the tradition of left-Hegelianism to be able to play off the thought of a procedural justification of norms going back to Kant, Horkheimer, Adorno, and Marcuse, who always pursued a reconstructive way of grounding their social criticism. The leading model of Marxist ideology critique said from the beginning that there must be in social reality itself normative ideas, by means of which the reality of capitalism could be justifiedly criticized. Already in the programmatic essay Horkheimer published in 1937 on the distinction between traditional and critical theory, the methodological principle is worked out that would determine the work of the Institute for Social Research from then on. Since Critical Theory as distinct from traditional approaches had to be conscious of its context of social development, as well as its political application, and thus was to represent a kind of self-reflection of the historical process, the norms or principles to which critique referred could only be those that were in some way anchored in historical reality itself.[5]

Despite their later turns and historical and philosophical revisions, the members of the Frankfurt School never really abandoned this methodological proposition; and for all his consciously coming closer to Kantianism, Habermas, too, remained faithful to it to the present day, unlike Rawls trying to relocate procedural rationality as a discursive practice of justification into the social reproduction of society. Of course, precisely Habermas's justificatory strategy makes it clear that the approach of reconstruction always meant more than what appears with Walzer as an ideal of a social criticism that operates locally. The procedure of criticism was to be left-Hegelian, not merely hermeneutic. This distinction must be briefly elucidated to bring out the first peculiarity that distinguishes the critical model of the Frankfurt School up to today.

Every reconstructive procedure of social criticism faces the problem that it cannot really justify what makes the ideals from its own culture chosen to be a reference point normatively defensible or desirable in the first place. That is, the moral principles that are contingently available in the value horizon of a given society initially lack any guarantee that they are in a certain way valid for its members. In this respect, such an immanent procedure, no different from genealogy, requires an additional step through which it would first be justified why the ideal raised by one's own culture should possess normative validity. It is this point at which a series of alternatives loom within the reconstructive model, so that different versions become possible. While Walzer equips the hermeneutic interpretation with trust in finding a moral minimum of reciprocal norms in every culture to which one can always be creatively connect,[6] Critical Theory uses a concept of reason that can justify the normative validity of the immanently raised ideals.

Here the starting point is the left-Hegelian premise according to which social reproduction occurs through forms of social practice in which the rational achievements of human beings are incorporated. It is further assumed that these rational achievements unfold according to progress that is realized through the learning process in connection with social action. At each new level of social reproduction, human rationality thus takes on a more highly developed form, so that the whole of human history can be spoken of as a process of the realization of reason. This still not completely absurd assumption forms a theoretical background against which the reconstructive procedure of critique contains a completely different meaning than Walzer's interpretation. For normative reconstruction must now mean uncovering in the social reality of a given society those normative ideals that offer a reference point for a justified critique because they represent the embodiment of social reason. Thus, with left-Hegelianism, the Frankfurt School solves the justification problem posed by every immanent form of social criticism by inserting a concept of social rationalization. As soon as it can be shown that an available ideal incorporates progress in the realization of reason, it can yield a justified standard to criticize the given social order.

Now, there is no question that the first generation of the Frankfurt School failed in the implementation of this extremely demanding critical program. The one-sided orientation toward the action type of work prevented them from developing a concept of social rationalization that could include the components of moral validity in a plausible way.[7] Here it is not a matter of the specific version, however, but only of the methodological structure of the left-Hegelian critical model. As discussed here, what is decisive for it is the special connection of an immanent procedure with a context-transcending concept of rationality. The critique of society can be based on ideals within the given social order that at the same time can justifiedly be shown to be the expression of progress in the process of social rationalization. To this extent, the critical model of the Frankfurt School presupposes if not precisely a philosophy of history then a concept of the directed development of human rationality.[8] Without a demanding theoretical program of this kind, it hardly seems to me possible to speak of a specific identity of Critical Theory that can somehow be distinguished from the other approaches to social criticism. Nevertheless, what has so far been said about the left-Hegelian heritage does not yet exhaust the critical model of the Frankfurt School. Instead, here an additional theoretical component appears that can be understood as the integration of a genealogical proviso. With it, I come to the third and final point of my reflections.

It was probably essentially the devastating experience of German National Socialism that gave rise to doubts among the members of the Frankfurt School about whether the ideals adduced for critique in fact still possessed the meaning with which they originally developed. Before this, a certain solid trust had prevailed that the normatively reconstructed principles of social reality possessed a firm kernel of meaning that also determined their practical context of application. Now, however, the establishment of the National Socialist system of domination showed that, under the social validity of an ideal, a social practice could also develop that was as far from its original moral meaning as imaginable. To understand the methodological status of the doubt that must have arisen under this historical impression, it is necessary to recall briefly once again the premises of the left-Hegelian critical program.

On this program, as we have seen, a given social order is to be criticized by means of normative principles that on the one hand are available as ideas within the social reality but on the other hand also represent an embodiment of social rationality. But this always presupposes that these principles possess a content that is sufficiently fixed to be immune to misuse. It is now this second premise that must have been retrospectively thrown into doubt for Critical Theory in order to do justice to the experience of National Socialism. The meaning of normative ideals or principles had proved to be much more porous, open, even vulnerable, than had been predicted by the original critical program. A moral norm, accordingly went the conclusion, does not as such prescribe out of itself how it should be socially applied. Rather, its meaning can be transformed as a result of imperceptible shifts of meaning, so that, in the end, it loses the normative kernel that originally justified its development.

In view of this conclusion, it can no longer be surprising that at the end of the 1930s, Critical Theory underwent a systematic convergence with Nietzsche's genealogy.[9] For in their best parts, his moral and psychological writings anticipate precisely the theoretical misgivings that the Frankfurters developed in exile. At the same time, Horkheimer, Adorno, and Marcuse did not simply replace their left-Hegelian critical program with the idea of genealogical critique as skeletally outlined in the first part of this essay. Rather, if I see it correctly, they built genealogy into their reconstructive model as a kind of metacritical standpoint. What resulted out of this synthesis of Hegel and Nietzsche as a model of social criticism can be described in very few words as follows: To each attempt to carry out an immanent critique of society under the premises of social rationalization must belong the genealogical project of studying the real context of application of moral norms. For without the addition of such a historical test, critique cannot be sure that the ideals it adduces still possess in social practice the normative meaning that originally distinguished them. To this extent, social criticism that has learned from the dialectic of enlightenment simultaneously delineates the norms at its disposal from two sides. On the one hand, the norms must satisfy the criterion of being socially incorporated ideals at the same time as they are the expression of social rationalization; on the other hand, it must be tested whether they still possess their original meaning. Today, it is no longer possible to have social criticism that does not also use genealogical research as a detector to ferret out the social shifts of meaning of its leading ideals.

What thus emerges at the end of my reflections it the irritating circumstance that Critical Theory in a certain way unites all three of the models distinguished in this essay into a single program. The constructive justification of a critical standpoint is to provide a conception of rationality that establishes a systematic connection between social rationality and moral validity. It is then to be reconstructively shown that this potential rationality determines social reality in the form of moral ideals. And these moral ideals, in turn, are to be seen under the genealogical proviso that their original meaning may have socially become unrecognizable. I fear that what Critical Theory once meant by the idea of social criticism cannot be defended today, short of this extremely high standard.

FOUR

A PHYSIOGNOMY OF THE CAPITALIST FORM OF LIFE

A Sketch of Adorno's Social Theory

It is ill-advised to restrict oneself to Adorno's social-theoretical essays and papers in order to get to his analysis of capitalism, and it is no less mistaken to believe that one can obtain the elements of his conception of society in the form of descriptive, explanatory theory. To be sure, Adorno repeatedly let himself be led to speak of the structural transformations of capitalist society as if it were a matter of parts of an explanatory theory. The lecture on "Late Capitalism or Industrial Society?" is as exemplary of this tendency as the "Reflections on Class Theory" from the early 1940s.[1] But everything in such texts is not simply underinformed, strangely uninspired, and almost dogmatic. Above all, these texts create the impression that lucid analysis has been replaced by functionalistic explanation, where the individual psyche, culture, or law assumes the function of fulfilling capitalist imperatives.[2] Understood as elements of an explanatory theory, these sociological papers seem to lack any attention to the internal logics of spheres of social action, any trace of the innovative power of values, and any sensitivity to the resistance of subcultural interpretive models. It is therefore not surprising that Adorno's social theory decisively lost influence soon after the decline of the student movement. At the Frankfurt conference on the occasion of his eightieth birthday, the contributions on his sociological writings already stand out for their relative skepticism.[3] Shortly thereafter, their trail vanishes in the drifts of a theoretical landscape marked by post-Marxism and systems theory.

Of course, the misunderstanding already lay in the point of departure. Taking the sociological part of his work as a specialized part of an explanatory analysis of society meant dissolving its internal connection to his philosophy, as well as to his aesthetics. It resulted in setting up false competitions, thereby inviting comparison with much more complex social theories. Moreover, it lost sight of the fact that Adorno really wanted to see even his sociological analyses only as part of the hermeneutic of natural-historical disaster that he had presented as his theoretical goal in his 1931 Frankfurt inaugural lecture.[4] Adorno's central intention from the start was to reveal the second, reified nature of historical reality by using sociological analysis to expose the determining figures of action and consciousness. And he did not abandon it as he later came under disciplinary pressure to produce sociological or social-theoretical papers. His analysis of capitalism is therefore not an explanatory theory but a hermeneutic of a failed form of life. The components that nonetheless point in an explanatory direction, like his psychoanalytic theory or the culture-industry thesis, have the sole function of hypothetically explaining the rise of particular models of action and consciousness. The fundamental object of the analysis, however, is to understand them.

If this intention is placed at the center of Adorno's social theory, the context of the individual parts of his work immediately changes. What have traditionally been interpreted as the remnants of a metaphysical philosophy of history take on the task of genealogically interpreting the rise of our second nature in the reified, frozen life conditions established by capitalism. This sketch of the pathogenesis of the bourgeois world owed almost everything, as Adorno was happy to concede, to Georg Lukács's analysis of reification (discussed in section I). The sociological papers, in contrast, must, as their author suggested, be understood as contributions to a "physiognomy" of social reality. Adorno attaches this expression, which recurs like a leitmotif, to the aim of interpreting social reality's determining figures of action such that they can be understood as bodily or gestural expressions of the capitalist form of life (section II). Finally,

Adorno's social analysis includes a third level, which has the difficult task of holding open the possibility of transforming a frozen, reified reality: "Out of the construction of a configuration of reality," as he already put it in his inaugural lecture, "the demand for its real change always follows promptly."[5] Adorno relies on Freud's psychoanalysis to show that in psychic suffering and impulsive reactions there constantly lies a dormant interest in an unrestricted capacity for reason, the realization of which would be a humane form of life (section III). In the following, I seek to reconstruct these three levels of Adorno's social-theoretical work. I am most interested, however, in attempting to defend Adorno's analysis of capitalism for the present.

$$\backslash\!\!\!(\text{ I })\!\!\!/$$

Adorno had acquired the idea of a materialistic hermeneutic of natural history, which he never again admitted to, in his exchange with Walter Benjamin.[6] Unlike Benjamin, however, he early on gave this idea a rational-theoretical turn that decisively oriented it toward the German Idealist concept of reason.[7] For both authors, as for many of their contemporaries, reading the analysis of reification in Lukács's *History and Class Consciousness* was a key intellectual experience.[8] The influence the barely one-hundred-page essay exerted over the philosophical development of a generation confronted with the socially destructive effects of capitalism in the shadow of World War I can hardly be overestimated.[9] The thought that the social spread of commodity exchange had led to a deformation of human practice because it forced subjects to take an objectifying attitude not only toward nature but also toward themselves and their fellows had opened Benjamin and Adorno's eyes. From then on, they both perceived the social and historical world of modernity as a space frozen into a "second nature," where human relationships had lost their transparent meaning, mediated by practical reasons, since the very experience of nature had been transformed.

Benjamin and Adorno were also in agreement about the methodological consequences of this historical starting point for philosophy. If, with the spread of the commodity form, the modern world had fallen into a process of reification, neither Georg Simmel's life philosophy nor Edmund Husserl's phenomenology, neither Martin Heidegger's analysis of Dasein nor Max Scheler's material analysis of values, could cope with the "crisis of idealism."[10] For, in their basic concepts, if this shorthand is allowed, these currents already miss the fact of historicity, so that they cannot take into account the emptying of meaning that results from an essentially structural social transformation. To be adequate to this regression of the social into nature, what was instead required was a philosophical method that considers social events as what they are: a blind ensemble of events that has become incomprehensible. And Benjamin and Adorno agreed that this initially meaningless "nature" of capitalism could only be decoded by a specific form of hermeneutics that shifts the given empirical material through possible constellations until figures emerge that reveal a cipher with objective, meaningful form.

What specifically this hermeneutic idea meant was of course disputed by the two from the start. As is well known, Benjamin tended toward the view that such sensual figures could be products of the collective unconsciousness itself, which contained the archaic potentials of a pictorial imagination. On his account, all that was therefore required was the methodologically skillful reconstruction of such dreamlike pictures to detect the dark secret that commodity fetishism had caused in the social life of capitalism.[11] For Adorno, in contrast, the philosophical task of interpretation was very different, both closer to and farther from hermeneutic method. Adorno remained much closer to hermeneutics when he insisted, against Benjamin, that interpreting the meaningless, enigmatic reality was the theoretical business of the interpreter alone. Anticipating his later critique, his inaugural lecture already announced:

The historical images . . . are not simply self-given. They do not lie organically ready in history; no showing (*Schau*) or intuition is required to become aware of them. They are not magically sent by the gods to be taken in and venerated. Rather, they must be produced by human beings and are legitimated in the last analysis alone by the fact that reality crystalizes about them in striking conclusiveness (*Evidenz*).[12]

The concept of production in the last sentence, however, already brings to light the distance Adorno was to maintain from contemporary hermeneutics, which is largely associated with Wilhelm Dilthey. Since, under the pressure of generalized commodity exchange, social reality has become an intentionless ensemble of events, there can no longer be any historically mediated meaning in which researchers can imitatively immerse themselves. What is needed is a constructive "juxtaposition of analytically isolated elements" in order to sort through the "incomplete, contradictory and fragmentary" text of the social and finally produce figures or indicators of the objective meaning of the historical condition. Many of the methodological formulations Adorno uses to specify this idea of "interpretive grouping" remain vague and are of little help. However, the fact that in this context he speaks repeatedly of "key categories, before which reality springs out" indicates that the Weberian category of the "ideal type" is in the background of his reflections.[13]

Even a brief look at the corresponding text by Weber makes it clear that hardly a methodological thought in Adorno's inaugural lecture had not already been formulated by the author of *Economy and Society*. In Weber's essay on "Objectivity," we read, in almost word-for-word correspondence with Adorno, that the ideal type should be understood as "the synthesis of a great many diffuse, discrete, more or less present and occasionally absent *concrete individual* phenomena . . . into a unified *thought* construct." This conceptual construction, Weber continues, has only an instrumental function: "by the thinking accentuation of certain elements of reality," it serves to reveal the so-called "objective possibility" of the "cultural significance" of a process.[14] With the exception of the concept of "cultural significance," to which I return in the following discussion, Weber's methodological proposal tallies completely with Adorno's reflections. Even the "figures" he introduces as the aim of the work of philosophical interpretation are the result of an exaggerated "construction" of reality on the basis of empirical material. The "elements of a social analysis," as he puts it, should be "grouped . . . in such a manner that the way they come together [makes] a figure."[15] The conceptual construction of this figure or "ideal type" requires, as Adorno says, using the same word as Weber, an "exact imagination" that "reaches beyond" the given empirical material insofar as it emphasizes, neglects, and on the whole reorders the "aspects" within it.[16] In Weber the corresponding thought is that the ideal-typical construction requires "imagination," which allows the assembled elements to appear as adequate to reality, as "objectively possible."[17] Finally, the two authors also agree on the practical goals of research involving such ideal types or figures. Just as we read in Weber that ideal types should not be "hypotheses" but should only "offer guidance to the construction of hypotheses," so Adorno writes that the constructed figures represent "models by means of which the *ratio*, examining and testing, approaches a reality which refuses to submit to laws."[18] Later in Adorno's social-theoretical discussions, we come across many formulations that point much more strongly in this Weberian direction: namely, that ideal-typical constructions of reality establish a kind of guideline for orienting empirical hypotheses.

But what is the equivalent in Adorno's methodological reflections for the idea of "cultural significance," which played such a central role in Weber's justification of the "ideal type"? Only with this question do we reach the core of the program Adorno lays out in his inaugural lecture: a materialistic hermeneutic of the capitalist form of life. As is well known, Weber follows neo-Kantianism when he asserts that ideal-typical concepts serve to reveal the cultural significance of particular processes or phenomena. In this context, "cultural significance" means the suprapersonal, historically given value perspective by means of which the chaotic multiplicity of individual data can be organized so that relevant bundles of events and chains of action can stand out.[19] The example Weber enlists for illustrative purposes is chosen as if aimed directly at Adorno's later example:

> One can delineate the utopia of a "capitalistic" culture, i.e., one in which the governing principle is the investment of private capital. This procedure would accentuate certain individual concretely diverse traits of modern material and intellectual culture in its unique aspects into an ideal construct which from our point of view would be completely self-consistent. This would then be the delineation of an *"idea"* of *capitalistic culture.*[20]

If in 1931 Adorno already intended to delineate such a comprehensive ideal type, its value basis would certainly not have been merely the cultural interpretation of capitalism. In those years, he was already much too convinced of the correctness of Lukács's analysis of reification. The justification Adorno gives for his program of a constructive, ideal-typical interpretation of the "second nature" of capitalism is completely different and based, instead, on Hegelian premises. With Lukács, he is convinced that the rational developmental of the human species has been disrupted by the generalization of commodity exchange in such a far-reaching way that living conditions as a whole under capitalism have taken the form of objectified relations. The assertion of such a regression of the social into nature-like relations is not the result of a particular value perspective; rather, it arises from the failure of all conventional theoretical approaches. As for Lukács and Horkheimer, for Adorno the motif of a crisis of contemporary philosophy and social science plays a justificatory role. Because the historically given models of thinking have all systematically failed to grasp the specificity of the modern way of being, it can be shown by elimination that only the hermeneutic approach is adequate to the phenomenon of reification. The evidence of a necessary failure of all post-Idealist theories with the phenomenon that affects every subject in the present supplies Adorno with a sufficient reason to assume the superiority of his own position.

But what is especially significant about the Hegelian premises of his hermeneutic approach is that they compel him to make a direct parallel between social conditions and the constitution of reason. This equivalence is no easy undertaking, since he must show that the social pathology of reification is intrinsically connected to a deformation of the human capacity for reason. Indeed, in his "Reification and the Consciousness of the Proletariat," Lukács had already taken a stab in this direction, insofar as he sought to understand objectifying action as a kind of interruption of any comprehensive practice through which the human being is embedded as a being endowed with reason in a reality that is for its part rational. But due to its Idealistic premises about reason, Adorno never really subscribed to this idea. He therefore tried repeatedly to give it an independent justification. Among the many places in his work in which Adorno offers an explanation of why the generalization of commodity exchange signifies a deformation of human reason, the most productive still seems to me that which operates with the concept of "imitation." In the long ninety-ninth aphorism of *Minima Moralia* ("Gold Assay"), there is a short sentence that could serve as the key to a corresponding theory: "The human is indissolubly linked with imitation: a human being only becomes human at all by imitating other human beings."[21] From this passage, which generally agrees with the observations of recent social anthropology that accord imitation a central place in the development of the human mind,[22] we can reconstruct why Adorno saw the reification of commodity exchange as the cause of a deformation of reason.

Only through imitative behavior, which for Adorno originally goes back to an affect of loving care, do we achieve a capacity for reason because we learn by gradually envisioning others' intentions to relate to their perspectives on the world. For us reality no longer merely represents a field of challenges to which we must adapt; rather, it becomes charged with a growing multiplicity of intentions, wishes, and attitudes that we learn to regard as reasons in our action. Adorno does not restrict this ability to perceive the world, as it were, "from the inside out" to the domain of interpersonal behavior. To the contrary, he sees our special, imitation-based capacity for reason precisely in experiencing the adaptive goals of speechless beings, even things, as intentions demanding rational consideration. He is therefore convinced that any true knowledge has to retain the original impulse of loving imitation sublimated within itself in order to do justice to the rational structure of the world from our perspective.[23]

Now, Adorno sees the institutionalization of commodity exchange as connected to the spread of an action schema that makes the ability to rationally respect others' intentions recede. For him, reification signifies a "recentering" of man, who, according to the standard of exchange, unlearns how to perceive the world from the perspective of those intentions and wishes whose significance had originally emerged through imitation. To this extent, Adorno is in a certain way right to claim that the spread of commodity exchange simultaneously represents a deformation of reason: the pressure to act according to the action schema of exchange in ever more spheres requires people to concentrate their capacity for reason on the ego-centric calculation of economic utility.

It is this idea of a social pathology of reason that explains the methodological point of application of Adorno's ideal-typical interpretive procedure within his analysis of capitalism.[24] The renaturalization of social relations, even the reification that extinguishes our gift for imitation, prevents internal access to the phenomenal domain of the social from the participant's perspective. Researchers must make do with the perspective of an observer to whom the social world is given as a meaningless ensemble of experiences, populated by utility-calculating individual subjects. However, researchers also know the historical—indeed, objective—significance of this event, since they possess an insight into the social causes of the process of social regression. They therefore try to develop a method suited to perspicuously depicting the objective meaning of the courses of social action. This is the task that falls to Adorno's ideal-typical construction. By conceptually accentuating particular elements of social reality, this construction creates figures that exemplify the pathology of reason that has arisen through generalized commodity exchange. The heading under which Adorno carries out this program in his writings is a physiognomy of the capitalist form of life.

⊰(II)⊱

According to what has been said so far, what Adorno regularly calls even in social-theoretical contexts an "art of exaggeration" is only the result of ideal-typical concept-formation.[25] Particular features of a given reality are regrouped in a stylized way so that the social pathology of reason is powerfully represented. The idea that such conceptual constructions are a matter of "interpretation," a specific form of understanding, also acquires a precise meaning in this context. As soon as we manage to produce a particular "figure" with this illustrative function, we at the same time achieve an interpretation, since a whole ensemble of practices, attitudes, or rules becomes comprehensible as a symptom of a failed developmental process. All the concepts that run like leitmotifs through Adorno's analysis of capitalism have this kind of interpretive character. A multiplicity of social phenomena are assembled into a closed unity, a "figure" that, by regrouping them, shows that these phenomena are related to the manifestation of a deformation of our original capacity for reason. Adorno's analysis of capitalism is in its bases and its execution a depth hermeneutic of a pathology of human reason. The ideal-typically distilled and enhanced model of behavior represented by action oriented purely toward exchange value is to make comprehensible the extent to which the capitalist way of life has driven our rational capacities toward merely instrumental, egocentric application. Adorno's theory of capitalism may appear singular in this extremely close connection between social analysis and the diagnosis of reason.

This characterization does not yet explain, however, why Adorno himself did not understand his analysis of capitalism as a hermeneutic but, rather, as a physiognomy of our form of life. The ideas of "physiognomy" or the "physiognomic" recur throughout Adorno's work. They turn up in striking places in the interpretation of literature, to a large extent define the analyses of music, and likewise regularly recur in the sociological writings.[26] In the first place, these categories do not say much more than has already been explained with the help of the concepts "objective," "materialistic," and depth hermeneutics—namely, that Adorno's analysis of capitalism essentially consists in the attempt to draw out the fundamental property of our form of life, the social deformation of our rational endowments, by means of a stylized, ideal-typical construction of its surface appearances. But the concept of "physiognomy" also possesses a farther-reaching meaning connected to Adorno's conviction that mental abilities are reflected in the corporal nature of human beings. Gestures, mimicry, modes of practical intercourse in and with the world—all are always as much an expression of the special profile of rational activity as they, in turn, represent reaction formations to the pressures of nature. Because nature and mind are restricted in this way, for Adorno what is needed is an expansion of social analysis beyond its traditional object domain. Not only linguistic utterances or written texts but also the physical form of a way of life as a whole must become the object of an ideal-typical interpretation that seeks to break through the surface appearances to signs of a deformation of our reason. It would therefore be wrong to restrict Adorno's social analysis to his sociological writings in a narrow sense. His diagnosis of a recurrence of ornaments in architecture belong to it, as do his remarks on gestural one-sidedness in *Minima Moralia*.[27] Just as the traditional physiognomist used a template to deduce a person's character traits from his facial features, so the social analyst should approach the physical surfaces of social life with the help of ideal-typical constructions to bring out "figures" that allow a conclusion about the character of our form of life.

Of course, much more definitive than this "physiognomical" feature of his analysis of capitalism remained the intention of constantly applying ideal-typical concept formation in a way that reveals the fundamentally deformed condition of our rational capacity through the stylized phenomena. All the important categories Adorno employs beyond the central ones (capitalism, exchange, utility) are constructed to allow us, through their bundling of individual phenomena, to recognize the extent to which the appearance is a case of making imitative reason impossible. Adorno's analysis of capitalism may well consist in nothing other than the attempt to construct a whole network of such ideal-typical categories, whose interplay can illustrate, to cite Weber, the "idea of capitalistic culture." How Adorno managed to draw out his key sociological categories into a diagnosis of reason can be exemplarily explained with the concepts of "organization" and "collective narcissism."

An initially striking feature of the construction of the concept of "organization," which holds a key place in the categorial network of Adorno's analysis of capitalism, has hitherto received too little consideration: the partial phenomena brought together in the "figure" are introduced as guidelines for an experience that has an irreducibly historical character insofar as they are only meaningful for the present or modernity. The social analyst, who sees the natural relations of capitalism before him, is thus not so alienated from his society that he does not know of its historically particular orientations and expectations. Rather, the findings he must draw together into an illustration of social pathologies always also have an experiential starting point that can only be explained historically. In the case of "organization," Adorno begins with the observation that today the "organizational overshadowing of ever more spheres of life" causes a feeling of powerlessness above all because it collides with the historically grown expectation of individual freedom. Only in a social epoch in which, he writes in nearly word-for-word agreement with Hegel, the "potential" of individual autonomy has become generally "visible" is the spread of bureaucratic organization accompanied by a feeling of growing powerlessness. But two developmental tendencies of modern organization that contribute to this orientation, which enter into the construction of the ideal type, can be explained only with rational-theoretical concepts. On the one hand, the rational goal that setting up an organization as "conscious creation," as technical "instrumental union," was to serve has become less and less clear in the course of mere "functioning," so that it finally becomes detached from its original "legitimizing basis."[28]

Today, Adorno observes, the instrumental "tool" of organization has become an "end in itself" without subjects having a chance to influence or direct it. But only the flipside of this process allows Adorno to arrive at the finding he puts at the center of his category development in order to complete the bridge to the diagnosis of reason. The more the goal takes on a life of its own within organizations, so that mere functioning becomes routine procedure, the clearer becomes their members' tendency to arbitrarily exclude particular groups. "Inherent precisely in all-inclusive organizations," writes Adorno, "is paradoxically the quality of exclusion, particularity. . . . That one can be excluded from an organization belongs as much to the concept of organization as the exclusionary processes bear traces of the domination exercised by group opinion." It is this last phrase that explains why administrative "arbitrariness in regularities" is a symptom of a deformed reason in the first place; for according to Adorno, exclusion rests on a principle that seals itself off against "what does not resemble the prevailing group opinion."[29] Precisely the tendency to exclude the dissimilar is the vanishing point that allows Adorno to sharpen the category of "organization" into a diagnosis of reason. It is precisely the inability to imitate strangers and thus to give up one's own, particular standpoint that marks the distance of prevailing instrumental reason from its original potential. In Adorno's concept of "organization" three phenomena—day-to-day powerlessness, the reversal of means into ends, and the growing tendency to arbitrarily exclude the "dissimilar"—are thus grouped into a single figure, which, through stylization, is to reveal the extent to which our contemporary form of life owes itself to a pathological deformation of human reason.

Adorno's aim of carrying out his analysis of capitalism as a diagnosis of reason through ideal-typical enhancement emerges even more clearly in his social psychology. Here all the central categories based on Freud's psychoanalysis are arranged so that they bring together various modes of behavior and character traits into a single type that demonstrates the regression, based on economic pressures, of the ability to take the other's perspective. This can briefly be illustrated by the concept of "collective narcissism," which plays an essential role in Adorno's late social psychology.[30] As with the concept of "organization," here too Adorno begins from the phenomenon of a mere orientation, for which he again uses expressions like "powerlessness." More forcefully than in other places in his work, however, it becomes clear with collective narcissism that this diffuse mood arises out of concrete experiences of a real loss of autonomy. The evident distress of "technological unemployment," he writes in "Remarks on Politics and Neurosis," "the economic impossibility of mastering life with one's own power," and thus in general the growing feeling "of being superfluous in the dominant social mechanisms,"[31] lead together to a massive feeling of individual powerlessness. If this collective orientation is the first phenomenon taken up in constructing the concept of collective narcissism, the second stems from the social-psychological finding that today in early childhood socialization, the development of stable object relations increasingly goes awry. Instead of flowing into "love for others," libidinal energy is steered toward the ego.[32]

Whatever the empirical soundness of these parts of the concept—and here considerable doubts can certainly be registered—for Adorno they establish the necessary, indeed causal, link between the initial phenomenon and a third element of his social psychology.

Because in the developmental process the ego is experienced as too weak, as powerless, the individual seeks narcissistic "compensation in an omnipotent, bloated collective image that, however, in this deeply resembles his own weak ego." By this, Adorno did not mean subjection to the authoritarian leader of a totalitarian movement but, rather, the mechanism of "stubborn identification" with an "in-group."[33] Thus, again in the concept of collective narcissism, partial phenomena are put together in such a way that as a total figure they allow us to see the intrinsic connection between particular modes of behavior and a deformation of our reason. The tendency to insist on one's own group's convictions through "lack of affect" with regard to others is, in the form of collective narcissism, at the same time the expression of a regression of imitative reason.

Now, it would probably be easy to show the extent to which the other key concepts of the analysis of capitalism represent ideal-typical constructions as guides for illustrating a social pathology of reason. The concepts of the "culture industry" and "half-education," for example, are constructed so that the phenomena they gather are revealed at the last stage as manifestations of how imitative behavior is made impossible.[34] And each time the ideal-typical figures are conceived so that they can be used as pointers for developing empirical hypotheses. Rather than treat further examples, however, in the last section, I briefly discuss how Adorno connected his ideal-typical procedure with evidence of an insuperable potential for resistance.

Adorno never lost sight of the question of whether the pathologies of our living conditions can, despite all the restrictions on our reason, be overcome. To be sure, he always greeted any speculation on real historical transformative powers with great skepticism, since to a certain extent he saw all forms of practice as already permeated by instrumental attitudes.[35] And the category of "context of delusion" [*Verblendungszusammenhang*], which plays a central role in his sociological and topical writings, makes his doubts concerning the chances of collective knowledge of capitalist reality unmistakable. Nevertheless, in many of his works, one often comes upon passages borne by the confidence that subjects can still experience the deformation of their reason in a specific way. The key to this trust in the fundamental ability to experience "reification" is found in Adorno's category of "suffering." Of course, it is no more a merely empirical observational concept than the ideal-typical "figures" treated in the preceding sections.

The concept of suffering that Adorno employed is not meant in the sense of an explicit, linguistically articulated experience; rather, it is "transcendentally" presupposed everywhere there is the justified suspicion that human beings have to experience loss of their distorted self-realization and happiness through the restriction of their rational capacities. Adorno owes the thesis that every restriction on reason, every loss of our rational potentials, implies psychic suffering to Freud's implicit anthropology. Adorno shares Freud's conviction that we are disposed to react to a restriction of our rationality with a somatic feeling of suffering.[36] It is on such feelings, which possess a weak cognitive form as unconscious feelings or "impulses," that Adorno bases his confidence that the failings of the capitalist way of life can still be experienced.

One would look in vain for an express justification of this line of thinking in Adorno's writings, however. There are references to the unavoidability of somatic impulses of suffering in numerous places, but a justification of their normative or social-critical revaluation is always left out. It is therefore the task of a supplementing interpretation to retrospectively provide arguments that can justify the systematic role of the concept of suffering within Adorno's analysis of capitalism. Here it seems advisable to bring increasingly complex presuppositions into play until finally the suspected connection between suffering impulses and resistance can emerge.

The ideal-typical figures of Adorno's analysis of capitalism are regularly interrupted by references to the suffering reactions of subjects. Indeed, according to the interpretation laid out in this essay, it even seems that such references belong to the content of phenomena reconstructed in this way: that, for Adorno, an ideal-typical representation of the capitalist way of life without suffering impulses of this kind would not even be possible. From a methodological point of view, this means that in his montages of groups of phenomena he wants to guard against the impression that the capitalistic organization of life could ever close itself off into a smoothly self-reproducing functional whole. The fact that the functioning of certain manifestations of capitalism is just as "typical" as the suffering they generate should mean that, to the contrary, the reproduction of this society necessarily always produces defensive reactions and discontent. To be able to go from this observation to asserting the ability of subjects to resist, however, Adorno has to charge his concept of "suffering impulses" with additional meanings that by no means belong to conventional linguistic usage. It must be shown that these kinds of impulses possess a cognitive content whose kernel consists in the intention or desire to overcome the pathological life conditions. In my view, Adorno manages to enrich his concept of suffering by imperceptibly equipping it with components of Freud's psychoanalysis. Owing to this categorial supercharging, suffering as an impulse with which subjects react to capitalist living condition becomes the prereflective desire to be freed from conditions that fetter our potential for imitative reason.

Adorno must interpretively deepen the concept of "suffering" in two analytically distinct ways in order to arrive at this conclusion. First, he is forced to give the impulsive reaction he designates as suffering a cognitive content that contains the perception of a restriction of reason. Like the neurotic symptom in Freud, these kinds of suffering impulses as a whole must be equipped with a prereflexive consciousness, a sense of the fact that the exercise of rationality is restricted or blocked.[37] Adorno expresses this first step in the formulation that every bodily impulse possesses an "internal" form of reflection: "The physical moment [of suffering] tells our knowledge that suffering ought not to be, that things should be different."[38] This sentence already anticipates the second step Adorno must have taken in order to be able to construct an immanent connection between "suffering impulses" and subjective resistance: the feeling of pain must rudimentarily include both the knowledge that one's own potential for reason can only be realized in a restricted way and, at the same time, the wish to be freed from this felt deformation. Here, too, Adorno implicitly follows Freud by taking over his idea that neurotic suffering motivates a "need for recovery."[39] Transferred to the critique of capitalism within which Adorno speaks of the "suffering" of subjects, the result of this line of thinking is that the negative feelings of a deformation of reason always bring with them a wish to be freed from social pathologies. To this extent, to put it more strongly, suffering impulses guarantee subjects' ability to resist the instrumental demands of the capitalist form of life.

At this point of his interpretation of capitalism, Adorno brings to bear yet another thought that shows up everywhere he speaks emphatically of childhood. Adorno assumes, as we have seen, that human reason develops by way of childlike imitation of loved ones; only the mimetic imitation of the other's perspective affords the young child the opportunity to decenter his own perspective to the point that it outweighs his own, and he can thus forge ahead to rational judgments on states of affairs. Now, Adorno seems to assume that these early childhood experiences, in which our thinking develops through love, have a continued existence as trace memories through the socially compelled instrumentalization of our minds. Even the adult who acts in total conformity with the instrumental pressures of the capitalist form of life retains a weak memory of the origins of his thinking in early moments of empathy and care. It is a residuum of experience of this kind on which Adorno in different places bases his confidence that, despite their deludedness, subjects still possess an interest in the liberation of their reason. The memory of childhood can, in the midst of all instrumental ways of life, always awaken the desire to be freed from the social restrictions imposed on our mental capacities. If this is the decisive thought that lies buried behind Adorno's defiant confidence, his physiognomy of the capitalist form of life is anchored in a normative picture of childhood.[40]

FIVE

PERFORMING JUSTICE

Adorno's Introduction to *Negative Dialectics*

Anyone who reads the introduction to *Negative Dialectics* will quickly
ascertain what Adorno has in mind when he speaks of his text as a
"web" or a music-like "composition" (21/44).[1] The roughly fifty-page
chapter has no derivation of a thesis, no step-by-step exposition and
justification. Rather, it presents itself as an artfully woven net of a
few, constantly varied thought motifs. If it were not enough that
there seems to be no rising line of argumentation, the flow of text is
barely graphically interrupted. Altogether in just three places are
larger spaces left between the very long paragraphs, suggesting a
certain new beginning. Even in its external appearance, the introduction thus resembles less a scholarly text than a piece of modern
prose. The sentences constantly repeat the same few basic ideas,
varying them with ever-new nuances, without justifying a thesis or
advancing an argument.

A text with these properties presents a nearly insuperable challenge for the commentator. As soon as one tries to work an argument out of the compositional web, no small part of the expressive
character of the substance of what is presented is lost. Conversely,
every attempt to do justice to the style of the text in commentary in
the end empties into mere paraphrase. In view of this difficult situation, it may seem advisable to give up any respect for the aesthetic
qualities of the introduction and to treat it in as sober and discursive

a manner as any other philosophical work. Such a procedure consciously risks a certain hermeneutic carelessness by heedlessly pulling apart what Adorno artfully brings together in a synthesis in each paragraph. Proceeding in this way, three isolable theses can be distinguished in Adorno's introduction that are justified with different arguments in different places.

First, Adorno claims that today it is necessary to move from the Hegelian dialectic to a new form of dialectics he calls "negative." Second, he supposes that this new, historically necessary form of dialectics will better do justice to the "object of knowledge," as well as the "subject of knowledge." Third, he believes that only such a method of philosophical thinking can assume the function of critically transcending the social conditions of the present. Of course, this sequence does not correspond to the order in which the theses logically depend on one another. Indeed, atmospherically and quantitatively in the introduction, the thesis of the necessity of a transition to negative dialectics has the greatest weight, but understanding it assumes the last thesis concerning the function and task of critical philosophy in the present. Thus, in my reconstruction, I follow this "logical" sequence by presenting Adorno's definition of the tasks of the philosophy in the present (section I), then turn to his representation of negative in contrast to "positive" dialectics (section II) in order finally to outline the further, essentially stylistic consequences of the new concept of dialectics (section III).

Before we can even begin to peel away the individual argumentative layers of the introduction, we need to recall briefly the context and aims of *Negative Dialectics*. Adorno must already have been engaged with plans to write a philosophical justification of the methodological procedure of his work since the early 1950s and his return from exile. Here he apparently had in mind the difficulties many of his writings had being understood, insofar as they asserted subjective feelings as self-evident in the analysis of texts or concrete states of affairs. The attempt to reach generally valid statements about facts and norms by articulating purely individual experiences probably represented the essence of Adorno's philosophical method from the beginning. As he began assembling sketches and outlines for a book with the title *Negative Dialectics* in the late 1950s, he thus had in mind providing a comprehensive justification for this idiosyncratic procedure. In the finished work that finally appeared in 1966, he shows, in three parts dealing with classic problematics of the tradition, the extent to which the necessary "concretion" in philosophy can only be achieved by way of a negatively composed dialectic.

Now, as concerns the fifty-page introduction to the text, it is not at all easy to get a clear idea of its intention or aim. The short prologue does say that it is to lay out the concept of "philosophical experience" (2/10), but this does not begin to cover the huge number of themes and reflections that are broached here in a peculiarly elliptical way. If we disregard Adorno's definition of his task, which seems a bit willful, the impression arises that here an anticipation of the intention and meaning of a negative dialectics is provided in advance of its concrete realization. This is supported not only by the fact that through its labyrinthine paths the text already collects all the elements necessary for a justification of the procedure but also that, in a certain way, it itself already practices this procedure in the form of its presentation. To this extent, it may make sense to understand the introduction as at once a justification and a presentation of Adorno's philosophical methodology.

All the arguments Adorno adduces in the course of his text for the necessity of such a new procedure in the end have their basis in a particular view of the current tasks of philosophy. Of course, he far from systematically defines a task in this kind, let alone presents it as a basis for further analyses. But the fact that the very first sentence of the introduction touches on reflections of this kind nonetheless supports the idea that they have a kind of argumentative priority. Adorno combines a "social-historical" with a philosophical-historical reason when he comes to speak of the transformed role of philosophy in the present. The historical reflection that, as mentioned, appears in an early version right at the beginning of the text refers with an obvious allusion to Marx to the missed moment of a "realization" of philosophy (3/15). Here

Adorno leaves open what exactly is to be understood by such a "realization," but the context makes it clear that he means the nonoccurrence of a social revolution that could have transformed social reality into the ideal of a society free of domination described by Marx. From this failure and still in the same context, Adorno draws the consequence that philosophy must change its role because it can no longer claim to contribute to the rationalization of the world. "After philosophy broke with the promise that it would be one with reality or at least struck just before the hour of its production," it must, as he puts it, "ruthlessly criticize itself" (3/15).

Nevertheless, the justification introduced is surely too narrow a basis for this important conclusion. For why should the historical fact that a single philosophical project (left-Hegelianism) has failed in its attempt to practically realize reason make it necessary for philosophy as a whole in the future to restrict itself to pure self-criticism? Adorno seems to want to force on the entire discipline of philosophy a conclusion that at best applies only to the singular tradition of the left students of Hegel. Probably to close these sensitive justificatory gaps, in connection with his first, historical argument, Adorno always brings into play another consideration that can best be called "philosophical-historical." The substance of this line of thought can already be found in his 1931 inaugural lecture,[2] but what is laid out there as a critical review of contemporary (German) philosophy is here presented in its own right as a mere reminder of a generally familiar logic of philosophical development.

According to this view, Hegel's system represents at once the zenith and the turning point of the history of philosophical system-building, since on the one hand it represents its immanent claim to conceptually penetrate the whole of reality in its clearest and most audacious form, while on the other it fails so dramatically that all subsequent approaches have to be understood as ways out of the "crisis of Idealism." Were the introduction's numerous excurses in the history of philosophy compiled, together they would yield precisely this picture of a movement that turns on the point of Hegel's failure and now, instead of ever more comprehensive knowledge of the totality, approaches the most precise possible disclosure of concrete phenomena. In his text, Adorno thus presents Bergson,

Husserl, and Sartre (6/20, 6/21, 30–31/59–60), whose philosophical approaches appear to him as failed attempts to obtain direct access to reality that is as conceptually undistorted as possible in reaction to rational Idealism.

These fragmentary sketches of a history of philosophy are connected to the first, social-historical argument insofar as they make the failure of the Marxian ideal of revolution into the fateful moment of all philosophical endeavors that are to be taken seriously. The nonoccurrence of revolution draws the final line, not only under all projects to improve the world but also under that of the desire internal to all philosophy to date to mold reality according to the standpoint of the knowledge of reason. Essentially, Adorno does not let even a systematic gap emerge between Hegel and Marx, since the latter's revolutionary purposes only put into practice the goal of giving reason form in reality. Thus, the failure of the revolution seals the fate of all efforts flowing out of Hegel's system to conceptually grasp the whole of the world.

Now, in the introduction, all these scattered reflections according to which the real, classical idea of philosophy has reached its negative consummation in Hegel and Marx have the sole function of allowing the conclusion that Adorno is after from the beginning. If the philosophical project of realizing reason has failed practically as well as theoretically, according to the thought repeated many times in the text, philosophy must in the future restrict itself to mere self-criticism, since only in this way can it remain faithful to its own concept. There is, of course, in the step thus outlined also an essentialist strain that characterizes Adorno's understanding of philosophy as a whole. Anyone who is not convinced that all philosophical efforts revolve in the end around aligning concept and actuality, spirit and reality, will accordingly also not share the conclusion from its failure that it must restrict itself to the critical investigation of all conceptual claims. But Adorno believes that since Hegel's downfall, sealed by Marx, there is no longer any way open to philosophy other than the self-criticism of its previous presuppositions. He holds neither the postmetaphysical naturalization of Hegel or Kant[3] nor the reconstruction of a parsimonious concept of rationality[4] but only the uncovering of the principled limits to all conceptual endeavors to still be philosophically possible after the failure of rational Idealism.

This program is not as narrow and one-dimensional as the category of "self-criticism" may make it appear, however. Adorno has in mind less a simple investigation of the epistemological reasons for the failure in principle of all conceptual knowledge of totality than that self-criticism itself should once again be given a systematic point by, reversing Hegel's procedure, being carried out as a "negative" dialectic. The sketch of the idea this implies represents the core of the introduction to *Negative Dialectics*.

Adorno seeks to carry out the self-criticism of philosophy that has become necessary in the form of a negative dialectic. The presupposition of this strategy is the assumption that Hegel's system represents not just any escalation or high point but the real culmination of all philosophical endeavors. For without a premise of this kind, he could not justify why the self-criticism of philosophy should specifically take the form of a negatively applied dialectic—and not, for instance, the form of a therapeutic liberation from the pictures that hold us captive (Wittgenstein) or a critique of all statements that cannot be verified (the Vienna Circle). Adorno, who was well aware of precincts of this kind, seeks a self-critical turn of the dialectic because for him it in a certain way makes up the essence of all philosophy, all endeavors to grasp reality as a rational whole.[5] But wherein lies the peculiarity of such a negative dialectic that claims to be the appropriate shape of a self-criticism of philosophy?

The first step Adorno undertakes to introduce the program of a negative dialectics has only an indirect character and consists in distinguishing as precisely as possible the systematic properties of all positive dialectics. This attempt to determine the terminal form of Hegelian philosophy, closed in on itself, runs like a red thread through Adorno's whole work.[6] In the introduction, Adorno repeats only what he had already explicated in other places as the system character of absolute Idealism. As soon as the dialectical method—namely, the proof of the "insufficiency" of a conceptual determination with regard to the object to be grasped—is practiced with the goal of demonstrating that the whole of reality is rationally constituted, it is compelled to exclude "everything qualitatively divergent" (4/17) and becomes a closed system. Adorno is thus not convinced that this tendency to conceptual truncation and closure is internal to the use of dialectics as such. Rather, it is only driven or provoked to it when, as he puts it, it is used with the aim of "thinking," of capturing reality, since with this "the appearance of identity" goes along with "thinking according to its purest form" (4, trans. modified/17). To this extent, Adorno distinguishes between a problematic application of dialectics he often calls "positive" or "idealistic," and an appropriate "negative" application. The use that is undertaken with the aim of the rational determination of reality is positive, while the negative use is free from such "identifying" aims.

Before asking what can be envisaged under the procedure of a dialectics determined in this way, two further considerations Adorno enlists with regard to positive dialectics should first be mentioned. It should already be clear from what has been said so far that his concept of such a positive dialectics is very comprehensive and by no means restricted to the Hegelian system. For him, it seems to be the case that any use of the dialectical method that is not based on the insufficiency of conceptual determinations but, instead, takes it as the occasion for an alignment of concept and reality that presses ever further can be called positive. It should therefore be no surprise that Adorno does not see an alternative to the idealistic figure of dialectics in its "materialist" turn, since in both cases the attempt is made to rationally penetrate the world. As he brusquely puts it in one passage, the "nonidealistic form" of dialectics "degenerated in the meantime into dogma just as the idealistic ones degenerated into a mere token of education" (5, trans. modified/19).

Of special significance for what is then called "negative" dialectics is another of Adorno's reflections concerning the system character of positive dialectics. In a central passage of the introduction (13–14/31–32), there is an attempt to explain the penchant for system building, and thus the dialectical penetration of reality, genealogically. Here, with a cursory reference to Nietzsche (13/31), Adorno develops proposals for how such a totalizing use of dialectics can be understood on the basis of certain archaic drives. The content of the explanation—which in the end boils down to the thesis already put forth in the *Dialectic of Enlightenment* that the systematic need for complete knowledge of reality is due to an atavistic "rage at the victim" (14/33)[7]—is of less interest than the fact of its detailed consideration, which takes up several pages. Perhaps it is justified to see in this an indication of the circumstance that Adorno understood such a genealogical demonstration as an immanent component of his own procedure. A negative dialectic must then, unlike its positive alterative, always attempt to bring to light the preintellectual, drivelike, or practical roots of all spiritual phenomena.[8]

This supposition is confirmed when we turn to the reflections Adorno devotes to the procedure of negative dialectics itself. So far, we can only infer from the opposition to positive dialectics that here the demonstration of the insufficiency of conceptual determination must be assessed not as a deficit that can be overcome but as a real result. In a certain way, thought should not seek to expel the finding of this disproportion; rather, it must try to fathom its consequences for its own position in the world. Naturally, this starting point presupposes some assumptions about the existence of a linguistically or intellectually unmediated "given"; without a premise of this kind, Adorno could not claim that we have knowledge of an insuperable disproportion between concept and object, thought and thing. Nevertheless, one searches the introduction in vain for arguments for this far-reaching thesis, which has been discussed again and again since Kant. Instead, Adorno seems to trust in the intuition that we must get into a position of complete immanence with respect to our linguistic or intellectual operations if we do not somehow presuppose the givenness of an independent world.[9] If this were not enough, Adorno goes beyond asserting an immediate givenness by repeatedly interspersing hints about its rudimentary properties. This objective world, for whose cognitive apprehension the concept proves to be inadequate or "insufficient," is to possess the character of a sum of qualitative "individuals," "particulars," or "heterogeneities" (for example, 6/20, 7/23, 8/25).

Of course, Adorno is cautious enough not to engage in further determinations of these presupposed givens. But it nonetheless remains unclear in his argumentation whether he would like to understand their designation as something qualitatively individual in the sense of an epistemologically unavoidable limit or as an ontological characterization. In any case, this assumed "nonconceptual" (8/24) or "nonidentical" (9/25) forms the first reference point in view of which Adorno positively elucidates his idea of negative dialectics. In his own words, there is the thought that once the philosophical premise of an identity between rationality and reality is dropped, there is a completely transformed relation to the "object."

Much of what Adorno accomplishes in this context has already been indirectly mentioned or arises from it as an immediate consequence. If the starting point of negative dialectics is the idea of taking the individual object as infinitely more complex and heterogeneous than any of its potential concepts, then, for Adorno, the position of thought changes with respect to its object. The latter can no longer be intellectually subsumed under a single "scheme" (9/25) or categorially tailored to a particular standpoint but, rather, when possible, registered in as many of its aspects and qualities as the indispensable "medium of conceptual reflection" allows (9/25). It is not easy to envisage more precisely what kind of modification in our cognitive attitude a change of this kind would involve. If one draws together Adorno's different formulations in the introduction, however, and also takes into consideration how strongly he sometimes tends toward normative phrases—"do justice to" (26/53)— the impression soon arises that for him it is a matter of determining intellectual or epistemological virtues. Something should change, not with the substance of the process of knowledge itself or with its dependency on a linguistic medium but, rather, with the orientation or attitude with which we perform it. We are to devote our cognitive attention, instead of to purposefully attaining results, as completely as possible to precisely apprehending all the qualitative properties that may otherwise still inhere in the object. The normatively colored expressions Adorno uses for the epistemic virtue of concentration on the object include "differentiation" (28, trans. modified/55), "nonviolence" (27/53), "precision" (32/62), and, again and again in the text, "intellectual experience."

The suggestion that we understand the transformed relation to the object as the virtue of a strongly receptive attitude that is open to different aspects goes along with the vehemence with which Adorno criticizes all attempts to place the process of knowledge itself on a completely other basis that is independent of language. Not only here in the introduction but in the most varied places in his work, he holds out Bergson's intuitionism as the most striking example of this false sublation of the classical model of knowledge. Bergson had indeed correctly and skillfully outlined the inadequacies of a conceptual knowledge that always remains dependent on abstraction, but he drew from this the completely misleading consequence of delivering knowledge over to an irrational source, intuition. For every "cognition," as Adorno continues decisively, "requires the rationality which he [Bergson] so despised, precisely if it is ever to be concretized" (6, trans. modified/20). But if this is so, if every cognitive achievement remains dependent on the medium of linguistic rationality, then the altered relation to the object can only consist in bringing a higher degree of responsiveness, differentiation, and precision to achieving conceptual knowledge. And, accordingly, what Adorno says about the role of the "nonidentical" in negative dialectics goes beyond recommending an intellectual attitude in which greater attention is given to the qualitative horizon of any object.

Now, Adorno draws conclusions from the negative turn of dialectics not only for the relation to the object but also with regard to the knowing subject. The altered kind of self-relation that has to follow from the insight into the insufficiency in principle of conceptual knowledge is the second positive theme of his demonstrations. To be sure, the transformations Adorno has in mind are much more comprehensive and complex than those he depicted with regard to the object to be known. It may be due to the greater accessibility of individual self-experience that here the yield of the analysis proves to be so much more differentiated and fertile. First, the fact that the prospect of conceptually penetrating reality is given up results in a tendency to decenter subjectivity. The subject that no longer believes it is able to conceptually appropriate the world conversely knows itself to be codetermined by it and must therefore forfeit a part of its previously assumed sovereignty. Adorno finds a series of different formulations for this structural transformation of subjectivity (17/38, 24/49, 26/52) that all flow into the idea that, with the turn to negative dialectics, the subject loses its capacity for autonomously making meaning. Instead, since it always presupposes a piece of ungrasped reality, the subject "becomes aware of itself as something mediated" (24/49). "Decentering," an expression Adorno does not use in the introduction, thus means two things here: on the one hand, that the subject can no longer grasp itself as the center of reality in the sense of its conceptual constitution; on the other hand, that as a result of this loss, it must learn to understand itself much more from the outside, from the conceptually unmediated world.

The already mentioned thought that, according to Adorno, a genealogical level of reflection always belongs to the performance of negative dialectics also falls in the context of this second meaning of "decentering." As soon as the subject is required to grasp things more from the periphery of its conceptually undisclosed environment, it must also at the same time become aware of the origins of its own thought in the "preintellectual" (14/33). For the real source of all our convictions and ideas lies, as Adorno repeatedly asserts bringing together Nietzsche and Freud,[10] in the prerational layer of cathexis, early-childhood fears, and longings. To this extent, the genealogical intuition according to which the provenance of our intellectual achievements dwells in deeper, drive-dynamic layers of our life is an immanent component of the insight into the insufficiency in principle of all conceptual operations.

Only the next step in the argument, however, represents the real explosive core of the reflections Adorno devotes to the transformed position of the subject in the world. To this point, his observations have still moved through familiar terrain. The thought of a decentering of the subject had come into the world a considerable time before Adorno through psychoanalysis and the theory of language, while the idea of a genealogical revision of our rational achievements goes back to Nietzsche.[11] Where Adorno now goes far beyond the insights of these currents is the paradoxical-sounding claim that precisely from the decentering of the subject must follow its revaluation as the decisive medium of all objective knowledge. The sensitivity of the disempowered subject is, on this line of thinking, the epistemological guarantee that the qualitative properties of the object will be perceived. Adorno apparently conceives of this connection, which constitutes the core of his reflections on the changed position of the subject, as follows: As soon as the subject has seen that it is not in a position to rationally penetrate reality, it at the same time attains through the loss of its meaning-giving sovereignty a new "uninhibitedness" in its trust in its own experiences. For now, released from the compulsion to unify its knowledge, it can pursue all the stirrings of its senses triggered by the uncontrollable world of objects and events in an open and differentiated way. This growth of differentiation and sensitivity leads the subject to develop the precision in registering its perceptions that is the precondition for an experience of the "nonidentical," qualitative horizon of all objects. Thus, from the subject's loss of sovereignty that goes with the turn to negative dialectics follows the revaluation of its subjective experience as a central medium of knowledge (26/52).

It is clear that Adorno brings precisely this argument into play to justify his own procedure of systematically using subjective experience. If, indeed, it is the case that the qualitative, essential properties of reality can be apprehended more clearly the more strongly their resonances are registered in individual feeling, then all serious knowledge requires the methodological inclusion of subjectivity: "In sharp contrast to the usual scientific ideal, the objectivity of dialectical cognition needs the subject more, not less" (25/50). Accordingly, along with a genealogical level of reflection, the procedure of negative dialectics always also includes a layer of argumentation on which the phenomenon to be dealt with is presented in light of its effects on the subjective sensitivity of the individual researcher. Only through this thematization of subjective experiences, Adorno is convinced, is the object presented in its factual objectivity, since qualitative properties also belong to it that are accessible only to differentiated experience, not to the schematizing concept.

Obviously, with this inclusion of individual experiences, the possibility of subjective arbitrariness enters into the cognitive process, and Adorno is also clear about its dangers. The ideal of scientific objectivity seems for good reasons to be tied to the precondition of neutralizing subjectivity, since only such precautions can vouchsafe the general verifiability of statements. If we drop the barriers to adding individual impressions and feelings, on the conventional view, knowledge loses its truth claim, since it becomes the mere plaything of subjective opinions. Adorno makes an argument against this scientific ideal that depends on a combination of epistemological and moral considerations (26–27/50–51).

We have just seen the epistemological consideration, which bears more weight. It says that the subjective impressions and sensations an object triggers in the subject of knowledge necessarily belong to an appropriate representation of any given object. Nevertheless, we have also seen that Adorno only grants such subjective experiences knowledge value when they are sufficiently differentiated, precise, and lucid. Accordingly, he can only ascribe the capacity for truthful, comprehensive knowledge to those subjects who possess a sensorium that corresponds to standards of this kind. Adorno defends himself against the objection that this social limitation entails the danger of an "undemocratic" elitism with a moral argument (26/51). Those who possess a sufficiently differentiated capacity for experience have the duty or task to name the properties of objects that are only given subjectively, "representative[ly]" (26/51). With a certain sense for stylization, this argument can be understood as a plea for an advocatory epistemology:

> To those who have the undeserved good fortune not to be completely adjusted in their inner intellectual composition to the prevailing norms . . . it is incumbent to make the moral and, as it were, representative effort to express what the majority, for whom they say it, are not capable of seeing or, to do justice to reality, will not allow themselves to see. The criterion of truth is not its immediate communicability to everyone. (26–27, trans. modified/51)

Of course, this line of thought depends on a premise that cannot be further vetted here—namely, the sociological claim that the majority of subjects, owing to tendencies toward a loss of personality, are no longer capable of qualitative, attentive experience. If this presupposition is conceded—though little speaks for it empirically—it may seem to make complete sense to grant only sufficiently sensitive people a right to representatively articulate contexts of reality that are accessible only to differentiated experience.[12]

With this reference to the epistemological value of privileged experiences, we have stepped outside the circle of implications that Adorno sees connected with the expression "negative dialectics." As soon as we achieve the insight into the insufficiency of conceptual determinations, along with the altered conception of the object and the decentering of the subject, the relation to knowledge as a whole changes. The subject aware of its "preintellectual," natural origins would bring so much trust to its own experiences of its environment that it would be able to perceive the multiplicity of aspects in which objects are significant that remained hidden behind conceptual onesidedness under the domination of positive dialectics.

Adorno draws consequences from the turn to negative dialectics not only for redetermining cognitive relations but also for the way that philosophy as a whole is presented. The considerations he devotes to this nexus of the style of philosophical argumentation together represent the third thesis that can be discovered in the text of the introduction. There are two primary themes that Adorno discusses in relevant passages: he is preoccupied with the questions of, on the one hand, the language to be used to describe a self-criticism of philosophy with the form of a negative dialectic and, on the other, the form in which a theory of this kind is to be carried out. For the solution of each problem, there is in the text of the introduction a corresponding concept that makes it possible to get an overview. The terms adduced for the language of negative dialectics are "expression and stringency" (12/29), whereas its form of presentation is called "model analysis" (18/39).

Simply the connection of the two opposed concepts "expression" and "stringency" makes it clear that Adorno seeks to determine the character of his philosophical language out of the same principle that guided his reflections on knowledge. Just as any real knowledge must include the resonance of the object in subjective experience, so in his view must philosophical language not lack the element of subjectivity. When it is experienced "in the closest contact" (11/29), the object compels an affective response in the subject that achieves "expression," or presentation in the expressive level of language. Of course, this moment of expression cannot gain the upper hand within philosophical language, since, according to Adorno, it would then degenerate into the mere bearer of a "point of view" (12/29). Rather, its expressive element always requires control through an effort of theoretical exactitude, vouched for in the text by the concept of "stringency." Adorno is thus convinced that philosophy finds the appropriate language when subjective feeling still resonates in the chosen concept without impairing its capacity to precisely determine states of affairs, and the formulation he enlists for this stylistic ideal accordingly speaks of a synthesis of "expression and stringency." Whether Adorno himself satisfies these demands in the language of his negative dialectics—whether in his own terminology he is, in fact, able to fuse expressive content and objective determinacy—is a not a question to debate here. There is no doubt, however, that in the following text he is always concerned to expose the expressive content of the central concepts of the philosophical tradition that attest to the emotional affects that have flowed into them.

In a certain way, this last reference already says something about the form of presentation in which Adorno would like to put forth the development of his *Negative Dialectics*. To this point, we know from the introduction only what reflective levels a thus transformed dialectics should be able to include. And in reading the introduction, we have of course experienced how it proceeds, not in the usual form of a linear presentation of arguments but in the idiosyncratic form of an ellipse, so that all the considerations brought forth seem to stand equally near to an intellectual center. But the introduction should also convey, only by way of anticipation, the idea of a negative dialectics; possibly completely different interpretive principles are to apply to it than underlie the main part of the book, the carrying out of the program. So how does Adorno present the performance of a self-criticism of philosophy that has the form of a negative dialectics?

The idea Adorno follows in answering this question is that of "model analysis," or a "model of thinking" (18/39). Both concepts signify first of all that "models" are to show how the operation of negative dialectics is to be performed. And "model" here probably means that in exemplary cases of philosophically central ideas it is shown how differently the phenomena they grasp present themselves when they are disclosed not from the perspective of total conceptual mediation but with the guide of conceptual insufficiency. Nonetheless, in the text it remains relatively unclear how we are to envisage the carrying out of such model analyses in detail. Only a few hints are given that can be understood as elucidations of a concrete procedure (18/39–40). Probably here, too, Adorno holds to the Hegelian maxim, according to which the method underlying principles can only be revealed in the implementation itself. All the same, if we recall what has been said so far, we can discern in broad outline what such model analyses have to contribute as ways of performing negative dialectics.

As a self-critique of philosophy, model analyses never apply to a phenomenon itself but only to its philosophically inherited formulation. Since the way a particular state of affairs has been conceptually mediated within system thinking is condensed in ideas of this kind, they form an exemplary starting point for a dialectic that proceeds negatively. By understanding the conceptual syntheses with which the corresponding state of affairs is determined in the philosophical system, the critical procedure must then transcend the traditional determinations in the direction of extraconceptual components—the nonidentical—in at least two places. First, the negative analysis can follow the conceptual mediation of a phenomenon back to the point at which its rootedness in "preintellectual" responses and cathexes appears genealogically. In this way, it can become clear that philosophical ideas do not belong to an autarchic, independent sphere of human rational achievements but, rather, result from the hitherto inscrutable impetus of human beings' natural impulses. Second, the critical procedure can pursue the conceptual mediations of a phenomenon to the point where its qualitative properties start to emerge in the resonances of subjective experience. In this way, too, it becomes clear to what extent the usual determination has cut off the nonmediable peripheral zones of the state of affairs by reducing it to the conceptual.

These two transcending movements together probably form the basic content of what Adorno calls "model analysis." It is to show exemplarily in particular cases to what extent the conceptual determinations of central ideas of the philosophical tradition do not do justice to the intended state of affairs because they deny their origin in situations of originary drive satisfaction, as well as qualities that are only accessible subjectively. In its performance, negative dialectics thus only lines up thought models of this kind; it is, as Adorno puts it, "an ensemble of model-analyses" (18/39). Nonetheless, by performing such analyses, a normative intention unfolds whose content Adorno describes in his introduction with the concept of "reconciliation": the practice of "negative dialectics" tries to thematize indirectly in the phenomena "what, though its preparation to the object, was lost" (13/31), "restituting to the pieces" (13/31) the wrong that identity-thinking has inflicted on them. To this extent, as Adorno must probably be understood here, the practice of the dialectical self-critique of philosophy is always also the practice of a restitutional justice.

SIX

SAVING THE SACRED WITH
A PHILOSOPHY OF HISTORY

On Benjamin's "Critique of Violence"

Like many of Walter Benjamin's texts, this essay is of highly vex-
ing subtlety because in the course of the argumentation, without
any noticeable transition, it carries out what begins with a sober, almost academic central question as a religious meditation. Written
at the turn of 1922,[1] at a time when the twenty-eight-year-old author
was still strongly under the influence of reading Ernst Bloch's *Spirit
of Utopia*,[2] the study apparently takes up a question that preoccupied many of his contemporaries in the immediate aftershocks of
the Russian and German revolutions. What kind of legitimacy, so
the central challenge for legal theory and political philosophy
at the beginning of the Weimar Republic ran, could violence claim
that arose outside of all contexts of constitutional justification
in revolutionary uprisings? Benjamin does not restrict himself to
the narrow circle of the more or less legal-philosophical questions
connected with this, however, but exceeds them within a few pages
in the direction of a completely different problematic he calls
"philosophico-historical" (238).[3]

His real theme, clearly, is not the place of violence in modern law.
Moreover, he does not simply concern himself with the question of
the violence of law, which he takes to be self-evidently answered in
the positive. In the end, what occupies him is a source and form of
violence that is of such a revolutionary kind that it can prepare an

end for the violent institution of law as a whole. As the text soon reveals, for Benjamin, the only candidate for the basis and origin of such a transforming violence is the God of the monotheistic—indeed, Judeo-Christian—tradition. Thus, the essay "On the Critique of Violence" is, not unlike so many of his earlier and later writings, a religio-philosophical tract.

The essay's intellectual beginnings fall in the period in which Benjamin, having successfully completed his dissertation, was urgently concerned with finding an appropriate place in the intellectual life of Germany. As a result not just of his regular changes of residence—in 1919, he still lived in Bern; that winter, in Vienna; in 1920, he returned to Berlin—but also his professional insecurity, no clearly discernible lines of attack can be made out in the new graduate's projects. Thus open to most disparate developmental impressions, as would remain the case throughout his life, Benjamin worked on a detailed, unfortunately lost review of *The Spirit of Utopia*, wrote the essay on "Fate and Character" during a short vacation in Lugano, and probably toyed with the first thoughts of founding a journal.[4] Nevertheless, out of this multiplicity of activities, a comprehensive, more compact project seems to have taken form whose basic theme was to be politics. In any case, Benjamin informed his friend Gershom Scholem of plans of this kind in letters, referred to initial sketches, and, through occasional references to books he was reading, let the intellectual outline of the whole be glimpsed.[5] Of the three manuscripts on which Benjamin reported to Scholem in connection with this project, however, only one, the essay "On the Critique of Violence," was preserved by publication. The other two, the first and shorter of which was to be devoted to "Life and Violence" and the second and longer to "Politics," can be counted as lost.[6]

To answer the question of the theoretical interest with which Benjamin set about composing his essay, we must cast a brief look at his intellectual self-understanding at the time. The student had already definitively split from Gustav Wyneken, his model and teacher from the time of the youth movement, for political reasons at the beginning of World War I. The central place the reformist educator had occupied in Benjamin's intellectual network had without doubt been taken up by the powerful figure of Gershom Scholem. But Benjamin's turn to the political left had no more brought about a renunciation of the "religious decisionism" that stamped his intellectual youth than had his split from Wyneken.[8] He continued to believe that the collapse of the present into mere mean-ends thinking could only be opposed if the inner-worldly presence of a noninstrumental, divine being could be credibly demonstrated. Indeed, the two motifs that flowed together in this religiously based cultural critique had frequently acquired new accents in the course of Benjamin's student life, but they remained the fixed points of his thinking. Dealing with social reality, especially with the state of culture, had, on the one hand, led him to the conviction that what fundamentally ailed contemporary society was treating all its affairs from the perspective of means-ends calculation. This diagnosis stood opposed, on the other hand, to the therapeutic intuition that these instrumentalized relations could only be burst open by identifying cultural images that, in their reflexive self-referentiality, resembled God in their sovereign withdrawal from all instrumentality.[9] It is this second motif that explains the striking discontinuity that characterized the thought of the maturing Benjamin far beyond his student days. The fixation on the thought that the overcoming of the encrusted present was to be expected only from the sphere of the intrinsic, and to that extent divine, must have driven him to ever-new attempts to get hold of a sphere with these properties. In this way, the young author first developed language as a medium that could bear traits of the self-revelation of God before then turning to literature and literary criticism to find related characteristics. And it is more than mere speculation to surmise that it was in the field of politics that Benjamin now made the third stage along this intellectual path.

This vague conjecture can be further narrowed down if we take account of the domain of scholarly literature to which Benjamin increasingly turned after the end of World War I. In the letters he regularly sent to his friends Scholem and Ernst Schoen between 1918 and 1921, along with literary works and Bloch's *Spirit of Utopia*, we find reference above all to three authors whose field of influence lay nearer or farther to the domain of political theory: Charles Péguy,[10]

Georges Sorel,[11] and Erich Unger.[12] If the latter is as good as forgotten today, the writings of the two others are still of more than merely historical interest. Péguy, initially a socialist, later a patriotically disposed Catholic, recently achieved a late fame; his penetrating contributions have been regarded as a valuable building block for a theory of the public significance of religion.[13] For a time, he maintained lively contact with Sorel, whose writings met with steady interest throughout the whole of the twentieth century, based on their common enthusiasm for the heroic energy of the masses.[14]

The books of these three authors Benjamin enthusiastically encountered are united by their tendency to hold the concept of politics as far as possible from the pursuit of interests so as to equip it with the potential to radically disclose new intellectual and moral orders. Decisive differences emerge between them with regard to the question of what can count as the source of such an explosive power of the political. For Sorel, it is the pictorial ideas of a just future that, as revolutionary energies, fire political action,[15] while Péguy sees resources of this kind in mystical religious experience.[16] But, according to Isaiah Berlin's felicitous formulation, it can be claimed that despite all their differences, the three authors agree on an "anti-utilitarianism" that seeks to grasp the political more as the expression of a visionary morality than as a means to an end.[17] And it must have been this common intention to pry the political from the grasp of the means-end schema that aroused Benjamin's interest after the end of World War I.

Of course, his enthusiasm for these political writings may not have been limited to their common opposition to utilitarianism. In line with the reflection Benjamin had pursued at the end of 1918 in his "Program of the Coming Philosophy,"[18] it also lay in the three authors' attempts to localize the noninstrumental character of the political in a domain of experience that bore clearly metaphysical traits. Whether for Sorel in mythical consciousness, for Péguy in magical experience, or for Unger in a "metaphysical atmosphere,"[19] for all of them a real form of political action is rooted in an experience that abruptly interrupts the continuity of social life by making something hitherto unknown appear. And the three authors further agree that this new something must possess the mental contours of a radically transformed moral and social order. It is hard to imagine that Benjamin did not perceive such a political concept of the extraquotidian as a chance to explore the field of the political, as well as the model of religious intrinsicness. The idea of breaking through all goal-setting, of the connection to a world-disclosing experience, of an exit out of historical experience—all this came seamlessly together in the metaphysical concept of the political, so that it must have appeared to Benjamin as a suitable basis for a factual expansion of his approach.

Now, the engagement with these three authors only explains the kind of concept of the political that Benjamin wanted to concentrate on in his project, not why in the period after the end of World War I he believed he had to turn to the field of the political in the first place. Neither his work on the religious-revelatory character of language nor his studies of the self-referential structure of literary criticism had thus far, it could be said, reached a satisfactory or even a felicitous end. In different ways, the intention thus emerges in Benjamin's letters from the immediate postwar period of returning to one of the two lines of research as soon as possible. Nevertheless, for a period of two years, he seems to have largely deferred these plans in order to first devote himself to the project on politics. In any case, the discipline and energy he put into working through this new area far exceeded what he had left over in the same period for the two older fields of study. To explain this short-term displacement of the focus of his research, we can probably only draw on his intellectual biography, which, of course, by its nature leaves much room for speculation. With the experience of the outbreak and failure of the revolution of 1918, his increasing awareness of the urgency of the Palestine question, which he had encountered through Scholem, and, finally, the unavoidable experience of the pauperizing consequences of the capitalist economy, we can surmise, Benjamin's conviction grew that breaking out of the apparently pathological contemporary society was only possible by concentrating on a radical redefinition of political action. The focus of his research interest, in short, was displaced to the field of politics because it seemed that only in this common sphere could sufficient forces be mobilized to explode the congealed living conditions.

The touchstone of this explanation, of course, is the question of whether Benjamin really arrived in such early years at the conviction that his decision for a religiously nourished regeneration of the world required a connection to the medium of collective action. Indeed, in his youth, he had been filled with the idea of a common practice, but he had shared with Wyneken the view that only youth educated in the religion of art, and thus a "social movement," could bring about the overthrow of existing instrumental thinking. But traits of spiritual aristocracy so unambiguously adhered to this concept of "collective" that it could not lead to the usual associational horizon of the idea of political action. With the turn to politics as a research topic, however, Benjamin seems suddenly to have set aside all tendencies to this kind of educational elitism. For now, five years before he got to know Asja Lacis and ten years before he got to know Bertold Brecht, all at once the imaginary world he had in mind with the concept of common practice is populated by the proletarian masses. A multiplicity of external and internal impetuses can be distilled for this turnaround in his thought, above all the influence of Bloch's *Spirit of Utopia*.

However ambivalently Benjamin may have reacted to the 1918 book—as mentioned, the manuscript of his review has unfortunately been lost—according to all available testimonies, it must have made such a lasting impression that his imaginative world could not have remained unmoved. Among the many ideas that may have especially impressed the twenty-six-year-old Benjamin in this intellectually overloaded book with its expressionistic tone, first and foremost is probably the eschatological charging of the Marxist concept of revolution. This reinterpretation went along with a social localization of the religious hopes and energies that virtually made the proletariat appear as the innerworldly vanguard of a return of God.[20] How strongly this kind of sacralization of the working masses may have affected Benjamin can be made clear by the fact that he essentially never gave it up. When in the future he spoke of the awakening of proletarian class consciousness, something of the religious tone he had probably encountered for the first time in *The Spirit of Utopia* always resonated. In any case, this Blochian thought seems to have met with such passionate agreement in Benjamin that it laid the basis for a displacement of his field of social perception. Whereas he had hitherto been able to imagine a practical implementation of the religious impulse of his cultural critique only in the form of pedagogical and educational reform, with the proletariat a social factor now enters his thinking that allows him to think much more of an institutionally transformative political practice. It is this turn that must have called into life Benjamin's plan to devote himself to the theme of politics. He carried it out by ensuring, with the help of the writings of Péguy, Sorel, and Unger, that he could discover in the political the structure of religious intrinsicness.

Now, the essay "On the Critique of Violence" is nevertheless surprising in that it seems to pay only slight attention to the phenomenon of politics as such. The foreground of the argument is determined by two concepts that, in a traditional way, come to stand at the opposed ends of any meaningful analysis of the political. Following the modern tradition, any rational politics finds its limits in "violence," while in "law" it finds its legitimate starting point. In his essay, Benjamin tries to accomplish nothing less then precisely reversing the polarity of these two concepts, so that violence appears as the source and fundament of politics and law, to the contrary, as its endpoint. The function of this proposed reinterpretation is to be able to interpret politics as an event that is in itself free of ends, detached from all human purposes, and to that extent is "religious."

METHOD AND CONSTRUCTION OF CRITIQUE

One of the possibilities that offer themselves for unlocking Benjamin's uncommonly difficult, multifaceted argumentation in this study is to start with the final paragraphs. Even if the author may have refrained from issuing a recapitulation in the traditional manner, this section nonetheless offers a kind of summary conclusion with regard to its goals and execution. "The critique of violence," the introductory sentence of the last paragraph reads with declaratory simplicity, "is the philosophy of its history" (251). Every single word here, as always with Benjamin, is of equal weight. That the phenomenon of violence is to be approached with a critical intent is already stated by the title of the whole. Benjamin liked to use the concept of "critique" to designate the character of his works; it often appears in the most prominent places in programmatic passages,[21] unashamedly playing on the heritage of Kant's critical philosophy. The difference from Kant, however, consists in the fact that, from the beginning, Benjamin felt that the spectrum of experience to which Kant had tailored his critique of knowledge was too narrow. Opening one's view to experiences that were not brought under the meager schema that opposed an epistemic subject to its object was to expand the object domain of the critique of knowledge in such a way that communicative and even religious consciousness could also be legitimately counted within it.[22] For the project of a critique "of violence" this means not letting the critical analysis be trapped in judging the phenomenon only under those aspects that Kant's cramped concept of experience allows one to emphasize. To this extent, with "violence," too, one must consider that level of experience that does not fit into the classic subject-object schema but, rather, explodes its instrumentalism in one or another direction.

To be sure, it is not clear in this context what all Benjamin wanted to include under the concept of "violence." Only right at the beginning of the essay, in the second sentence, does he give a short, restrictive definition that is probably to hold for the rest of the text. "For a cause, however effective, becomes violent, in the precise sense of the word," we read here, "only when it enters into moral relations" (236). Here Benjamin tightly binds the use of the concept to the presupposition of a transformation of human life practice. Only that which works on interactive relations in such a way that they are morally affected is to be regarded as "violence." It is not entirely clear on first view where exactly Benjamin draws the boundaries with this definition. Indeed, the masculine violence he seems to exclude from his text remains, mostly within the boundaries of private family relations, but it, too, has transforming effects on the moral relations between the sexes. Just as problematic is the case of natural causes like earthquakes and erupting volcanoes, which on a corresponding scale can certainly exert a compelling effect on a community's ethical relations without Benjamin including them in his text as "violence." In view of this kind of fraying, Benjamin's definition must clearly be understood more narrowly, so that under "violence" only those compelling powers are to be included that not only affect "ethical relations" but also are themselves equipped with ethical validity. Accordingly, in his study, he restricts himself to analyzing forms of violence that possess sufficient moral legitimacy to be able to compel ethical transformations in a society.

All the same, with this conceptual clarification, nothing has yet been said about how the "critique" of such a morally construed "violence" is to be carried out methodologically. The casual allusion to Kant, implied less by the mere concept of "critique" than by the earlier essay on the "coming philosophy,"[23] helps us little, since Kant's critique was devoted only to spheres of knowledge, not to social formations. Benjamin's answer to the question of the method of a critique of violence is laconic: it is a "philosophy of its history" (202).

The second sentence of the last paragraph already briefly explains what is meant by the thought that a critique of violence is to be carried out only in the form of a history of philosophy devoted to it. If to this terse explanation we also call on the passage earlier in the text where Benjamin refers to the necessity of philosophico-historical view (238), we get the following, not implausible argument: All "critique" must assume the task, Benjamin seems to want to say in connection with Kant, of judging the "value" or the "standards" or "distinctions" applicable to the object domain to be investigated. It can only reach such a "discriminating" [*scheidende*], or, as he also says, "decisive [*entscheidende*] approach" (251) if it does not simply reproduce the use (or application—*Anwendung* [238]) of the kinds of standards or distinctions that have historically been made in the corresponding domain. Were critique to restrict itself to grasping only the "temporal data" of the application of a domain-specific standard, it could very well contribute to the analysis of its internal "meaning" (238) but not advance to a judgment of its value. This kind of judgment of given standards requires attaining a "standpoint" (238) outside the "sphere of its application," from which "light" falls on the sphere as a whole. This standpoint is offered only by the philosophy of history, which allows a distance from the "rising and falling ... forms" (251) such that it makes its variations transparent as the principle of a single "historical epoch" (252). With the thought that a particular standard is the expression or product of a limited epoch, there arises the prospect of a transcendence of the given, of a "coming age" (252) from which the value of sphere-specific classifications and criteria can be appropriately judged.

Before carrying this argument in the closing paragraphs over to the particular sphere of violence, it probably makes sense to reexamine the plea reconstructed here for a philosophico-historical view independently of the wording of the text. The self-evidence with which Benjamin here transfers the task of judging the standards and distinctions prevailing in a particular sphere to the history of philosophy probably owes something to the model of Georg Lukács's *Theory of the Novel*, though Fichte's and Schelling's historical-philosophical speculations, on which Lukács had drawn when he characterized the novel as the expressive form of "the age of absolute sinfulness,"[24] also play a role in Benjamin's formulations. What is methodologically significant about this kind of philosophy of history is that it seems to allow one to make a negative judgment on the present without basing it explicitly on a value judgment. Here the reference to a normative standard is replaced by constructing a past or future that is characterized as successful or free of evils to the extent that it offers a privileged perspective from which the "true," negative traits of one's own age can be discerned. In the philosophico-historical tradition on which Benjamin apparently drew in his argumentation, such a breakdown of history into different ages is made possible by assuming a God that has withdrawn from the human world in order to return to it in an indeterminate future. Here the present is always understood as a middle epoch in which, owing to the absence of God, a condition of "corruption" (Schelling) or "sinfulness" (Fichte) reigns, and which, of course, cannot be perceived as such by human subjects.[25] To this extent, the methodological assumption of a standpoint to be found historically outside this context of delusion is the epistemological precondition for being able to judge the actual "value" of all the institutions and practices of the present.

As problematic as these historical-philosophical background assumptions might appear today, they doubtless represent the theoretical basis for Benjamin's critique of violence. The reference to an external standpoint, which is to be taken in order to be able to judge the "value" of sphere-specific standards, thus includes the challenge of putting oneself in a historical point outside the delusive context of the present. For only from such a transcendent lookout can we see where the standards and distinctions practiced today break down or fail. Since the sphere Benjamin wants to investigate is that of "violence," he therefore has to try to identify the character of the standards that prevail in this sphere in the present from an external perspective of this kind. And already in the sentences that immediately follow the methodological prelude to the last paragraph, Benjamin announces the hypothesis that leads his investigation. The standards and distinctions that determine the treatment of violence today all come from the institution of law, which, for its part, is locked into in the conceptual scheme of means and ends.

In the last paragraph of his text, Benjamin clarifies what this fundamental statement means in detail only in the case of some central concepts, but the determinations he uses are so decisive for the whole essay that they can be used as guiding threads for further reconstruction. To begin, Benjamin underlines his conviction that, in the present, violence can only be thematized in the form of law by naming two forms of violence that can only be thematized as ethical factors: "A gaze directed only at what is close at hand can at most perceive a dialectic rising and falling in the lawmaking and law-preserving forms of violence" (251). Here we already find two of the three or four concepts on which, like weight-bearing columns, the whole of Benjamin's argumentation rests. In the present "epoch," there seem to be only two forms of violence, both of which are extremely closely tied to the institution of law: lawmaking violence on the one hand and law-preserving violence on the other. For Benjamin this thesis includes an assertion about the structural peculiarity of law, as well as about the limitations of violence in the present.

With regard to law, it should be said that, contrary to its official self-representation, it structurally depends on the application of coercive force, since its institutionalization ("making") and reproduction ("preserving") can only be guaranteed through the threat or exercise of violence. And with reference to the phenomenon of violence itself, the thesis means that violent acts in the contemporary age can only in a narrow sense be thought of as a function of law.

Just a few sentences after these definitions, we find the third concept on which Benjamin's analysis is based. The thought begins with a step transcending the contemporary age, by referring to the possibility of an interruption of the domination of law. In such a condition, Benjamin indicates, violence would no longer be locked into in the means-ends scheme of law; rather, it would possess the "pure" form of a "divine" creation. This third concept, too, that of "pure" violence, comes in the context of the last paragraphs only as a reminder of the previous analysis and is therefore once again explained in just a few words. From this, it emerges that the attribute of "purity" is to designate the opposite of all means-ends relations, and "pure" violence is thus to be free of all goal-setting and instrumental considerations. Moreover, it is significant that a few sentences before the end of his study, Benjamin brings, alongside the "divine," a second, human figure of pure violence into play, which he designates as "revolutionary" (252). He claims, in the murkiest possible way, that its "possibility" "furnishes truth" when the "existence" of a pure violence beyond law is "assured" (252).

With these three or four categories of violence, the conceptual network on which Benjamin bases his study is outlined in order to be able to deliver a philosophico-historical critique of violence. The starting point seems to be an analysis of the distinctions by means of which we can attempt to get hold of the phenomenon of violence in the contemporary age. Then everything that is conventionally called "violence" collapses into the two forms of lawmaking and law-preserving violence, both of which owe their legitimation to the unquestioned domination of law. In a way that still is not entirely clear, Benjamin further claims that the peculiarity of law consists in proceeding strictly according to the schema of means and ends. To this extent, for him, the two forms of violence that are thematically admitted must be grasped either as means or as ends within his system of reference. Now, Benjamin believes that he can only reach an effective judgment of the "value" of this distinction by putting himself in the perspective of another, "coming" age, the most outstanding quality of which named here is the suspension of law. To be sure, in the last paragraphs, we repeatedly find the expression "divine" for this future period, but what seems decisive for his normative intention is the circumstance that, with law, the domination of the means-ends scheme also expires.

It is clear that Benjamin alternately designates the forms of violence that are to mark the "new" age as "divine" and "pure." Both expressions were doubtless used to emphasize the nonteleological, probably expressive character of acts with coercive effect. In the last two sentences of his text, this thought of an opposition of "impure" contemporary and "pure" new forms of violence is taken up again, as Benjamin undertakes an attempt reminiscent of the young Heidegger to coin old-German words. Here "lawmaking" violence is designated as "executive" [*schaltend*], "law-preserving" violence as "administrative" [*verwaltend*], and the "pure" violence of a coming age as "sovereign" [*waltend*] (252). But before clarifying all three concepts, it is necessary to examine the meaning of "law" in this text. For the whole critique Benjamin seeks to undertake on the currently prevalent classifications of violence is based on the premise that these are anchored in the institution of "law."

BENJAMIN'S CONCEPT OF LAW

In the study "On the Critique of Violence," "law" takes over the function of standing for the spiritual structure that is supposed to thoroughly stamp the contemporary age. With this, Benjamin anticipates an assessment that Georg Lukács would make three years later when, in the most famous essay in *History and Class Consciousness*, he presents modern law as a product of capitalist reification.[26] Even if Benjamin was still far from attributing the laws that govern the form of modern thinking to the Marxian concept of "reification," his characterizations of the peculiarity of legal regulations nonetheless initially and generally correspond to those of Lukács. Both theorists are convinced that the legal sphere constitutes a pure "formal calculus with the aid of which the legal consequences of particular actions . . . can be determined as exactly as possible."[27] To be sure, Benjamin uses another pair of categories to define this abstractness of the law more precisely than those that lie at the basis of Lukács's critical argumentation. While the author of *History and Class Consciousness* relies on the opposition of "form" and "content" to charge modern law with increasingly "turning away from the material substratum" of social living conditions,[28] Benjamin describes the same situation as a consequence of the integration of any and all social relations into a means-ends schema. What for Lukács constituted an emptying out of content in favor of juridical form is for Benjamin the intrusion of legal instrumental thinking into the noninstrumental sphere of ethical existence. With this sharpening of the problematic of utilitarianism, the author of "On the Critique of Violence" shows himself in his theory of law to be a faithful student of Georges Sorel, whose polemical attacks on modern law he takes up, adjusting them to contemporary legal theory for his own purposes.

As already discussed, Benjamin had become familiar with Sorel's book *Reflections on Violence* in advance of his study. From it, he became acquainted with not only the idea of a morally justified proletarian violence, which flows into the famous idea of the general strike, but also the extremely sharp polemic against the institution of law that plays a significant part in the text. Unfortunately, it is not known whether Benjamin could have been familiar with other of the Bergson students' works, in which the critique of law is much more clearly substantiated. In any case, Sorel may have been the author that led him to the thought of a parallel between the legal system and the contemporary state of consciousness. In Sorel's text *Reflections on Violence*, law plays a role only insofar as it is set up as the formal medium of legitimation the ruling classes use to secure and develop the legitimacy of a social order that is useful to them. Translating power interests into the apparently neutral language of legal formulas means outfitting them with a moral impression of general validity that makes them respectable and convincing precisely to the oppressed classes.[29] In opposition to any authentic morality, which is the expression of values and ideas of honor acquired in early-childhood socialization, law is therefore for Sorel merely an instrument that serves the amoral interests of maintaining power.[30] If this already indicates the distinction he draws here between "sublime" morality and instrumental law, Sorel worked out this opposition in shorter, much more striking writings, primarily before his masterwork. In these he always emphasizes the fact that the legal system as a whole is useful only for the preservation of the social order, while the morality of the oppressed masses possesses the revolutionary power to interrupt the continuum of the history of political domination and open an epoch of true freedom.

Of course, Benjamin did not take up the highly ambivalent proposals that emanated from this idea at the beginning of the twentieth century directly and unaltered in his study on violence.[31] But Sorel's thought that there is an unbridgeable chasm between law and morality, between the general validity of laws and the demand for justice, surely ripened into the conviction that, as a medium of social organization, law represents a problematic, even pathological, institution. The central reason for this problematization is not, as for Lukács, the empty formalism or abstractness of law. Rather, the mere circumstance that something should be useful, and thus in the end serve a purpose, is as such already evidence of its inferiority, since then it cannot be the expression of true ethical life or justice. Ethical life of this kind, we can further infer, is always free of all determination of ends, for it does not take interests into consideration, without which ends cannot be defined. Almost like for Kant, only that which possesses moral validity in itself is ethical, so that it may not be restricted to certain ends. For Benjamin, here a faithful student of Sorel, an "epoch" that articulates its ethical issues in the language of law is therefore of lesser quality, since it allows the means-ends schema to dominate in the wrong place.

Before Benjamin could reach the formulations with which his text presents the basic character of law, in addition to his reading of Sorel he also had to be aware of some contemporary treatises on legal theory. To be sure, he consistently employs highly idiosyncratic constructions when revealing the restriction of law to a mere means-ends schema, but the kinds of expressions he chooses, the examples and historical connections he adduces, nonetheless show a certain degree of familiarity with the literature of the day. Above all, Benjamin must have engaged intensively with a work of legal theory that today enjoys a legendary reputation, even if it is mentioned neither in his letters nor in his works. I refer to the two-volume *Der Zweck im Recht* [*The End in Law*] (first edition 1877, second edition 1884), in which Rudolf von Jhering sought to establish a foundation for legal theory. Wherever Benjamin goes into legal theoretical matters in the narrow sense in his study, he seems to rely on this classic work. To be sure, he does not take over the full compass of von Jhering's arguments, and neither, of course, does he share von Jhering's generally affirmative understanding of law. But in his choice of concepts and his fundamental definitions the correspondences are so enormous as to eliminate all doubt. In von Jhering's *Zweck im Recht*, we find the basic thesis that all law serves the end of "securing the living conditions of society," with respect to which the choice of legitimate means is only a dependent variable.[32] We encounter in a slightly modified formulation the distinction between "natural ends" and "legal ends" on which Benjamin draws in a central place to justify his reflections.[33] And finally, we find, in an almost word-for-word correspondence, the same definition of the role of violence in law that forms the basis of Benjamin's study when he introduces the two forms of lawmaking and law-preserving violence.[34] Even more, in his book von Jhering also anticipates the idea that would be decisive for Benjamin's purposes, that a domination-free alternative to the coercive institution of law can be found built into the voluntary altruism and intersubjectivity of "ethical life."[35] The moral practices that von Jhering, just like Benjamin (249), has in mind here are the moderating conventions of decorum and politeness.

When we further pursue this opposition of ethical life and law, which is central to the architectonic of von Jhering's investigation, we come upon a deeper distinction that may also have determined the implicit background of Benjamin's argumentation. For von Jhering, the comprehensive end of law, the task of maintaining the social order, arises from the fact of human egoism, which creates a constant conflict of individual interests. He sees social conventions, in contrast, and thus everything Benjamin calls forms of "nonviolent agreement" (244), embedded in the human tendency to selflessly make the concerns and purposes of the other one's own. To this extent, for von Jhering the sphere of law is far inferior to the moral power and authenticity of ethical life. The former can only serve the end of conflict prevention by means of authoritarian coercion, whereas the latter is itself an organic expression of the moral make-up of human beings. It very probably this connection of law to egoism that reinforced Benjamin's thoroughly negative conception of law. The idea he took from Sorel that law is merely an instrumental institution for the maintenance of social order was further sharpened by its connection to the egoistic nature of human beings. As a whole, law thus represents for Benjamin a "rotten," even pathological, institution because it replaces social living conditions with a means-ends schema that, in the end, serves egoistic individual interests.

From this negativistic image of law, we see that Benjamin is not really concerned with the internal paradoxes of justifying law. For him, the urgent problem is not, as the secondary literature often claims, the iterative indeterminacy of law that today stands at the center of deconstructive approaches to law.[36] Nor is his attention primarily directed to the circumstance that all law is based in an exercise of unlegitimized force. All these are indeed perspectives that Benjamin thematizes in the course of his argument, but for him they do not constitute the core of the grounds on which he criticizes law as a form of sociality from a philosophico-historical point of view. This basis is rather, as indicated, to be seen in the circumstance that law as such serves ends, which themselves are set by the expression of the egoistic nature of human beings.

VIOLENCE IN LAW

The preponderant part of Benjamin's study—the first eighteen pages of the twenty-four-page text—is devoted almost exclusively to the attempt to determine the role of violence in the medium of

Saving the Sacred with a Philosophy of History

law. Of these eighteen pages, the first three are allotted to locating violence in legal relations in the first place, while the remaining fifteen analyze the specific place of violence in the "contemporary European" (238) legal system. Already in the fourth sentence of his study, Benjamin apodictically states about law what we have gotten to know as the theoretical fallout of his preoccupation with Sorel and von Jhering: "With regard to the first of these [the system of law], it is clear that the most elementary relationship within any legal system is that of means to ends" (236). At this point, we do not know how Benjamin will judge such a restriction to the means-ends schema as a whole, as he tries to analyze the criteria that result from a sphere made up in this way for judging violence. His approach thus consists in seeing how the legal standard of the conceptual pair means and end can be applied to a variable like violence. Benjamin does not set about this task directly, however, but uses the hermeneutic device of canvassing leading doctrines for answers. Largely in agreement with what today is still the finding of legal-theoretical historians, he distinguishes between the traditions of natural right and legal positivism in order to use both as historical variants of the application of the mean-ends schema to the phenomenon of violence.

Benjamin believes he can make short work of the natural law tradition. Without more precisely distinguishing between the highly various approaches to natural law,[37] it is obvious to him that that here a test of the lawfulness of violence can only be carried out with a view to its instrumental role. Since the architectonic of this theory forces it to regard the establishment of a violence-free condition as the legitimate end of a legal order, the exercise of violence can then only be judged according to whether it serves as an appropriate means for implementing this pregiven end or not. With this, the natural law tradition, as Benjamin presents it, possesses no other criterion for normatively judging violence than that of instrumental appropriateness. He is convinced that not even the question of whether as a means it satisfies ethical standards can be satisfactorily answered because it lacks a noninstrumental, moral point of view. It would take us too far afield to examine whether Benjamin's objection is justified. Even a brief glance at the argumentative history of natural law would probably show that the normative commendation of particular, rational legal ends is often also carried over to the evaluation of the means that may legitimately used to implement them. But such differentiations within the natural right tradition are decidedly not in the foreground of Benjamin's concerns. He is solely interested in showing that the tendency to see violence as a "natural datum" (237) of human beings is built into treating it as a mere means. The argument by which Benjamin reaches this conclusion results from the premises of his interpretation of natural law. Precisely because this tradition places everything on replacing man's violent natural condition with a morally legitimate legal order, it must covertly make violence into a natural "raw material" (ibid.) that cannot be ethically repudiated as long as it does not serve to implement unjustifiable (legal) ends. Referred back to the question that concerns Benjamin in these first pages— the role of violence in law—this means that in the natural law tradition the means-ends schema has led to a paradoxical neutralization of violence.

It becomes clearer still what Benjamin is aiming at with this critique when he moves on to his analysis of the positive law tradition. As with the treatment of natural law, in the second step, too, not a single author is mentioned by name. Instead, the whole current is subjected to a very general, virtually schematic characterization. Accordingly, "positive legal philosophy" remains caught in the problematic circle that emerges with the reciprocal dependency of means and ends. However, its advantage over the natural law tradition for Benjamin consists in the fact that it is in a position to provide a noninstrumental criterion for judging a specific use of violence. In contrast to natural law, as Benjamin sympathetically summarizes, positivism binds the legitimacy of the legal end to the warrant for the means required to carry it out. The lawfulness of a public order is no longer to be measured by the fulfillment of particular "natural" ends; instead, conversely, the lawfulness of the means vouchsafe the legitimacy of the legal order (237). Such a "proceduralization," as we would say today, compels positivism to give standards for judging legal means that are formulated independently of all imaginable ends or goals. In the "historical school" that

Benjamin probably has primarily in mind here, this task is solved by using the extent of the historical confirmation of legal means as an independent criterion. For the phenomenon of violence, this sort of solution means that its legal use is to be approved as long as it historically proves itself in the form of de facto agreement and effective practicability. Now, Benjamin is far from endorsing this criterion of historical sanctionability as such. Indeed, as we have seen, for him the whole attempt to master violence by containing it within the legal means-ends schema is suspect. But of the solutions legal theory offers to subject violence to such a schema, he unambiguously favors historical positivism because it is connected to declaring a standard: "On the other hand, the positive theory of law is acceptable as a hypothetical basis at the outset of this study, because it undertakes a fundamental distinction between kinds of violence independently of cases of their application" (237).

The result of this limited or relative valorization of legal positivism for the progress of the investigation is that on the following pages Benjamin is almost exclusively concerned with the legal-positive standard of sanctionability. The answer that natural law can offer to the place of violence in law has already been discarded, since, according to Benjamin, it has no criterion for judgment at all. Thus, to answer the question of how violence can be judged within the legal system, there remains only the positivistic theory that, with the idea of historical sanction, at least offers a standard for evaluating violence as a means. The fifteen pages that follow this preliminary positioning of violence in the two authoritative legal traditions thus consist of an examination of the distinction that legal positivism makes between historically sanctioned and nonsanctioned violence. More precisely, as Benjamin puts it, it is a question of "what light is thrown on the nature of violence by the fact that such a criterion or distinction can be applied to it all" (237–38). Benjamin laconically justifies the fact that this examination is carried out only within "European" legal systems with reference to the insuperable difficulties of a comprehensive analysis that includes different cultures. But the real reason for the restriction can probably be regarded as the historical circumstance that precisely in Europe at the time, there was scarcely another more politically explosive question than that of the legal legitimacy of non-state, revolutionary violence.

LAWMAKING OR "EXECUTIVE" VIOLENCE

All the considerations Benjamin enlists in the following parts of his investigation stand under the premise of the hypothetical validity of the positive-legal distinction of sanctioned versus nonsanctioned legal violence. When it comes to the goals of the middle section, we can therefore suspect that, for Benjamin, it is a matter of showing the necessary collapse of such a criterion of legitimacy in order to demonstrate the unavoidability of a circular determination of law even in positivism. To be sure, it is not easy to see how the author proceeds in detail to produce the evidence he aims at. The text oscillates between invoking concrete legal problems and systematic considerations without it ever becoming sufficient clear which is to offer the weight-bearing and which the dependent argument. Probably it will be in the interest of clarity in reconstructing this to retain the bifurcation Benjamin gradually establishes in the course of his demonstration. Accordingly, the collapse of positive-legal standards first emerges in the fact of a lawmaking violence, then also more broadly in the fact of a law-preserving violence.

The argument Benjamin seems to use in the first step of his demonstration amounts to the claim that the positive-legal standard of historical sanction would permit far too many cases of violence that is disruptive and hostile to order to be able to hold as the normative basis of a public legal order. Thus, we can infer, when the danger of such de facto legitimation arises, the state always has to monopolize all violence and draw arbitrary, nonsanctioned boundaries. It is relatively easy to imagine the list of concrete examples Benjamin took from contemporary legal reality to support his thesis. Although the end of childrearing is de facto—measured by the recognition of the population—considered as a private matter outside the law, these "natural ends" threaten to be implemented with such an "excessive measure of violence" (238) that the state sees itself prompted, without any historical legitimation, to pass "laws relating to the limits of educational authority to punish" (ibid.). The historical circumstance that "the 'great' criminal" has not seldom "aroused the secret admiration of the public" (239) also seems to Benjamin to belong to the same category. Sympathy comes in his case, he is convinced, less from the deed itself than from the violence whose order-exploding character must be so threatening to the state that here, too, it foregoes any proof of historical sanction and violently attempts to the enforce its monopoly.

The same motif—the law-threatening tendency that seems to be inherent in all de facto–sanctioned violence—is also decisive for Benjamin's third example. Just the fact that two pages (239–40) are devoted to depicting this case calls attention to its exceptional significance for the text as a whole. The right to strike, Benjamin claims, represents a still clearer example of the impossibility of consistently applying the standard of historical sanction. For here a right to use violence is granted under the pressure "from below" of the workers; this right, under certain circumstances, can change into so pronounced a danger for the constitutional order that the state finds itself compelled to use lawmaking violence in spite of any procedural principles. Probably in no other example in the text does Benjamin's intention in his immanent refutation of legal positivism emerge more clearly. He wants to show that in assuming the positive-legal standard (for which there is no alternative), the constitutional state always comes into contradiction with its own procedural principles, since it can only meet the threat of violence, which it itself necessarily allows, with a lawless use of violence.

All the same, precisely this case of the right to strike gives Benjamin a series of interpretative difficulties, leaving the text strewn with explanations and clarifications. Thus, for example, it is not at all obvious that the legal guarantee for the strike is to be interpreted as a "right to exercise violence" (239), as Benjamin seeks when he speaks of the "objective contradiction" of the law. If a strike is instead seen as the mere omission of certain actions—namely, work activities—so that there can be no talk of the use of violence, then the point Benjamin attributes to this legal institution does not apply.

Without engaging with the extensive discussion in the legal theory of his day, Benjamin disposes of this alternative without further ado by appealing to the "view of labor" (239). The workers, he argues without suffering objections, must see in the "right to strike . . . the right to use force in attaining certain ends" (ibid.). The thesis, which is no less important for his purposes, that it is only a short step from a work stoppage to a use of violence that threatens to "overthrow" (240) the legal order as a whole represents just as great a problem for Benjamin. He needs this argument in order to be able to claim that, in terms of its own bases, with the right to strike the constitutional state has to produce an "internal potential for violence" whose dynamic in the end compels it to use lawless state violence. The device with which Benjamin manages these challenges consists in the rather bold idea of regarding the revolutionary general strike as the practical and legal consequence of a (permitted) work stoppage. In the "simultaneous" (240) strike on all (national) firms, he claims, implicitly following Sorel, the proletariat brings a subversive violence to bear that can still be understood as a "use" (ibid.) of the right the constitutional state granted it in allowing the strike. To this extent, the general strike is a legal product of the same constitutional order it now seeks to overthrow by availing itself of the right to strike. And the state, in turn, can only react to this danger, we can again infer, by violating its own principles by arbitrarily seizing on the "violence" of lawmaking.

It is not difficult to see that with the whole argument concerning the "right to strike," we have an extremely fragile, if not specious, construction. Benjamin himself admits that he only succeeds in demonstrating a necessary self-sublation of law if the interpretation of the "view of labor" is given equal standing. Only by taking up this perspective—which is, moreover, merely attributed—can the right to strike be understood as allowing the legal use of violence, and the general strike, for its part, as its radicalized performance. What Benjamin therefore achieves with his demonstration is proof not of a "logical contradiction in the law" (240) but only, as he himself guardedly concedes, of an "objective contradiction in the legal situation" (ibid.). It further appears that something contingent clings to the reference to the "general strike," since it is not a regular or even a necessary occurrence in the history of the modern constitutional state. Thus, the demonstration in a certain sense lacks closure, which could only consist in the claim of a necessary conversion of sanctioned violence into subversive violence. Benjamin, to give him credit, sensed these weaknesses in his argument, for at the end of this section he writes that remaining objections are to be rebutted by "a consideration of military force."

With the concept of "military force," Benjamin designates in this context the ability of "external powers" (241) to make "new law" in the defeated country after they have won a war. Benjamin also wants the case of such a "law of war" to be understood as evidence for the tendency of the modern constitutional state, according to its own procedural premises, to have to recognize foreign lawmaking when it is neither in its interest nor under its command. One could immediately object that this further example does not serve Benjamin's aim particularly well, since it refers to relations between states, not to a single state legal order. But Benjamin confidently overrides misgivings of this kind by looking only at the effect of the external legal intrusion on domestic legal relations. In his presentation it can thus seem as if the case of a legal order imposed as a result of losing a war is comparable with that of the right to strike being forced by the struggling proletariat. In both cases, the constitutional state has to accept the lawmaking potential of external powers because its procedural principles forbid it from contradicting the de facto sanction of force. Benjamin believes that with this fourth example he can conclude the first round of his internal refutation of modern law. Although he does not offer an explicit résumé, the result of his argument can probably be summed up to the effect that the dominant legal positivism's criterion for the legitimation of violence fails because it has to recognize uses of violence for legal goals that explode the system. But if this is so, as the thesis can be more pointedly formulated, then the modern legal order always allows itself to be abrogated: either it has to surrender its sovereignty to external legal powers or mobilize a violence against them that possesses no constitutional legitimacy.

LAW-PRESERVING OR "ADMINISTRATIVE" VIOLENCE

The section on law-preserving violence fulfills for Benjamin only the propaedeutic function of immanently testing whether, in the given legal order, any "value" (237) inheres in the ends-means schema in its positivistic interpretation. The negative answer this question has received so far anticipates the direction in which Benjamin now steers his argument. With the same sharp tone he had struck before, he lists further legal cases that are to make clear the necessary collapse of any positivistic standard. At issue, however, is no longer violence for "natural ends" (241), as applied to childrearing, the strike, or military occupation, since there it was a matter of goals that were not further legally codified. Instead, in this new section, Benjamin takes up forms of violence whose legal legitimacy is out of the question from the start, since it is applied "as means to the ends of the state" (ibid.), that is, in its constitutional function. The critique of this "law-preserving" violence, Benjamin immediately emphasizes, is, despite all the "declamations of pacifists and activists" (ibid.), no small undertaking. For it is to be treated neither with reference to an original freedom of all human beings nor by appealing to the "categorical imperative" (ibid.), for in both cases it is denied that the constitutional state "acknowledge[s] and promote[s] the interest of mankind in the person of each individual" (ibid.). How, then, is such a claim—which entangles the state's use of law-preserving violence in a circular determination of means and ends and thus always undermines the constitutional order—to be justified?

The first answer Benjamin gives to this implicit question comes with a view to the death penalty, which then in Germany was still prescribed only for the crime of murder. Again, a minor inference is required to see Benjamin's argument in this context. Like all forms of punishment, the constitutional state must claim the death penalty as a means that serves to maintain the legal order by threatening the potential criminal with the use of violence for the end of deterrence. But with the execution of this particular penalty, it quickly emerges that here this end only provides the curtain that conceals the real function: the sanctioning of law. To this extent, in carrying out the death penalty, the law-preserving violence of the state regularly turns into its opposite, a violence that manifests itself: "For in the exercise of violence over life and death, more than in any other legal act, the law reaffirms itself" (242). For Benjamin, this finding seems to be a first corroboration of the thesis that modern law cannot clearly fix means and ends even with regard to law-preserving violence. On closer examination, the death penalty, which is thought of as a means of safeguarding the law, emerges as a form of legal violence that falls into the domain of lawmaking, since it achieves nothing other than symbolically reinforcing the legal order. To be sure, it is not entirely clear whether this argument actually supports the thesis Benjamin wants to assert. If the real function of carrying out the death penalty turns out to be the reassertion of the law, that is, we cannot speak of a displacement of means and ends but only of a concealment of the real end. The argument serves ideology-critical purposes, but not to demonstrate a basic indeterminacy of means and ends.

But the excursus on the death penalty is only meant as a bridge to the general discussion Benjamin devotes to the theme of law-preserving violence on the next page. The example by means of which he pursues his thesis concerning the indeterminacy of means and ends is that of the police. For him, they represent the most striking instance of law-preserving violence because they are permitted to use violent means to ensure the maintenance of the legal order. Benjamin is so sure of himself in this case that he does not even try to lay the ground for his argument but poses it at the beginning of his observations as a premise. In its mien as in its powers, the police mix the task of securing the law with producing new legal goals in such an "unnatural," "ignom[inious]," even "spectral" (242) way that "the separation of lawmaking and law-preserving violence is suspended" (243). In the rushing sentences with which this thesis is then elaborated, Benjamin outdoes himself with the assertion that this interleaving of functions leads to an even greater "degeneration of violence" in "democracies" than in absolute monarchies (ibid.). Whereas in the latter the police, on this argument, feel bound in their authority by the "supremacy" of the ruler, in the former they are "elevated by no such relation" (ibid.) and so can come more quickly to abuse and arbitrariness.

This line of thought obviously owes itself to vivid impressions of police abuses of power at the time. The excited tone, the choice of adjectives, the open antipathy—all reveal that Benjamin must have been very precisely informed about concrete cases of such transgressions from contemporary sources. The empirical bases of the argument provoke the question, however, of whether the surely innumerable examples can be generalized into a principled thesis about the removal of constraints on police violence in the constitutional state. Benjamin does not seem to have more in hand than the dubious observation that democratic regimes lack the exemplary authority to bind their personnel. The question of whether such excesses are an essential or only a contingent characteristic of police action under constitutional conditions does not even enter his mind. That it could perhaps be completely otherwise, that with time precisely democratic societies could develop civil resources to control the police and the military, lies outside his imaginative horizon.

Thus, Benjamin's pleadings on law-preserving violence as a whole rest on problematic foundations. The thoughts on the death penalty do not really thematize an indeterminacy of legal means, only a concealment of de facto ends. The reflections on the police owe themselves to a generalization of historical experiences whose systematic significance remains untested. To this extent, only the section on lawmaking violence serves to justify the thesis Benjamin pursues with his "immanent" critique of the legal system. There it could be shown that the constitutional state on the European model is not in a position to unambiguously determine legitimate forms of violence, since from the perspective of de facto validity, new, system-bursting sources of violent lawmaking always have to be recognized. The section that then deals with law-preserving violence, in contrast, contributes very little to the thesis on the indeterminacy of constitutional norms, for beyond the two dubious examples, no considerations on the generalizability of their content are developed.

NONVIOLENT ALTERNATIVES TO LAW

The critical considerations that the "ultimate insolubility all legal problems" (247) in the case of the European legal system are meant to call to mind are followed by a series of diffuse trains of thought that bring the idea of "purity" into play for the first time. Their function is apparently to help prepare for the section in which Benjamin will set to work assessing the age of law from the transcending perspective of a future ethical life. In this context, the observations concerning the possibility of nonviolent forms of social agreement represent a transition. As the previous pages have shown, Benjamin believes that every use of violence as a means is necessarily affected by the problem that accompanies legal relations as such. He therefore then turns to the question of whether under given conditions there could be a way of reconciling social interests that does not call for employing legally legitimized violence. In this justification for the following change of perspective, we once again clearly see what Benjamin takes as the summary of his discussion of law. The legal relation is a social medium that fails in its task of mediating social contradictions because, within the framework of the means-ends schema, it cannot clearly fix the application of the means of violence at its disposal. To what point Benjamin wants to extend this critique of law is shown by the context (244), in which he locates Parliament as a symptom of legal pathology. In the style of the then-widespread critique of parliamentarism, he says with an appeal to Erich Unger that the tendency toward parliamentary compromise shows how deeply all legal orders are rooted in violence.

Even if this critique of parliamentarism must appear somewhat questionable today, since it reveals an astonishing proximity to the antidemocratic thinking of Carl Schmitt,[38] in the text it is thrown in as hardly more than an aside. For what really interests Benjamin here, leading him to refer just once to Parliament as a foil, are the aforementioned forms of social agreement that arise without any use of violence. Benjamin now introduces these nonviolent media of interest-mediation by first referring conventionally to emotional "virtues" (245) that allow one empathically to assume the other's perspective. Wherever reciprocal attitudes of "courtesy, sympathy, peaceableness" and "trust" predominate "among private persons" (244), he explains, it is possible to agree nonviolently without the intermediation of law. The next step, in which Benjamin undertakes to designate such forms of affectively based understanding as "pure" means, is equally understandable. For here, "pure" preliminarily means only the absence of violence, so that, retaining the language of means and ends, such forms of understanding can be understood as "pure" or simply "nonviolent" means to the end of problem-solving. Benjamin then expands this consideration of peaceful instruments of social agreement in a third step by calling them functional equivalents for empathetic virtues, or, as he puts it, the existence of a "culture of the heart" (244, trans. modified). He is convinced that wherever such capacities to take on others' perspectives are lacking, insight into common basic interests also ensures that conflict is settled nonviolently; the "fear of mutual disadvantages" (245) is the exemplary case to which Benjamin here refers in an almost Hobbesian manner.

If all these examples of nonviolent conflict-solving independent of law still move within the private sphere, the next step leads to a discussion of the field of transindividual conflicts, represented by struggles between "classes and nations" (ibid.). Here in a later passage (247), we find a reference to skillful diplomatic negotiation, which can without difficulty, in analogy to private agreement, be understood as a nonviolent instrument for dissolving conflicts between states. But Benjamin is primarily interested in a completely different instrument of public conflict management that can no longer be understood as completely free of violence. The proletarian general strike, he writes, supported by repeated citations of Sorel, "as a pure means, is nonviolent" (246) because it does not "cause" the "upheaval" as much as "consummate" it (ibid.). The least that can be said of this surprising turn in the argument is that is seems highly ambivalent. For here, "pure" can no longer mean "nonviolent" but, rather, something like "free of ends"—thus, the performance of an action for its own sake. Benjamin makes the fact that he tends to employ the expression "pure" here to mean the absence of any attachment to end-setting clearer still, when in the next sentence he emphasizes the "anarchistic" character of the proletarian general strike. While the traditional defeat of the workers, of which he had already spoken in his discussion of the "right to strike," represents a mere "lawmaking" enterprise on account of its programmatic intent, the authentic general strike lacks any ambition toward such a social-political transformation, which is why it "purely" creates all its meaning out of "destroying state power" (ibid.).

Shortly after this significant passage, Benjamin begins to summarize his reflections on the place of violence in the means-ends system of law (247). Here it becomes clear that he now means to conclude his observations on the age of legally deformed ethical life. If we once again schematically cast an eye over the general construction of the eighteen-page section, it becomes clear that the preceding reference to the revolutionary general strike brackets the change of perspective that, as we know, is to open up a view of an age beyond law. After Benjamin had shown that under legal positivism the use of violence in legal relations cannot be unambiguously fixed and therefore occurs without any final basis of legitimacy, alternatives were initially shown within the existing, legally determined systems of order that can resolve conflicts of interest without violence. Within the framework of this attempt to thematize such "pure" means of social understanding, the "proletarian general strike" was also mentioned, whose "purity" resulted less from the fact of nonviolence than from the way it was performed, its freedom from all instrumentality. This discernable displacement expresses the direction in which Benjamin will search in the last part of his essay for a form of violence that no longer belongs to the "confines" of the "conditions of existence" (247) he has discussed so far and is therefore free from the means-ends relation of law. This violence, which the proletarian general strike exemplifies under existing conditions, can no longer serve as a means for an ethical end but must itself be an expression and a form of performing ethical life. In the final part of his essay, which makes up scarcely more than six pages, Benjamin works to explore such a "pure" form of violence.

PURE OR "SOVEREIGN" VIOLENCE

The key to understanding the thought that makes up the goal and endpoint of the whole essay is found precisely where the analysis of legal violence is brought to an end. Here Benjamin repeats one last time the thesis, now sufficiently familiar to us, that violence in legal relations cannot be justified because in the end its justification as a means cannot be fixed. He then closes the sentence with a rhetorical question that contains nothing less than a hint of another model of thinking:

> How would it be, therefore, if all the violence imposed by fate, using justified means, were of itself in irreconcilable conflict with just ends, and if at the same time a different kind of violence arose that certainly could be either the justified or the unjustified means to those ends but was not related to them as means at all but in some different way? (247)

In a certain way this last formulation can no longer really be surprising, since in dealing with the "proletarian general strike" a form of violence has already been anticipated that cannot be understood without further ado as a means to an end. Instead, precisely the repeated references to Georges Sorel should make it clear that what is at stake here is a kind of social protest whose violence is not a means to achieving an anticipated end but, rather, the expression of moral outrage. Benjamin seems to want to generalize this so far merely outlined thought in order to be able to bring a concept of violence into play that is free of all instrumental connotations. In the same passage, he also speaks of how on such an alternative conception it is now a matter of a "nonmediate function of violence" (248). It almost sounds like a proposed definition, then, when Benjamin, with the example of "everyday experience" (ibid.), explains how we should imagine an immediate form of violence of this kind: "As regards a man, he is impelled by anger, for example, to the most visible outbursts of a violence that is not related as a means to a preconceived end. It is not a means but a manifestation" (ibid.). It is this concept of "manifestation" that stands in the center of the essay's last pages. With it is meant a kind of violence that is no longer a means to an end, but the expression or demonstration of a correspondingly shaded will.

Fundamentally, however, more happens in this passage of the text than Benjamin's sober explanation, which takes up just a page, reveals. With the transposition of the concept of violence from an instrumental to an expressive concept, Benjamin not only turns to another aspect of violence; he transcends the whole historical framework in which his argumentation has so far moved. For after all has been said, this kind of noninstrumental form of violence can have no appropriate place in the age determined by law, since in such an age all ethical relations between people are organized according to the legal means-ends schema. To this extent, in this passage Benjamin carries out the change of perspective he had announced fourteen pages before with the reference to a "philosophico-historical view of law" (238). The introduction of the expressive model of violence allows him to assume a standpoint that is so far outside the given legal order that it enables a judgment of the whole sphere of legal standards "with regard to its value" (ibid.). If one wanted to reduce this change of perspective to a handy formula, it could perhaps be said that here Benjamin makes the transition from an "immanent" to a "transcending" critique. As long as his argument was restricted to the merely instrumental concept of violence, that is, legal relations could only be immanently criticized on the basis of their constitutive means-ends schema and the internal indeterminacy in their treatment of violence exposed, whereas taking into account the manifestation character of violence of violence now makes it possible to survey the limitations of the legal sphere as a whole from a transcendental lookout point.

Understanding Benjamin's further course is admittedly made more difficult by the fact that he opens the next section with a restriction that concerns the character of expressive violence. Even this no longer mediated form of violence "has," in his lapidary formulation, "objective manifestations" (248) that can in no case be exempted from critique. Benjamin makes this suggestion more concrete in the next sentence by naming "myth" as a "most significant" (ibid.) source of false figures of a violence that manifests itself and is worthy of critique; and the opposition of a "mythic violence" of this kind and a truly "pure immediate violence" (249) forms the architectonic backbone of the reflections with which Benjamin closes his essay. To understand what this opposition is about, it is probably best to turn to each form of expressive violence before dealing with the reasons for their inferiority and superiority.

As has already been seen, "mythic violence" does not belong to the age marked by the predominance of law. Because it possesses a manifestation character, it cannot be regarded as a means for just ends and accordingly not be assigned to legal relations. Benjamin claims that the violence that played a role in the mythical tales of antiquity is a manifestation or expression of the "existence" (248) of the gods. In exercising such violence, the gods demonstrate that they possess power or domination over human beings by virtue of their supernatural powers. For Benjamin, this demonstrative violence is nonetheless not entirely without reference to legal relations, since he is convinced that in a certain way it allows law to develop as an ordering system in the first place. The gods, he says with reference to the legend of Niobe, punished the woman who committed the outrage of challenging them by making principles whose contravention led necessarily to punishment. From this extremely audacious genealogy, the evidence for which lies not in historical occurrences but in mythical stories, Benjamin draws the far-reaching conclusion that law owes its origin to an act of the sheer demonstration of power. In order to show the rebellious people who really had the authority to draw normative boundaries, the gods produced legal principles that were nothing other than the expression of their fury: "Lawmaking is powermaking, assumption of power, and to that extent an immediate manifestation of violence" (248). From a methodological point of view, this genealogical finding, for Benjamin, completes the enterprise of a critique of violence. For now, the initially merely immanent analysis is presented as the result of a transcending observation that allows us to see how the "value" of the legal sphere as a whole is to be judged.

Benjamin sums up the result of his abyssal view of law by calling again on Georges Sorel. According to Sorel, from the beginning, the law serves—and precisely this makes up its "value"—the "pre-rogative" of the "mighty" (249) to arbitrarily draw normative boundaries that allow them to safeguard their privileges under the appearance of "equality." To this extent, as Benjamin summarily puts it, all violence that circulates in legal relations goes back to "the mythic manifestation of immediate violence" (ibid.). In another, simpler formulation—which, however, underscores its vulnerability—the thesis can also be rendered as follows: a condition for the operation of legal violence is a hidden connection to the monopoly over physical violence that has the greatest interest in holding onto power.

Benjamin now makes the transition to another, positive form of expressive violence by asking about the ethical power that in the future will be in the position to once again break through the "fate" (248) of legal relations produced by myth. This new broadening of perspective is undertaken in just two sentences, but they mark out such a central course for the essay that their complete reproduction is unavoidable:

> Far from inaugurating a purer sphere, the mythic manifestation of immediate violence shows itself fundamentally identical with all legal violence, and turns suspicion concerning the latter into certainly of the perniciousness of its historical function, the destruction of which thus becomes obligatory. This very task of destruction poses again, ultimately, the question of a pure immediate violence that might be able to call a halt to mythic violence. (249)

In the next sentence Benjamin then answers his own question by introducing the ethical quantity that, by reason of its "purity," is superior to all the forms of violence discussed so far: "Just as in all spheres God opposes myth, mythic violence is confronted by the divine" (ibid.). Here, for the first time, we see the whole table of categories that have underlain Benjamin's essay in the guise of a normative schema. Indeed, the concept of "divine violence" had essentially already appeared on the previous page (248), but only now can we see its significance for the closing of the argument as a whole. At this point, it is probably helpful to interpose a schematic overview of the now-completed categorical framework before finally thematizing the philosophico-historical role of "pure divine violence."

By now, it is not hard to see that Benjamin introduces the fundamental concepts of his essay in a chronological order that is in inverse relation to their objective or historical significance. The decisive opposition on which all the concepts used before "genealogically" depend is only brought into play in the last one-quarter of the text. Here what is at stake is an opposition between two immediate, self-manifesting forms of violence whose difference consists in the fact that the one can be called "impure" and the other "pure." Benjamin designates such expressive violence as "impure," then, when it is exercised with regard to external ends, so that it is no longer merely the demonstration of a will or a feeling. For him, this kind of violence, which is indeed immediate but at the same time "impure," appears historically with the outbursts of rage of heathen gods, who, according to the mythical accounts, despite their affective arousal always soberly pursued power interests. In the conceptual construction Benjamin develops in his essay, this mythical violence stands at the beginning of a process that leads via the differentiation of mean-ends thinking to the general establishment of legal violence. As soon as legal relations are completely institutionalized, the legitimacy of violence can only be evaluated by means of instrumental criteria, with the consequence that the constantly recurring reversal of means into ends that follows from the connection of law to power can no longer be seen. It is the mythological dead hand of this reliance of law on power interests that Benjamin finally holds responsible for the fact that the implementation of legal relations gradually deforms all ethical forms of life by subjecting them to the domination of the means-ends schema. According to Benjamin, even the few alternatives that still remain within these ruined living conditions to solve conflicts of interest without the interposition of law are stained by a displacement of the ethical by the dominance of interests.

When we now envision this genealogical axis in a column of concepts at whose head is the category of impure immediate violence, we must then imagine a parallel column that captures a completely different genealogy, since at its head is the category of pure immediate violence. Benjamin seems to designate an immediate, expressive form of violence as pure, then, when its manifestation is not clouded by the consideration of external ends. To this extent, the exercise of such violence possesses something self-referential, since it expresses only what underlies it as a source in the form of a will or a feeling. In this text, Benjamin apparently attributes the ability to exercise this kind of pure violence only to God. And because his will is good and right, as Benjamin does not explicitly highlight, God's expressive demonstration of violence is the pure expression of justice (248). Here, of course, the question arises of whether Benjamin can also enter other concepts in this column under the heading of "pure violence," so that, as in the case of the first column, a genealogical axis can be discerned.

Against this stands not only the fact that under the domination of law all possibilities for a continuation of this violence seem to be excluded but also that there can hardly be worldly successors for divine violence. Of course, scattered references to the special quality of the violence embodied by the proletarian general strike suggest that Benjamin does not want to accept these two misgivings. For him, there is clearly no doubt that sporadic demonstrations of pure violence are also possible in the age of law and thus that God's justice has left a genealogical trace. Benjamin glimpses the first form of such a return of divine violence on Earth, as I said, in the revolutionary general strike of the proletariat. It, too, possesses a self-referential character, since its violence manifests only the untainted moral will the proletariat possesses by reason of its social situation. To be sure, Benjamin leaves it unclear which particular experiences of the working class are to have enabled the development of a will of this kind. But we can suppose that on this point, he follows Sorel's suggestion, which, in an idiosyncratic synthesis of Nietzsche and Proudhon, assumes an authentic, "sublime" producer morality.[39]

The considerations that Sorel, in connection with his discussion of the producer morality, further devoted to the value of family morality probably also represent one of Benjamin's sources for a further instantiation of pure violence under innerworldly conditions.[40] Taking up again a thought that already played a role at the beginning of his text when he spoke of the nonlegalizable character of parenting (238), Benjamin now writes in the context of explaining pure immediate violence: "This divine violence is not only attested by religious tradition but is also found in present-day life in at least one sanctioned manifestation. The educative violence, which in its perfected form stands outside the law, is one of its manifestations" (250, trans. modified). This initially surprising proposal, which surely reflect elements of the young Benjamin's endeavors in educational reform,[41] can probably best be understood by strictly respecting the parallel to divine violence.

No different from the will of God, Benjamin seems to want to say, the will of the parents or guardians is exclusively directed toward the well-being, the salvation, of those entrusted to them, their own children or pupils. Thus, the violent expressions with which they react to possible misconduct are a pure demonstration of benevolent justice. If this argument is referred to the passage where Benjamin spoke of the "natural end" of educational violence (238), it could be feared that here his talk of "strik[ing]" (250) is meant entirely literally. The blows with which the father punishes the child's malefactions are manifestations of a just wrath and, to that extent, as such justified testimony of pure, indeed "sacred" (251), violence. With this illustration, it becomes clear why Benjamin insisted so decisively at the beginning that educational violence according to its whole structure is cut off from juridification. For from his perspective, the penetration of legal categories into the sphere of childrearing necessarily leads to its perversion, since then what previously bore his seal of approval as a moral manifestation becomes a mere means.

With the reference to educational violence, we have named all the social phenomena Benjamin evokes in his text as testimonies to a secular persistence of divine violence. Unlike the powerful story by which he attests to the legal relations that arise from myth, the genealogical trace of this form of violence is distinguished by the highest degree of discontinuity and is thus only barely visible. Alongside childrearing, in the end only the proletarian general strike appears as a further instance to feed the hope for a return of divine ethical life. Notwithstanding, Benjamin does not close his text with the thesis of a definitive loss of the "the sacred" (251). In a final turn that probably most clearly betrays the political intention of his whole project, he, instead, assesses the weak, porous continuity of a violence that is at once pure and immediate as evidence of the inevitability of revolution. Only a few lines before the end of the text, he thus writes: "But if the existence of violence outside the law, as pure immediate violence, is assured, this furnishes proof that revolutionary violence, the highest manifestation of unalloyed violence by man, is possible, and shows by what means" (252, trans. modified).

The revolution Benjamin his in mind in this sentence cannot be imagined as a mere political overthrow; nor is the overturning of private capitalistic relations of primary significance. What Benjamin has in mind and what forms the secret goal of his whole article is, rather, the idea of a sort of cultural revolution that would bring down the centuries-old system of legal relations altogether. The critique of the legal means-ends schema, initially carried out only from an immanent perspective, then from a transcending, historical-philosophical one, has led to the insight that the legal violence that dominates everything, and has penetrated into every last corner of everyday ethical life, finally serves only to maintain the established order of power. In the end, Benjamin is convinced, we can only be liberated from this spell of law by a revolution that, in a sacral way, immediately produces justice through the performance of violence. It is no wonder that an essay with this content—whose concept of law is terroristic, whose ideal of violence is theocratic, and whose idea of revolution is eschatological—has so far been interpreted only in ways that make it harmless,[42] appropriate it,[43] or render it one-sided.[44] The impulse that drives Benjamin's essay is a critique of law as a whole. He is convinced that any institution of society carried out according to the means-ends schema must reduce all human affairs to the balancing of individual interests. And the only moral power that the still only thirty-year-old author believes can—by reason of its purity, its absolute intrinsicness—free us from the fatality of law is the sacral violence of God.

SEVEN

APPROPRIATING FREEDOM

Freud's Conception of Individual Self-Relation

Only dogmatism can today still blind one to the fact that a string of premises of Freudian theory have in the meantime become highly questionable. Developments in infant research, in developmental psychology generally, but also in evolutionary biology, have cast doubt on central and basic assumptions of the psychoanalytic view of young children. Beginning with the assumption of a primary narcissism, in which the infant is still supposed to experience its environment exclusively as its own work, through to the claim that girls typically have penis envy, much of what was still considered relatively secure fifty years ago has been discredited.[1] Even drive theory as a whole, which was, after all, the biological foundation of Freudian theory, today sees itself open to legitimate doubts. If one also adds to these growing concerns the revisions that have meanwhile been made to Freud's work within the psychoanalytic movement itself,[2] then in 2008, two years after his 150th birthday, one can indeed say that never since Freud's death have the future of his original theory and its chances of being productively continued been as bad as they are today.

The zeitgeist also seems to agree with this extremely skeptical assessment. Not only can one hear on all sides that the number of patients prepared to undergo psychoanalytic treatment is dwindling; not only was laying into Freud's work more or less a journalistic fashion until shortly before the just celebrated birthday.[3] Rather, subjects themselves seem to be increasingly growing out of psychoanalytic culture because they are required to constantly readjust to an uncertain future and so hardly still feel an incentive or the necessity to occupy themselves with their own past. The social benefit of a time-consuming, activity-obstructing return to the history of one's individual formation has obviously lapsed, so that in our culture psychoanalytic ideals are also becoming increasingly discredited.

A widespread reflex reaction these days to this situation of growing doubt and marginalization, indeed of a downright threat to its existence, is for psychoanalysis to retreat forward—namely, into a core area of recent natural science. The central components of the original theory—the interpretation of dreams, the idea of repression, and the structural theory—are no longer to be defended on their own territory but to receive confirmation in the framework of the practically exploding neurosciences. If one is to believe some of its leading representatives, psychoanalysis hopes to be rescued from the long-simmering crisis by the results of brain research. But then there is a threat—and this is my thesis—of losing that element of Freudian theory which comprises its central legacy, one still valid today beyond all parts that have in the meantime surely become questionable: the insight that, to begin with, the human is always a divided, inwardly ruptured being, yet one which, thanks to its inherent interest in extending its "inner" freedom, has the ability to reduce or even overcome that rupturedness through its own reflective activity.

In all components containing this one anthropological idea, Freud added to the traditional image of humans an essentially new thought, the core of which is a respective extension of the idea of the human self-relation. The subject gains access to his psychic activities only from the inner perspective of an already familiar idea of his own freedom. The latter more or less forces him to turn retrospectively to the separated-off aspects of his own life history so as ultimately, by way of the remembering thus embarked on, to belatedly appropriate what had been separated off. It could also be said that only on the condition of a critical appropriation of her own process of formation does the human seize the opportunity provided to her for freedom of the will. However, access to this reflective movement is fundamentally blocked for brain research. Although it can perhaps make out such a movement's neuronal circuits thanks to its imaging methods, it cannot define the movement's performance itself because it lacks the condition for identifying in the brain the reflectively effective idea of one's own freedom. From the observer perspective of brain research, that feature of the human person disappears which had, almost as a matter of course, been its driving force for Freud: the self-activating anticipation of a freedom of the will, which, faced with subjectively experienced restrictions, motivates one to set about the process of working through one's own life history.

In the following, I attempt to reconstruct this complex, multi-layered conception of the individual self-relation by first setting out Freud's turn to the pathology of the "normal" personality. The further the founder of psychoanalysis developed his theory, the less he shied away from also drawing conclusions about the "healthy" subject's irrational centrifugal forces from his findings about the causes that generate neurotic illnesses (section I). From here, Freud saw himself forced to adapt his concept of repression and of defense to the conditions that had to apply to the apparently intact subject. In the second step, I therefore outline how on his view the causes are to be defined for the growing child's building up a reservoir of repressed, not further integrated, desires even in usual conditions of socialization (section II). With this normalization of repression, Freud faces the task of characterizing the reflective process through which the intact personality brings about the kind of psychic emancipation that analytic therapy is supposed to help attain in the case of the ill subject. The final step is to expand on how the conception of individual self-appropriation with which Freud attempted to solve this task is constituted (section III). Central to my deliberations is thus the extremely close connection Freud made between individual autonomy and reflectively coming to terms with the past, between freedom of the will and biographical "working though." I show that Freud never doubted, even for a moment, the possibility of "freedom of the will," but he made the step of appropriating one's own will a necessary precondition for it.

$$\sqrt{\left(\ \mathbf{I} \ \right)^{\mu}}$$

In his work, Freud did not just rely on assumptions about normal socialization processes to get information about the infant causes of neurotic illnesses. Rather, conversely, he continually drew conclusions from the peculiarity of individual neuroses for normal psychic life. This to and fro between pathological diagnosis and the analysis of normality, between etiology and personality theory, forms a conceptual thread in his work that gains more and more in independent significance with his increasing scientific maturity. In the end, his theory as a whole represents more of a contribution to revising our idea of human subjectivity than a proposed solution to special problems of psychic illness.

Already in his *Interpretation of Dreams* (1900), Freud draws on the dream as an example to study the nonpathological case of mental activity characterized by defense strategies. In the acute memory of his or her own dream, every person is confronted, on Freud's view, with a text that is made so alien by omissions and displacements that a key to understanding the self-produced meaning can no longer be found within it. Freud continued his preoccupation with such irrational clouding of apparently completely normal, healthy psychic life a year later as he set about writing his treatise on the *Psychopathology of Everyday Life* (1901). In this new context, he was concerned with initially completely inconspicuous faulty actions such as slips of the tongue and forgetting, but which even in the intact personality can take on such frequency and persistence that they can no longer be dismissed as mere coincidence. In such cases of compulsive repetition, everyday mistakes attain the character of symptoms permitting an insight into the deep-seated defense mechanisms by which even the normal person is molded. With a view to his further researches, Freud can therefore maintain at the end of his study that "the borderline between the normal and abnormal in nervous matters is fluid"—indeed, that we are all, as he laconically put its, "a little neurotic."[4]

From now on, Freud would no longer drop the perspective according to which a constant readiness to produce strange desires and conspicuous defensive attitudes also exists in apparently intact psychic life. He is constantly in search of the point at which the subject that comes across as completely normal manifests a behavioral expression possessing such bizarre, unintelligible traits that it points to the continued systematic influence of archaic residues in the individual psyche. An essential step in the direction thus outlined is represented by the short text on "Mourning and Melancholia" that Freud published in 1916 in the *Zeitschrift für Psychoanalyse*.[5] In his view, the mourning in which we cling to a lost love object in a hallucinatory manner departs only gradually from melancholia, in which we also experience a drastic reduction in our feeling of self-esteem in addition to the wish-fantasy. But it is less what separates these two states from each other that initially interests Freud in his essay than what links them. Both mourning and melancholia are psychic reactions to the painful loss of an object in which each time an "inhibition and circumscription of the ego" occurs in that in the wish-fantasy, the loved person's ongoing existence is hallucinated and hence extinguishes, almost without residue, commitment to the social environment.[6] The threshold to pathology is thus already crossed on entering the state of mourning, since, according to the conventional idea, fantasizing about nonexistent objects is a clear sign of the presence of mental confusion. And it is only scientific routine, Freud concludes, that prevents us from taking the corresponding step and adding mourning to psychic illnesses. Both the degree of the "painful loss" and the intensity of the wish-fantasies are in themselves clear indications that a tendency toward pathological denial of reality is already present in the clinical realm of the normal.[7] The usual functions of the ego, essentially those of keeping a check on reality, are suspended because the subject is animated by the primitive wish to maintain communication with the lost love object.[8]

These brief reflections basically contain more by way of consequences than Freud himself would like to admit. He does not actually move the conventional boundary between normality and pathology but shifts the potential for expressing pathological behavior into the sovereign territory of the "normal" personality itself. Each subject, including those otherwise perfectly adept with reality, is supposed to be able to be sporadically sought out by wishes that would not stand up to being checked with reality. Instead, their particularly primitive character, the fact that they ignore the differentiation meanwhile erected between inner and outer, is a clear indication that they must stem from unsurmounted relics of early childhood.[9] This view is explicitly confirmed in a short essay that Freud published in the same year as the essay on "Mourning and Melancholia" titled "A Metapsychological Supplement to the Theory of Dreams."[10] There Freud deals with the processes that make it possible that in certain affective states taken to be normal, such as mourning, being in love, or sleep, the same kind of hallucinatory satisfaction of wishes can take place that we recognize from states of neurotic illness.

Of interest here are not the details of the complicated reflections Freud develops in his essay but just the rough schema by which he orients himself. The question is, How is it to be explained that the same happens in those relatively usual situations as what otherwise goes on only in an accentuated form in pathological conditions? In his answer, Freud starts by assuming that in the states of dreaming, being in love, or sleep, the psychic forces in the subject that usually take care of examining reality are paralyzed, due either to the intense excitement or greatly reduced attention. In this way, an "undressing" of the "psychic" takes place that allows the hallucinatory mechanisms of early childhood to take possession of the ego.[11] This "not only brings hidden or repressed wishes into consciousness; it also represents them, with the subject's entire belief, as fulfilled."[12] The normal adult is thus also familiar with situations in which the mere wish for an object suffices to experience it mentally as the source of an actual satisfaction. In such states, the boundaries between inner and outer, between ideas and reality, are cancelled so that the early, primitive mechanism of hallucinatory satisfaction of wishes again grasps a place.

All the texts mentioned, starting with *The Interpretation of Dreams* through to the "Metapsychological Supplement," agree in discerning in intact psychic life the kind of rupture that is usually suspected only in the psychically ill. It can also be said that Freud anthropologizes the potential for conflict between repressed wishes by granting them a power over even the healthy subject: we all occasionally experience situations in which we are confronted with needs and wishes that don't really seem to fit into the rationally attuned network of our remaining wishes. What is peculiar about these desires, however, is not only the degree of their heterogeneity, their incompatibility, but also the fact that they go along with the fantasy in its—in itself impossible—satisfaction. Thus we obviously reactivate psychic mechanisms we might suspect of having dominated us in early childhood.

However, in the texts cited, Freud does not yet seem to possess any really convincing answer to the question of why repressions should also have played a role in the prehistory of the normal adult. In the case of neurotic illness, he had initially started with the assumption that the cause of such repressions must lie in traumatic events in early childhood which had been banished to the unconscious due to their threatening character. The symptom is supposed to reflect the compulsively returning recollection of a real occurrence, the catastrophic meaning of which the young child was able to protect itself from only by instinctively withdrawing it from consciousness. However, Freud soon replaced this realistic interpretation with a considerably more subtle hypothesis, according to which not an actual event but the wish for such an event forms the cause of repression: impulses that the child had to experience as dangerous because they threatened its affective equilibrium were shunted into the unconscious for reasons of self-protection, from whence they produced neurotic symptoms in later life.[13] But none of these explanations is suited to making understandable why the intact personality should repeatedly be plagued by repressed wishes. In such cases, there is no symptom of illness, there is no hint of suffering that is difficult to bear. We are concerned only with wishes that do not seem to fit, in either their content or form, into the system of adult endeavors. Freud only finds an answer to the questions linked to this once he realizes that a kind of intersubjective anxiety the healthy subject must have encountered in childhood has to be considered as the ultimate cause of repression.

⤙ II ⤕

The difficulties Freud has had until now in explaining that there is also pathological potential in the completely normal subject result from his assumption that repression sets in at a relatively extraordinary point. If only the young child that is confronted either with a traumatic event or a particularly intense, extravagant drive wish is supposed to have cause for repression, there is hardly any reason to impute a reservoir of unconscious wishes to an intact personality. For the fact that this person is without any degree of suffering, and exhibits no symptoms of any kind of illness, makes it more natural to suppose that here one is concerned with a completely normal, disturbance-free socialization process. If repression—that is, the exclusion from articulation—is bound to preconditions that could only apply to the unsuccessful process of formation, how then is it to be made intelligible that unarticulated, nonintegrated impulses should also make themselves noticed continually in the healthy person's psychic life? Freud thus lacks, it can be said, an idea of the normality of repression. He is unable to explain why there should be cause in every process of socialization to exclude certain drive impulses or wishes from future translation into language and to banish them into a realm of the unconscious.

Freud makes the transition to such a more comprehensive conception of "repression," one significantly better adapted to normality, in the second half of the 1920s when he begins to get clearer about the anthropological significance of anxiety for the young child. And it is no coincidence that it is in this phase of his output that deliberations take shape in his theory for the first time that point in the direction of the object relations theory later developed by Donald Winnicott and Melanie Klein. In this context, the text "Inhibitions, Symptoms and Anxiety," which Freud published in 1926 as a book in the International Psychoanalytic Press, assumes particular importance for our considerations.[14] Already with regard to the differentiation in content, anthropological breadth, and realism about the child's world of experience, this text stands out in Freud's work. Again his gaze is directed above all to the causes of repression in the neurotic, but the "comparatively simple neuroses of everyday life" are also given enough attention for the healthy person to remain included in the analysis.[15] In a certain way, a continuum is even created between neurotic and completely normal repression because Freud, obviously consciously, no longer attempts to determine the point at which the first turns into the second: that is, normal repression goes beyond the point at which the development of neuroses is supposed to come about.

The starting point for the argument is a self-correction that Freud undertakes so inconspicuously that it easily avoids being noticed. Until now, we read, he has explained the young child's anxiety as an affective result of the backlash of repression on its experience—namely, as an automatic transformation of the "cathectic energy of the repressed impulse . . . into anxiety."[16] Now, however, he must admit that it could also be exactly the other way round: the young child does not sense anxiety because it is repressing certain drive wishes; rather, the child represses because he or she feels anxiety about certain drive wishes. The modified premise, which now seems considerably more plausible to Freud, nonetheless raises the new problem as to where the anxiety is then supposed to stem from, which in certain, yet to be more closely designated, conditions occasions the child's repression. The "mnemic image" of such an affective state must already be somehow present in the child's psychic life,[17] if it is claimed that it is not repression that produces anxiety, but, the other way round, anxiety that produces repression. It is the question just outlined that Freud makes central to his text. On the next sixty to seventy pages, he concerns himself with hardly anything but the search for the origin of the anxiety through which the young child withdraws certain of its drive wishes from continuing articulation.

The hypothesis that initially most strongly captivates Freud is that of the trauma of birth. In 1924, Otto Rank had published a book in which it was supposed that, because of its protected well-being in the womb, the infant reacts to the act of birth with a kind of panic anxiety.[18] Suddenly exposed to the flood of stimuli breaking in from the world, the infant experiences a traumatic shock whose subsequent influence in all later states of anxiety attains validity through the affinity of the physical reaction patterns. The mere fact that Freud goes into this thesis in detail no less than three times reveals how intensely he must have felt it to be a theoretical challenge. In any case, he seems convinced that, among the various alternatives, the idea of an original trauma of birth initially provides the best key to explaining the young child's constant readiness for anxiety. However, wherever he comes to speak of Rank's proposal, Freud immediately hints at slight doubts relating to a certain disparity in the explanation: whereas young children always tend to attacks of panic anxiety when they feel left alone, the traumatic shock at birth lacks any relation to being left alone in such a way because "during its intra-uterine life" there were "no objects" whose disappearance might have been experienced as threatening.[19] In all its later anxious behavior, the child is directed toward a danger for which the trauma of birth could not have provided the triggering schema. For due to the fetus's lack of an object relation, the threat of being left alone is something that could not have been experienced in any way by the infant itself during the process of being born.

It is this grave objection that now paves the way for Freud's own intersubjective view. It is almost diametrically opposed to the trauma-of-birth thesis insofar as it recognizes the danger situation that the infant reacts to with panic anxiety, not in the interruption of the intrauterine existence but in being left alone by the mother who first appears afterward. It can indeed be said with Arnold Gehlen that Freud's starting point is the biological fact that human beings are carried by the mother for much less time than most other animals.[20] From this fact of "premature birth," both authors infer a relatively high degree of organic helplessness and lack of specialization that makes the newly born child heavily dependent on a protective environment right at the beginning.[21] For Freud, the dependency thus effected now results in the infant's more or less biological fixation on its mother, whose care and support is so vitally important for it that the first sign of her disappearance creates the paradigmatic schema of all that spells "danger." From now on, any hint of being left behind without the loved object is the signal to which the child reacts with the same kind of anxiety that befell it when it first experienced the mother's disappearance. The following passage, which today still demands admiration in view of its synthetic power, summarizes all these argumentative steps in a single train of thought. The biological point of departure, Freud says,

> is the long period of time during which the young of the human species is in a condition of helplessness and dependence. Its intra-uterine existence seems to be short in comparison with that of most animals, and it is sent into the world in a less finished state. As a result, the influence of the real external world upon it is intensified and an early differentiation between the ego and the id is promoted. Moreover, the dangers of the external world have a greater importance for it, so that the value of the object which can alone protect it against them and take the place of its former intra-uterine life is enormously enhanced. The biological factor, then, establishes the earliest situations of danger and creates the need to be loved which will accompany the child through the rest of its life.[22]

Precisely this latter formulation, which almost exactly anticipates a central idea of Winnicott's, might provide cause for further reflections concerning its consequences for Freud's entire theory. He speaks here, very unusually for him, not of the young child's "drive" but of its "need"; and the content or the direction of such an early need is allocated the expression "love"—a term that Freud finds a use for only very rarely in his theoretical writings. But for our purposes, it is of more interest how Freud now finds a bridge from this intermediate result back to his initial problem; for the question he actually wants to answer is to what extent a danger-signaling schema that is grasped as "primal anxiety" can cause the young child to exempt certain of its drive impulses from the further process of mental organization and to repress them into the unconscious.[23]

For Freud, the key to his answer is the idea that signals of a separation from the loved object can originate not only from the outer world but also from the inside. For then every wish the child senses, but which is at the same time experienced as incompatible with the continued existence of the love it longs for, must trigger in the child the old, original separation anxiety. If this is so, if the young child is also capable of perceiving its own wishes as warning signals of a possible loss of the loved object, then, according to Freud, it will more or less instinctively do anything to avoid the situation prefigured by the dangerous wish. And the only means it has to this end consists of relinquishing the disagreeable impulse, which is hence dropped as a wish and withdrawn from consciousness. The child, as Freud's line of thought can be summarized, represses all its wishes into the unconscious the pursuit of which it must experience as endangering the love of its reference person. So as not to be separated from its mother or another loved person, it builds up within itself a reservoir of unarticulated, primitively left wishes that henceforth continue to exist within it like a "foreign body."[24]

With these considerations, Freud has created a concept of repression that can also be applied to the completely inconspicuous, normal socialization process. Assuming the infant's constitutional helplessness, every child will sense a panic anxiety about being separated from the care-giving reference person and will hence try somehow to suppress such wishes as might endanger that relation, and like all others will thus finally develop in itself a potential for repressed tendencies. For Freud, this normalization of repression results in the consequence that the intact personality, too, is not free of the restrictions that are imposed on the psychically ill subject in an incomparably more intense manner. Like the neurotic, though well below the threshold to suffering, the healthy person is exposed to intervention by unconscious wishes that interrupt the "free intercourse . . . between all its parts" and occasionally force involuntary utterances.[25] Freud puts the endangerment of freedom of the human will at the center the consequences of these "restrictions of the functions of the ego."[26] The individual's ability to form a rational will that is transparent to herself and resolute has extremely narrow limits when alienating wishes constantly intervene or when intentions can no longer be implemented or, conversely, acquire an unwilled priority. In such situations, familiar to us all, our will constantly seems clouded because it is influenced by compulsions or dependencies whose origin we cannot see clearly. As relatively widespread examples of such disturbances of the will, Freud names the lack of desire to eat and inhibited work.[27] But, of course, much less spectacular cases can be also be drawn from normal everyday life that show how often the subject's own will is not under its command.

Now, the language Freud uses in these passages already shows that he does not want to present the compromise to freedom of the will as something constituting an immovable fact of human nature. Rather, to speak of such disturbances as forming "restrictions of the functions of the ego" means making the ego's normal prosperity, its functional efficiency, dependent on overcoming all such compromises. With his psychology's functionalist terminology, Freud appears to adopt a normative perspective in which human welfare is bound to the presumption of eliminating such clouding of the will as originates from its unarticulated childhood needs. The human can only enjoy its proper nature—that is, the capacity for freedom of the will—to its full extent when no restrictions are imposed on its functioning. Between the ego's functional efficiency and human welfare, one can also say, a link in conditions exists for Freud because he is convinced that only rationally weighing up wishes, values, and reality can guarantee successful living.[28]

However, at this point of an almost Aristotelian ethics,[29] the question arises as to what means Freud provides the individual subject to attain such a form of as unclouded a freedom of the will as possible. If the intact personality is already constantly caught up by wishes and tendencies that can appear nontransparent and alienating to itself, then it is completely unclear how the aim of a functionally efficient—indeed, free—will is ever supposed to be attainable. To be sure, for the psychically ill, Freud provides the instrument of analytic therapy to find a way out. Through the associative interpretations offered by the analyst, the patient is supposed to learn to attain insight into the early childhood causes of its symptoms and, in this way, to regain a certain latitude for its freedom of will. But what means of attaining freedom of the will does Freud recommend to the subject that, although free from the degree of suffering of the ill, is nonetheless also familiar with that clouding of its will that arises from repressions of the past? To this question, Freud provides an answer that only seldom rises to the surface thematically in his works. He is convinced, namely, that as a matter of course we have all always adopted an attitude toward ourselves in which we try to appropriate our own will by means of recollective work.

In the steps of his conception reconstructed so far, Freud makes use of the methodical means of a naturalistic self-objectification.[30] For the purpose of gaining knowledge, that is, he describes the pathological processes of repression or defense as though these were natural, causal processes that fulfill certain functions in the reproduction of human creatures. With the transition to the question of how subjects react to these restrictions in their ego's abilities, Freud shifts his perspective by now orienting himself according to the self-understanding of persons who feel themselves restricted. The reflective efforts by which ruptured subjects seek to free their willing from nonperspicuous influences can only be explored from the subjective inner perspective of the subject affected. From this new perspective, what could previously appear to be a lawlike natural process must now be comprehended as something produced by the subject itself—namely, as a form of repression attributable to itself. The account of the reflective process through which such a recovery is supposed to be possible forms the core of Freud's conception of the individual self-relation.

What is peculiar to this conception is surely that the determinations developed in it are presented not as normative ideals but as completely normal achievements every healthy subject is capable of as a matter of course. The human is for Freud less a self-interpreting being than one that critically scrutinizes itself, constantly looking through its own past to see whether traces of compulsions that have remained unconscious can be found in it. It would have been quite alien for Freud to hold it as a demand from the outside that the subject shows interest in its life history. Rather, he presupposes as self-evident that every person possesses a deep-seated interest in forming a will that is as free as possible by critically reappraising its own previous history. It may be that the demanding traits of his own personality are reflected in Freud's image of humans, which is conspicuously opposed to the pessimism of his cultural theory.[31] It may also be, as Thomas Mann has supposed, that here Freud's close link with Romanticism, which was also already concerned with the emancipatory potential of returning to contemplate one's own unconscious, comes to light.[32] In any case, it is certain that, from the beginning, Freud credited humans with the ability to attain a will that is as free as possible through its own intellectual efforts. To this extent, the conception of the individual self-relation he develops merely retraces the conscious processes that are supposed to take place pretheoretically in every subject.

The process Freud is interested in begins with a person sensing in himself or herself an alienating wish or a conspicuous, compulsively recurrent association of thoughts. None of these mental activities fits into the concerned subject's system of endeavors, and they all fulfill the condition of the individual not really being able to be understand them. Of course, noticing such a difference already demands adopting not merely an observer's perspective toward oneself but the perspective of interested attentiveness, even solicitude. If, that is, one's own wishes and beliefs were taken to be independent facts, as though they could be somehow discovered in one's inside, it could not be subjectively asked at all whether they result in an intelligible, or meaningful, interrelation.[33] Freud presumes, as I have said, that human subjects naturally have such an understanding attitude toward their psychic life. They do not behave indifferently toward their mental productions but, due to their "ego," persistently aim to integrate them into a rational whole. It can also be said that in the subject's relation to itself, to its mental activities, a constantly effective anticipation of a meaningful, intelligible connection between all its own wishes and beliefs is presumed. In addition, Freud seems to want to claim that this hermeneutic process of disclosure takes place in a form possessing features of an inner dialogue. Thus he often uses metaphors from the political world to sketch the idea that the psychic instances should, if possible, maintain a relationship of free exchange and commerce among one another.[34] In such a communication process the "super-ego" takes on, as he puts it in "Inhibitions, Symptoms and Anxiety," the voice of "ethical and aesthetic" critique, while the task of thematizing the necessity of adjusting to reality falls to the "ego."[35] And in the sense of integrability, all the wishes and beliefs that are approved by these two instances' dialogical test procedure can then count as rational.

Of course, as long as the wishes thus rejected are held only to be nonrational, they do not yet have to signify any particular irritation for the affected subject. We all develop intentions or endeavors often enough that on reflection quickly prove to be incompatible with reality or our moral conscience. To this must be added, first, the fact of constant recurrence or compulsiveness and, second, a high degree of unintelligibility, before such wishes provide occasion to deal with their origin and prehistory more intensively. To be sure, this return to contemplate one's own biography cannot be motivated by a degree of suffering. The healthy person dealt with by Freud's conception of the individual self-relation does not suffer in the clinical sense from its opaque, compulsively recurrent wishes but probably initially feels them to be merely tedious or obstructive to realizing its own aims. So, in order to be able to explain why such an intact subject should also be brought in this situation to deal with its life history, Freud must venture a risky step, for which he lacks a reliable justification. He has to impute to every person, whether healthy or ill, an interest in pressing for the production of a will that is as free as possible.[36] Returning to contemplate one's own process of formation, which Freud also ascribes to the normal subject as a reaction to confronting irrational wishes, is simultaneously the performance and the expression of this interest. We turn back to our life history in such moments because we want our willing to be free of elements that are unintelligible to us and not willed.

It is only with this return that a reflective process sets in that can be comprehended, with Freud, as appropriating the history of one's own formation. The intact subject starts retracing the development process it has itself experienced in order to explore the biographical situation in which the alienating, hardly intelligible wish might have arisen. Here different methods of reflection that are already intuitively familiar to us mesh with one another because we have already gotten to know them in our process of maturing as appropriate means of determining our personal identity. We have at our disposal different narrative schemata by means of which we can represent our life as a more or less conflict-ridden formation history, and from this standpoint we can try to discover retrospectively the point at which the individual elements of our current system of endeavors originate. Introspection and genealogy, narrative self-assurance and the reconstruction of individual wishes and intentions complement one another to allow the breaks that open up in our individual history of needs to become transparent.[37] To the extent that such a genealogy of our wishes is carried out, we then finally come across a pattern of interaction that dates back a long time, often fixed to certain key experiences that seem to be somehow barred from our memory; we don't really get further in our individual attempt at reconstruction, perhaps even feel a massive defense, sensing in any case a certain discomfort in daring to go back behind the blocked threshold of our biography. For Freud, this moment of "negation" represents the linchpin of our self-appropriation process.[38] For it is the question of whether we are in a position to penetrate the repression becoming manifest in the negation that decides the success of our effort to increase the degree of our freedom of will.

"Appropriation" is not a term Freud systematically used in his own theoretical language, but he could have accommodated it in his approach without difficulty, since it refers to the same achievement that he thought of as the direction in which the individual self-relation's moves. In the process of appropriation, we attempt to make something that is initially alien or unintelligible our own by comprehending it as something previously separated and, hence, ultimately belonging to our person.[39] The subject that has advanced in its biographical self-contemplation through to the point of a "negation" has, according to Freud, already almost reached the threshold of such an appropriation. For the negative, negating reaction already contains the pointer to a biographical location at which a certain wish was not pursued further out of anxiety about the intersubjective consequences—that is, was repressed into the unconscious and subsequently existed there in a disfigured, primitive form. Perhaps it could also be said that what else is needed in the reflective moment of negation is just individual resoluteness, perhaps also the help of friends or confidants, to intellectually elicit the biographical circumstances that at the time led to the separation of the today irritating, unfamiliar wish. Guided by the indirect hints contained in our memory's recoil, we recollectively prepare the way back to the past situation in which we have separated off an element of our will out of intersubjective anxiety.

For Freud, of course, the process of recovering one's own will is not yet completed with this intellectual realization of the causal circumstances. We must first still learn to accept for ourselves what cognitive insight yields before the process of appropriation can reach a successful conclusion. In a marvelous passage in his short essay on "Negation" (1925), Freud makes a distinction that aims precisely at this last step in which "remembering and working through" is completed:

> Negation is a way of taking cognizance of what is repressed; indeed it is already a lifting of the repression, though not, of course, an acceptance of what is repressed. We can see how in this the intellectual function is separated from the affective process. With the help of negation only one consequence of the process of repression is undone—the fact, namely, of the ideational content of what is repressed not reaching consciousness. The outcome of this is a kind of intellectual acceptance of the repressed, while at the same time what is essential to the repression persists.[40]

Unfortunately, Freud does not expand further in this passage, or in other passages of his work, on how the "affective process" is to be constituted through which the taking back of repression is actually completed. It also remains unclear with him which element of repression it is that must be assumed to be "affective" in the subject's concluding act of self-appropriation. More clearly than in other texts, Freud here initially distinguishes between an "intellectual," or merely cognitive, insight and an "affective" acceptance in the process of individual reappraisal. Whereas the first process ought to consist of learning to comprehend the circumstances of repression or what is repressed itself as a fact in one's own biography, the affective process would have to have the aim of retrospectively accepting this fact as a motivational element in one's own personality.[41] To this extent, the process of reflectively appropriating one's own will would only be concluded once the previously repressed fact of repression or what was repressed is accepted into the given system of endeavors in such a way that from now on they decisively shape our self-understanding, our view of the world and others.

If this is what Freud had in mind with his concept of "affective" acceptance, then it still has to be clarified whether what is to be accepted is more what was repressed itself or the fact that the repression took place at the time. In the passage quoted, Freud seems to want to say that what was repressed—that is, the intentional content of the repressed wish—must itself be retrospectively accepted for one's own self-understanding. But such a view would amount to the peculiar consequence that we are able to articulate and accept the object of repression even before we have emotionally accepted the fact of repression. I therefore believe that here we should deviate from Freud's view and understand affective acceptance of repression as the goal and endpoint of self-appropriation. Starting with the negation through to the affective level, we must learn to accept the fact that anxiety about losing the loved person had once necessitated us to repress a threatening wish. And it is the emotional admission of this anxiety that first allows us retrospectively to accept the performed separation as something we ourselves willed and thus to reappropriate it as something of our own. To be sure, such recognition of one's own anxiety does not by itself reorganize the previously repressed wish. But at the same time, it is the only way that we can learn after the event to mentally reorganize the content locked within it and to give this a propositional form.

In a formal respect, Freud's conception of the individual self-relation is thus very much like Kierkegaard's conception.[42] Although Freud was always rather skeptical about such philosophical extensions of his theory,[43] the central importance of his insight is lost if such comparisons are not drawn. Neither for him nor for Kierkegaard is attaining freedom of the will the result of a one-off, momentarily performed act of becoming aware. We do not become assured of our individual freedom through an instantaneous reflection that shows us that our endeavors and wishes are the expression only of our own will. For such self-assurance, what is needed is, rather, a protracted and strenuous process of working through and remembering in which we attempt, against persistent resistance, to appropriate retrospectively the previously separated elements of our will. Since the cause of the separation was always anxiety (with Freud, namely, anxiety about separation from the love object), we must hence succeed in accepting that anxiety as an integral component of our personality. To the extent that we succeed in such acceptance of anxiety in our system of endeavors, we purify our will of influences and elements that we could not understand as self-willed. The human self-relation, as Freud's great insight can be summarized, consists in the process of self-appropriation of one's will by affectively admitting to anxiety.

Translated by Andrew Inkpin

EIGHT

"ANXIETY AND POLITICS"

The Strengths and Weaknesses of Franz Neumann's Diagnosis of a Social Pathology

Franz Neumann's late essay, "Anxiety and Politics," represents one of the few available attempts to combine the diagnosis of a social pathology with an interest in questions of political justice.[1] The pathology under consideration in his study involves various forms of anxiety, while his normative reference point follows from the thesis that democratic will-formation presupposes a necessary measure of individual autonomy. The theoretical association by which Neumann connects these two levels of analysis presumably originated with Adam Smith and has since been further developed by only a few political thinkers, such as Michael Bakhtin and Charles Taylor. At stake is an elementary presupposition of individual autonomy, understood as the capacity to reflexively participate in processes of democratic will-formation: freedom from anxiety.

An analysis of those social pathologies consisting of unnecessary or superfluous forms of anxiety contributes directly to an examination of the normative preconditions of the constitutional democratic state: only those subjects free from the internal limitations of anxiety can enter into the political public sphere and therein act as democratic citizens. It follows from this formulation that only those forms of anxiety that do not function as affective mechanisms capable of indicating the existence of real dangers can be regarded as effectively inhibiting individual autonomy. While we consider such reactions of anxiety to be integral parts of a healthy personality, we are at the same time confronted with "neurotic" or "pathological" manifestations of anxiety that paralyze the individual, reducing his or her capacity for autonomous action. It is clear that Neumann is only interested in this second type of anxiety, which he suspects as a psychological impediment to democratic will-formation.

The distinctiveness of Neumann's approach stands in contrast to competing analyses in that he proceeds from a psychoanalytic concept of "anxiety." Whereas Bakhtin, for example, understands politically relevant forms of anxiety or fear as resulting from the disappearance of "carnivalistic" laughter in public places,[2] Neumann begins, conversely, by concentrating in detail on those affective mechanisms that foster the emergence of neurotic forms of anxiety. In the tradition of the Frankfurt School, he links this concern with individual anxieties to a social-psychological attentiveness to the neurotic features of "mass" phenomena. In the following discussion, I focus on the strengths and weaknesses of this approach. It is my conviction that Neumann's small study not only opened up a remarkably significant and often neglected field of research but also appropriately distinguished the conceptual and normative premises that should be taken into consideration today in the context of political psychology. At the same time, I believe that this starting point evinces considerable weaknesses that can be traced back to, on the one hand, its strong dependence on Freud's classic psychoanalysis and its continuation in the Frankfurt School and, on the other, the narrowing of its view just to the case of National Socialism.

In the following, I proceed by successively commenting on each of the theoretical steps Neumann takes to substantiate his theoretical agenda. I begin with an analysis of the concept of individual neurotic anxiety, which Neumann, following Freud, takes as the basis of his approach (section I). The second step, in accordance with Neumann's own procedure, deals with the psychological connection between the neurotic anxieties of individuals and the regressive loss of one's own ego as part of a mass in unbounded collectivities (section II). Only after I have clarified these two psychoanalytic premises do I concern myself with what Neumann calls the institutionalization of anxiety in "tyrannical governments" (section III).

I. ALTERNATIVE CONCEPTS OF INDIVIDUAL ANXIETY

Neumann initially outlines his approach by distinguishing between three types of "alienation"—"psychological," "social," and "political"—in order to be able to show that the first psychological form of alienation represents the most elementary one. In this contest, this simply means that the initial psychological form of alienation makes the other forms possible. From here, Neumann moves quickly to an identification of psychological alienation with neurotic anxiety, which, in the spirit of Freud, he tries to conceptualize as resulting from repressed libidinal drives. Even if the affects of anxiety possess a number of healthy functions that, in essence, exist either to protect the individual from danger or to facilitate cathartic experiences, a negative form can be clearly distinguished from them—one that leads to an immobilization of the ego functions and therefore to a paralysis of the subject. Having associated them with the repression of libidinal energy, Freud named this class of anxieties "neurotic."

My difficulties already begin with this starting point, since it is far too dependent on Freud's biological assumptions about a human drive-surplus. For Freud, this constitutive surplus arises from a deeply embedded and oppressive compulsion extant in all human beings that to a certain extent represses their drives. The resulting "neurotic" anxiety is thus an anthropological fate, so to speak, allowing little room for individual deviation. In contrast to this model, I prefer to understand the idea of neurotic anxiety as a secondary human reaction-formation, anchored in the dangers of lost intersubjective security.[3] Within the framework of such a model, which is based on the assumptions of object-relations theory, earlier situations of endangered intersubjectivity—as epitomized in the process of separation from the mother or other primary caregiver—are considered the cause of all subsequent forms of anxiety. To a certain extent, therefore, all forms of neurotic anxiety are anchored in an inability to completely overcome those earlier affective experiences in which we were required to recognize the independence of the concrete other. In this context, Michael Balint, one of the most interesting advocates of object-relations theory, has advanced the intellectually rich suggestion that the child can react with two different behavioral patterns to early traumas caused by the loss of the mother, who at the time is still (episodically) symbiotically given.[4] The first, "ocnophilic" behavioral reaction consists in an apprehensive bond with the object of love, out of which develops a continuous search for the pleasure of being held and a reluctance to relinquish the security-giving partner. By contrast, the second reaction model, which Balint calls "philobatic," takes the form of a swift search for new objects of love, accompanied by a desire for the stimulus generated by the loss of partners.

I am convinced that this distinction between two forms of coping with reactive anxiety would be more accommodating to Neumann's theoretical interests than the one-dimensional thesis that all forms of anxiety can be traced back to the original compulsion of surplus drive repression. For the object-relations theoretical conception not only possesses a clearer conception of what constitutes "irrational" human anxieties; not only does it explain why each additional stage in the developmental process of childhood is accompanied by new forms of an anxiety-laden endangerment of intersubjectivity. In addition, it is capable of differentiating between various patterns in the intrapsychic overcoming of such experiences of loss in a plausible way. In short, had Neumann followed the complex model of object-relations theory, he could have understood neurotic anxiety as an intrapyschic expression of the reaction model that Balint described as ocnophilic. Against the background of this alternative account of childhood anxieties, it also seems sensible to question the next step Neumann undertakes in the working out of his basic social-psychological thesis: the attempt to draw conclusions about the unconscious mechanisms of social mass formation from an explanation of neurotic anxieties.

II. INDIVIDUAL REGRESSION AND MASS FORMATION

The central concept with which Neumann achieves the transition from the stages of early childhood to the phenomenon of mass formation is "identification." Again in agreement with orthodox psychoanalysis, he assumes that the central mechanism whereby drive-conditioned anxieties are surmounted consists in a kind of projected identification by virtue of which the repressed portion of drives are transferred to a leadership figure—upon whom falls the role of hypnotist. Fearing its drive-surpluses, the neurotic subject deposits them, as it were, in the personality of a charismatic leader so that the power of the bond between him and the gathering mass is constituted by the "sum of repressed drive energy." To be sure, Neumann is careful enough not to make the mistake of reducing every type of group formation to the unconscious mechanisms of libidinal identification. Instead, he distinguishes emotional or affective types of identification from those free of affective components, which presumably are found above all in purely objective ties to formal organizations (the church, the army).[5] He is convinced that this second type of identification is exclusively rational and, hence, does not constitute an example of individual regression.

Neumann also differentiates between two forms of affective, or rather libidinal, identification: the first is found in small cooperative groups, while the second concerns the relationship of the masses to leadership figures. In Neumann's view, only such mass movements lead to a loss of ego powers, such that only they, on the basis of their regressive tendencies, can be described as "irrational." His suggestion is that such irrational types of libidinal identification are best described as "Caesarism"; they should be regarded as causally responsible for all regressive forms of mass-formation in the modern world. Let me address the strengths and weaknesses of this step in Neumann's argument.

Already the fundamental distinction on which Neumann bases his concept of group formation hardly seems to me generally persuasive. The distinction between forms of affective identification and those that function without the support of affective elements gives rise to the misleading impression that a group's bond could somehow be emotionless and purely based on conviction. Here a very traditional conceptual model, found earlier in Max Horkheimer, is probably at work on which affects or emotions are completely equated with irrational powers, such that group formations free from affective elements must be presupposed simply for conceptual reasons; for it requires a category that can designate types of group formation that do not arise merely from the aggregate calculation of individual interests but also are not the result of confluent individual regressions. Neumann is assisted in characterizing formative process of this kind of group, whose members are bound together in a nonregressive way, by the idea of an affect-free identification.[6]

This is the source of the downright confusing idea that there could be a form of binding to common goals or values that could get by, so to speak, without the addition of any feelings or affects—precisely the notion of an affect-free identification. If we retain the more convincing idea that each social group arises not as the sum of individually calculated interests but through some emotionally supported relationship of identification, however, then a distinction different from the one on which Neumann bases his thesis is required. On such premises, we must be able to distinguish between "normal" and "pathological" types of (emotional) identification with a group. Relevant suggestions for formulating a distinction along these lines today can be found, for instance, in the psychoanalytic work of Otto Kernberg, who differentiates forms of group cohesion according to which types of object relations are reactivated among the members at any given time.[7]

From this objection arises a corresponding reservation about Neumann's treatment of the mechanism of individual "regression." Here, too, he appears to be operating with a problematic, even misleading, opposition between the rational and the irrational, since he explicitly designates all forms of individual regression or the dissolution of ego boundaries "irrational" and therefore "dangerous." I take this equation to be unconvincing because we know of forms of ego-boundary dissolution that can be regarded as signs of mental health or vitality. Psychic phenomena like the tendency to merge with a beloved partner, complete immersion in a game with children, or the disorienting fusion with an enthusiastic crowd at the soccer stadium are certainly all forms of a retrogressive departure from previously established ego boundaries, but they cannot simply be designated dangerous and therefore irrational, since otherwise we would lose sight of their positive functions for recovered psychic creativity.[8] Since he shares with Horkheimer a psychological rationalism that regards every psychical dissolution, every opening for unregulated affects, as a symptom of a relapse into irrational behavior, Neumann is forced to obscure the existence of empowering and healthy forms of regression. Instead, it would be advisable to distinguish between "healthy" and "pathological" forms of psychic regression by means of the criterion of whether the dissolution of ego-powers is secondarily beneficial through increased creativity, or whether it permanently paralyzes their functioning. Here as well, the studies of Otto Kernberg could be of some help, since they distinguish various types of regression according to which of the wish-formation stages of early childhood are reactivated.

Now, only against the background of these seemingly necessary conceptual modifications can the phenomena that Neumann apparently considers indicative of what he calls "social" alienation be appropriately dealt with. He assumes that there are, in a more limited sense, social factors that can strengthen the tendency toward libidinal identification with a charismatic leader and thus generate a substantial psychic readiness for regressive dissolution into the masses. Foremost among these, he is convinced, is social anxiety concerning a loss of esteem grounded in the prospect of deprivation and decline.[9] This specific anxiety, which stems from experiences of comparison in society, strengthens the drive-anxiety established in early childhood by, in a certain sense, allowing—through the fearful anticipation of the wounding of one's self-esteem—neurotic tendencies to become the motivation for action. Where the reciprocal reinforcement of both anxieties has occurred, libidinal identification with a leadership figure then serves as a vehicle for acting out a resentment derived from wounded self-esteem.

Neumann could have been much more persuasive in developing this potentially fruitful train of thought if he had introduced the concept of neurotic anxiety in such a way that its correlation with social experiences of loss had been clarified from the outset. Had he drawn on the reflections of object-relations theory (as they had become rudimentarily represented at the Institute for Social Research by Erich Fromm) instead of Freudian orthodoxy,[10] then social anxieties could have been rendered explicable as traumatic anxieties reactivated through experiences of deprivation resulting from the traumatic loss of the constant, security-giving presence of the first, most intimate relation. Within such an explanatory model there exists a kind of psychological continuity between the early forms of childhood anxiety and the social experiences of loss in adulthood, the enduring core of which is constituted by the anxiety-laden endangerment of intersubjectivity. In contrast, Neumann has no theoretical means at his disposal with which to mediate between the two forms of anxiety. For the same reason, fears of deprivation in Neumann's theory appear to break into the psychological inner life of the subject as if from outside, unable to reach the fertile ground of a readiness for anxiety already established in early childhood.

III. SOCIAL ANXIETIES AND CONSTITUTIONAL DEMOCRACIES

At the third stage of his argument, it becomes clear that Neumann tailored his social-psychological explanatory thesis first and foremost to the fall of the National Socialist movement. In particular, he adds two further components to his previous interpretive schema, both of which he sees as typical of this particular form of mass movement. I refer to these only briefly before I draw some general conclusions.

First, Neumann assumes that historically muddled conspiracy theories can significantly intensify those neurotic anxieties that have already attained expression in the identification with a charismatic leader. Such libidinally invested leadership figures are for this reason in a position to intensify their own hypnotic power through historical narratives that pseudo-concretely project social dangers in a vague and diffuse way onto the intentions of a person or group. Whether it is Jesuits, Communists, capitalists, or, as in the German case, Jews, a collective is always supposed to be responsible for the injuries and privations under which the members of the mass movement have previously suffered.[11] Here Neumann is probably drawing on the results of Theodor Adorno's content-analysis investigations of the inflammatory radio addresses of Martin Luther Thomas in the United States.[12]

Second, Neuman identified the mechanism for intensifying mass formations of this type as institutionalizing anxiety through psychological terror and political propaganda. Since the libidinal substrate of the mass's fixation on the leader is not stable enough to endure over long periods of time, stabilization through such external influence is necessary.[13] Here as well, the mechanisms of intensification Neumann has in mind are undoubtedly taken from the National Socialist movement in Germany. They help explain only the particular case of permanent, state-sponsored terror through uninterrupted surveillance, pseudolegal punishment, and constant propaganda, but they certainly cannot make sense of those forms of institutionalized anxiety that function by subtler means of state terror.

On the whole, Neumann's approach is tailored so much to the exceptional case of German National Socialism that he is hardly in a position to make intelligible the entire spectrum of impaired political autonomy attributable to socially created anxieties. Instead of pursuing this critical line of inquiry further here, I instead conclude with a discussion of the implications of Neumann's approach. For our purposes here, it is useful to distinguish between theoretical and normative inferences.

On the theoretical level, it appears to me extremely useful to follow Neumann in trying to understand neurotically intensified mass anxieties as a kind of social pathology that can profoundly interfere with the individual's ability to participate in democratic will-formation. In order to autonomously form an opinion and be able to articulate it publicly, freedom from anxiety is indispensable, since anxiety impairs self-esteem, limits deliberative powers, and allows ego-estranging idol substitution. With this initial idea, Neumann goes far beyond the agenda of the central representatives of the Frankfurt School,[14] since he is interested in a normatively grounded diagnosis of social pathology that coheres with the presuppositions of a democratic public sphere. Socially produced anxieties are significant for him, not simply because they violate the preconditions for the development of a free subjectivity but because they, in turn, destroy the conditions of uninhibited will-formation in the public sphere.

Yet the explanatory framework Neumann presents is too narrow to allow him to fulfill his theoretical agenda. Because he concentrates from the beginning on the repression of drives as the source of neurotic anxieties, he fails to establish an internal connection with those anxieties caused by the experience of social endangerment. The theoretical gulf that emerges between the propensity for anxiety acquired in early childhood and the social anxiety of adults is too great for Neumann to productively carry out his original theoretical agenda. The fact that neurotic anxieties are supposed to arise from failed processes of drive repression fails to explain why adults experience the imminent loss of social status as so threatening that they tend to identify with leadership figures who help them find (as part of a mass) compensatory support for the injured self. In this respect, it would have been better for Neumann to have abandoned the orthodox explanatory framework of psychoanalysis and instead pursued psychoanalytic "revisionism," as represented, for instance, by Erich Fromm at the Institute for Social Research. As soon as one concedes that neurotic anxieties develop only secondarily through unsuccessful processes of separation from the object of love, it is easy to see the psychodynamic roots of anxiety in social endangerment.

As far as the normative consequences of Neumann's analysis are concerned, he ultimately leaves us with a choice between two alternatives, whose difference is found in the degree to which they rely on the democratic constitutional state to either moderate or help remedy the individual anxieties of its members. On the one hand, Neumann could, in the spirit of a "liberalism of fear,"[15] endorse the idea that the essential responsibility of the constitutional state is to demonstrate reliability to its citizens through guarantees of legal security and political predictability, thereby minimizing the development of paralyzing anxieties. In this case, by taking legal measures that instill confidence, policy would only negatively refer to the propensity for anxiety among members of society. In this scenario, the rule of law does nothing to promote the development of individual autonomy itself but, rather, has only a moderating effect on this propensity to develop social anxiety. On the other hand, Neumann has a considerably stronger alternative at his disposal, which exhibits paternalistic characteristics insofar as it would require positive steps concerning the development of individual autonomy: the propensity to develop social anxiety could be remedied by guaranteeing conditions of socialization that afford a high degree of reliability and security in intersubjective relationships. The path that Neumann would have taken in providing the constitutional state with legitimate means for coping with the democracy-inhibiting consequences of individual anxieties will remain forever unclear, for his essay on the relationship of "anxiety and politics" was, owing to his sudden death, the last publication he was able to author.

Translated by Chad Kautzer

NINE

DEMOCRACY AND INNER FREEDOM

Alexander Mitscherlich's Contribution
to Critical Social Theory

The first thing that can probably be said in retrospect about the significance of Alexander Mitscherlich is that today we perceptibly and sorely miss his studies, observations, and diagnoses. At present, there is no social-psychological thinker who can describe psychic transformations in individuals or masses with comparable subtlety, caution, or understanding. The analyses Mitscherlich devoted to the tendencies of a spiritual structural transformation in capitalism in the period between 1955 and 1975 tower far above everything we know today by way of comparable diagnoses in their thematic range, degree of conceptual differentiation, and depth of comprehension. At the time, probably only the social-psychological diagnoses of Arnold Gehlen could compete with those of Mitscherlich.[1]

Simply the multiplicity of empirical findings on which Mitscherlich tried to comment makes clear what an alert, restless spirit was at work here. His analyses dealt with rising drug consumption no less than rage on the autobahn; he diagnosed the tendency to collective "infantalization" and the separation of sexuality and eroticism very early on; neither the structural transformation of puberty nor the sudden spread of plastic surgery escaped his powers of observation—and with all this, we have not yet named the themes that make up the substantial core of his social-psychological works: the "inhospitability" of our cities, the German resistance to remembering in his day, and the unconscious dynamics of prejudice. His diagnoses are distinguished not only by their empirical flair or the breadth of the transformational tendencies they perceive, however, but also by their caution in applying basic theoretical concepts. Nowhere does Mitscherlich act like the orthodox Freudian who faces no task beyond merely applying the insights and assumptions delivered by the master to a changed reality. At the center of his analyses there is, instead, always the attempt to bring together everything available by way of knowledge from the fields of psychoanalysis, psychosomatics, and social psychology that could serve a satisfactory explanation of the findings being diagnosed.

In line with these characteristics of his writings—their principled openness to new developments and theoretical suggestions—there is finally a third quality that is striking about this work from today's perspective. In contrast to many social-psychological diagnoses we encounter in the present, for Mitscherlich in his far-ranging works, it is always also a matter of pursuing a moral-political concern. The author of *The Inhospitability of Our Cities* and *Society Without the Father* carries out his studies not so much in order to defend a particular theoretical approach as above all to investigate a public, emancipatory challenge.[2] All his works, however different their topics, revolve directly or indirectly around the question of what conditions of "inner freedom," of tolerance, are required for a democratic constitutional state to achieve continuity and vitality. This connection between individual self-relations and political culture constitutes the innermost motive of Mitscherlich's work. It grounds his diagnoses and investigations even where they take up such apparently remote themes as the aesthetic development of "happenings," the experience of space travel, or even the German autobahn. If in the following I briefly remind us of this, Mitscherlich's basic concern, it is because I remain convinced of its urgency and its undiminished relevance.

$$\ll | \gg$$

In a lecture he gave in Berlin in 1954 that would later become famous, Franz Neumann, shortly before his death, took up a question that had attracted attention much earlier in older democracies.[3] A democratic constitutional state, Neumann claimed, can be threatened not only by processes in the external world—corruption, the concentration of power, or class justice—but also by the inner constitution of individuals themselves. If they develop a certain tendency to apathy or cowardice born of irrational anxiety, individuals will not be able to apprehend the advisory and supervisory functions that democracy envisages for them in their role as citizens.

According to Neumann, "anxiety" is the greatest internal psychic obstacle for any form of democratic politics because it prevents citizens from realizing and exercising capacities that are indispensible for common will-formation. Neither the ability to place oneself in the life situations of other citizens nor the capacity to examine and sometimes set aside one's own interests can be developed under the domination of irrational anxieties. Neumann himself was unable to work out the suggestion contained in the basic outline of these reflections. Due to his sudden death a few months after the lecture, for him these path-breaking speculations remained a mere program. It could seem—indeed, the impression almost imposes itself—that after Neumann's death, one man made it his goal to make Neumann's tersely sketched thesis his own. For the work of Alexander Mitscherlich, like no other in the intellectual history of the first three decades of the Federal Republic, revolves around the relation between anxiety and politics—between the weakness of the ego and the demands of democratic behavior.

Of course, the theoretical roots of Mitscherlich's efforts lay in an entirely different domain from those that arose in Neumann's lecture. Whereas in determining the sources of anxiety Neumann was oriented to Freud in an orthodox way, Mitscherlich managed to engage with the irrational consequences of anxiety by outlining a psychosomatics. In his earlier, still-fascinating study on freedom and unfreedom in illness (1949),[4] Mitscherlich still moves completely in the world of medical anthropology, into which he had been introduced by his teacher Viktor von Weizsäcker. The theoretical sources he uses to explore the possibility of psychic causes of organic illnesses thus derive largely from philosophical anthropology as we know it from Arnold Gehlen or Helmuth Plessner. Nevertheless, even then the question of what the special course of psychosomatic illness says about the "communication" with one's own wishes and drives—what he would later call "inner freedom"—already stands at the center of Mitscherlich's interests.[5] Owing to his special biological position—namely, his lack of organic specialization and the resulting compensatory activity of the mind—among all creatures only the human being possesses the capacity for "freedom of being able to act."

However, it is this singular potential for freedom that at the same time enables him to unconsciously seek ways of avoiding conflicts that result from the pressure of disagreeable impulses that complicate his behavior. Only the human being, it could be said, strives to avoid suffering out of his own fear of internal conflicts. For Mitscherlich, then, neurotic illness is a privileged way of circumventing such psychic tensions through the "retention" of "psychic agitation" in an organ.[6] Instead of finding the communicative path of linguistic articulation, the disagreeable wish or conflictual impulse is projected onto an organ, where, as the unresolved remainder of one's own interior, it becomes the source of illness. To this extent, psychosomatic illness is, as Mitschlerlich puts it with a sense for speculative heightening, at once the demonstration and the loss of human freedom. On the one hand, the illness always represents an expression of freedom because it is rooted in the human capacity for psychic conflict avoidance and so to speak demonstrates it; on the other hand, it is always also the strictest limitation of freedom, since, in it, the [physiological] human body [*Körper*] regains its dominion over the [lived] human body [*Leib*].[7] In the neurotic symptom that afflicts the person suffering from psychosomatic illness, we see the extent to which the subject can lose its freedom of will, its "ability to will," out of the anxious wishes to avoid burdensome impulses.

The fascination for the peculiar, specifically human, dialectic that consists in the loss of freedom out of freedom, out of the free anxiety concerning internal conflicts, never left Mitscherlich. In the innumerable essays and studies that followed over the next thirty years, he concerned himself again and again with the causes of those tendencies toward infrapsychic conflict avoidance that already stood at the center of his early investigation of psychosomatics. All the same, at that time he had not yet established the connection to political culture, to the habitual requirements of democracy. This occurred first by way of a politicization of his thinking that went hand in hand with a turn to Freudian psychoanalysis. Thus, in the course of the 1950s the relation between anxiety and politics, between the individual self-relation and democratic culture, gradually moved into the center of his work.

Mitscherlich probably received the impetus for politicizing his thinking, for gradually integrating his medical and psychological interests within a democratic theoretical framework, from his engagement with the evidence of the National Socialist crimes. Above all, in working with the documents of the Nuremberg doctors' trial, which he edited and provided a commentary for together with Fred Mielke,[8] it became clear to him that willingness to carry out brutal, inconceivable experiments on humans presupposed a personality type that is incompatible with the demands of civilized humanity and democratic attitudes. In retrospect, the research into the social-psychological preconditions of National Socialism, which he never dropped, throws new light on the older studies on psychosomatic illness. What originally appeared only as a source of neurotic symptoms—anxiety concerning threatening and conflictual impulses—can now be seen on a more generalized level as the root of psychic dispositions that lead subjects to escape into the refuge of obedient masses.

By way of a detour through the exploration of personal pathologies that could lead to toleration or support of the violent National Socialist crimes, Mitscherlich thus arrived at the normative problematic that from then on would serve to orient his social-psychological and psychoanalytic works: What psychic dispositions must subjects be able to have, what kind of attitudes must they assume vis-à-vis themselves, in order not only to be armed against the temptations of a flight into the masses or subjection to an unburdening authority but also to be able to be resolute and engaged participants in democratic will-formation? Despite all suspicions about frivolous idealizations and reservations about merely normative speculations, can something halfway substantive can be said about those personality characteristics a subject must be able to possess in order to be psychically equipped for the many demands of mass democracy? The attempt to find an answer to this question runs like a red thread through Mitscherlich's social-psychological works. And the further we penetrate the underbrush of his many articles, positions, and diagnoses of the times, the more clearly the outlines of a single, highly subtle solution emerges.

Since the beginning of his turn to social psychology, for Mitscherlich the key to understanding the dispositions that make democratic participation possible is represented by the category of "tolerance."[9] To be sure, with this concept he does not primarily designate, as is generally customary, a behavior or attitude we are supposed to be able to assume intersubjectively with regard to the representatives of another culture, another alien (indeed, objectionable) value community. Rather, for him, such a social, interpersonal form of tolerance must be preceded by a process in which the individual subject learns to behave "tolerantly" and generously toward himself or herself. It is this phenomenon of inward tolerance that primarily interests Mitscherlich as a psychoanalyst and social-psychologist. In his writings, he develops the abilities that are connected to this kind of self-relation through an opposition to "anxiety."

For Mitscherlich, anxiety is, as we have seen, an anthropological constant insofar as it represents the emotional price human beings have to pay for their constitutive openness to the world. Released from all instinctive securities and placed in an open environment that must be mentally mastered, as he claims with implicit reference to Arnold Gehlen, human subjects, unlike animals, possess a deep-seated sense for the dangers that can stem from the pressure of conflictual drive energies that are difficult to control. As a rule, the first, quasi-natural reaction to this sensed danger is drive-defense: that is, the unconscious repression of the disagreeable wish through projection or displacement. And for Mitscherlich, the consequences of this kind of "banishment of anxiety" extend from the development of prejudice to subjection to the obedient masses. It would be something different—and this is Mitscherlich's central thought—if human beings learned early in their socialization to react to the seemingly dangerous drive energies, not defensively but initially perhaps with playful, later with increasingly understanding forms of "recognition."[10] Mitscherlich calls this kind of ability to put up with what, within me, is alien to me by way of wishes, needs, or longings, "inner tolerance" or "freedom." It is the infrapsychic precondition for the kind of interpersonal behavior that we reciprocally expect from one another when we ordinarily speak of "tolerance." Mitscherlich masterfully captures this presupposed relation in the title of his first essay on tolerance (1951): "As to myself—so to you" [*Wie ich mir—so ich dir*].

Now, Mitscherlich leaves no doubt about the difficulties that arise in connection with achieving such an attitude. Indeed, already in Freud, we find some indications of the processes that would be necessary to achieve a tolerant, generous attitude toward oneself in concepts like "working through" or "recognition."[11] And, of course, Donald Winnicott's work contains a multitude of suggestions concerning how we can imagine the way small children acquire the ability to disclose their own drive-lives through play.[12] But, on the whole, we nevertheless remain very much in the dark about what such an attitude of inward tolerance, of "inner freedom," could mean. Mitscherlich's work helps here to the extent that at least it lets us see the direction and the steps by which the process of acquiring this redemptive self-relation could be characterized. One hint that can be taken on the first level here is already contained in the idea of "communication" with one's own drives, which he refers to in various ways. In order to be able even to experience one's own disagreeable and often violent drives, a laborious process of articulation is first required in which what is hidden in the interior is linguistically expressed to another or to oneself. Without the fumbling, open attempt to express our initially alien wishes, we cannot take a posture of tolerance with regard to them.

But according to Mitscherlich, we are not done with this first step of articulation, since even drives and wishes that have been made linguistically conscious still retain their foreignness if they cannot also somehow be understood; thus Mitscherlich often also speaks of "understanding" "the alien world within."[13] A process of understanding of this kind probably means gradually learning to diminish the discordance and foreignness of the newly articulated wishes so that they are put in relation to the rest of the wishes that are transparent to us, to which they are thus referred. Such an effort to understand the inner alien has to embed the drives that are questionable to us into the web of known and familiar wishes. Only both steps taken together, however, articulation and understanding, then enable the attitude Mitscherlich calls inward tolerance: namely, the recognition of the frightening, discordant wishes as part of one's own biographically developed personality.[14] Now, Mitscherlich's writings often suggest a further third step in the development of inner tolerance that can probably be understood as achieving a corresponding form of behavior. He often says that a tolerant form of self-relation must always go along with a dose of "irony" that is based on remaining conscious of the ambivalent shades of all one's opinions.[15]

From here, from this normative aim of human personality development, Mitscherlich makes the bridge to the political theme of democracy. He is convinced that, in the end, subjects can only possess the ability to handle the challenges of a pluralistic democracy constructively and without coercion if they have learned to assume a tolerant attitude with regard to their own interior. As long as the chances for the spread of such forms of self-relation are slight, however—as along as subjects cling to the mechanism of anxiety defense—there will continue to be massive prejudice formation, hatred projection, and social exclusion, which are incompatible with the tasks of discursive will-formation. To this extent, the project of democratization is tied to the presupposition of a condition of inner freedom, and the best model for characterizing this condition has so far been provided by psychoanalysis.

TEN

DISSONANCES OF COMMUNICATIVE REASON

Albrecht Wellmer and Critical Theory

In his innumerable reflections on Beethoven's late style, recently compiled from his literary estate into a volume about the composer, Theodor Adorno repeatedly emphasizes the fading, the general withering of harmony as a characteristic trait.[1] The further Beethoven develops in his compositional opus, the more at ease he becomes with leaving behind the classical style of his middle period, the more clearly apparent—in the late quartets, the Diabelli Variations, the Bagatelles (op. 126)—are dissonance and polarization, which can mount even to a renunciation of tonality. To Adorno, this tendency for growing, uncurbed disharmony attests not only to an idiosyncrasy of Beethoven's musical development but also to a characteristic of the maturation of all great composers: emerging in their work is, with increasing age and technical refinement, almost always a preparedness to break with the "compulsion of identity" by renouncing harmonious constructions.[2]

By contrast, the developmental law for philosophical oeuvres, one might say without further ado, is quite different. Here the tendency increases with age for each author—Kant, Hegel, or Heidegger comes to mind—to harmoniously round out or even systematically close one's theory. In the philosophical tradition, there can scarcely be found an oeuvre that in its mature, late condition is not poorer on openly carried out tensions and polarizations than in its early conception. The theoretical accomplishments of our prize recipient present an exception to this rule. The intimacy with music that Albrecht Wellmer evidences in his philosophy manifests itself in that the maturation of his work follows the developmental pattern not of philosophical theories but of musical compositions: the further it progresses, the more lived history it subsumes, the more apparent are dissonances and tensions that originally remained submerged. Albrecht Wellmer's later writings articulate more open and unreserved fractures in its subject matter than the earlier works had ever permitted.

Adorno himself warns against interpreting this peculiarity of the late style of great composers, their tendency to renounce harmony, as an "expression" of an evolved subjectivity that has, as it were, become stubborn.[3] Such a perspective aiming purely at the psychological and personal quickly proves incapable of unlocking the content of the works themselves. Instead of carrying out a technical study of the compositions in question, it is satisfied with interpreting the enigmatic, fractured style simply as a testament to a personality that in its later days has become reckless and expressively uninhibited. If, in contrast, compositional content is taken seriously, according to Adorno, something quite different becomes apparent in late works: subjectivity, the impulse toward the integration of the individual, has so loosened its hold that they to some extent become free to articulate the "fissures and rifts" of what is objectively given.[4] In the late style of Beethoven, the "irreconcilability of reality" itself attains musical expression, precisely because the compulsion to identity is abandoned. "Harmony is avoided," according to Adorno, "because it produces an *illusion* of the unity of many voices."[5]

It seems to me that this conclusion provides a suitable key to unlock the developmental dynamics of Albrecht Wellmer's work. With each new writing, with each new article, the tendency in him grows to radicalize the fissures and fractures within that very communicative reason he had earlier considered the basis and motivation of the project of modernity. In place of hope for the reconciliation of an internally divided modernity comes an extremely sharp consciousness of the irresolvable tension among its different elements. Yet this decay of harmony, this renunciation of integration, is not an expression of a rigid subjectivity but the result of a progress in sober, even depersonalized intelligence. I mean this quite literally: in the course of the development of his works, Wellmer increasingly becomes carefree about connections of effective history, public expectations, and the media's attributions, to the extent that the theorization is free to articulate and bring out objective contradictions that had formerly remained obscured by the requirements of identity.

Today, in his mature work, Wellmer undertakes the risky task of both defending and limiting communicative reason: he defends the eccentric, intransigent subject against communicative assimilation and yet, at the same time, protects communicative understanding in its open-ended potential for reason against all relativistic, utopian, or fundamentalist temptations. Thereby, in a historically new and advanced stage in Wellmer's philosophical theory, Adorno's voice again makes itself heard. Bringing to bear again his sensibility for the nonidentical within the changed conditions of communicative reason should be seen as the fundamental concern of the philosopher Albrecht Wellmer.

The fortuities of a not entirely linear education placed Albrecht Wellmer from the start of his philosophical career in the intellectual zone of tension that has remained determining for him through the present. After the state examination in Kiel in mathematics and physics, the decisive influence on him to continue his studies in philosophy was likely the intellectual force field of Hans Georg Gadamer's hermeneutics. But after only a short study at Heidelberg, Wellmer was drawn to Frankfurt, where Adorno taught philosophy and sociology with growing success. Above all, the latter's theoretical presence in the musical life of the Federal Republic must have moved the new graduate, himself highly musically gifted and fascinated by the new music, to switch over to the center of Critical Theory.

What at this point really captivated him philosophically and initially forged his path was the perfectly independent and original approach with which the young Jürgen Habermas attempted to set the first generation of Critical Theory on methodologically solid ground. Only four years younger and having come of age in the natural sciences, the doctoral candidate must have been enthused right away by the Habermasian idea of determining anew, in a journey through the modern, contemporary theory of science, the epistemic location of a critical theory of society.[6] In these years, Wellmer acquired what in retrospect can be considered the source and foundation of Critical Theory's linguistic turn: on Habermas's suggestion, he familiarized himself with the history of analytic philosophy from Russell to Wittgenstein, occupied himself with methodological debates in both the natural and the human sciences, and pursued the epistemological self-reflection of the social sciences. Wellmer then devoted his dissertation, in the spirit of Adorno, to be sure, yet in fact in close cooperation with Habermas, to Karl Popper's theory of science.[7] The pioneering thesis, later elaborated by Habermas in *Knowledge and Human Interests*, according to which scientism results from a "hypostatization" of methodical procedure whereby the natural sciences attain technically useful knowledge,[8] is here for the first time epistemologically justified.

In the following years, while serving as assistant to Habermas in Heidelberg and Frankfurt, Wellmer deepened his knowledge of the analytical theory of science. For all his dedication to the student movement, whose democratic aims he would later justify in a very courageous and far-sighted discussion of the terrorism of the Red Army Faction,[9] he was above all preoccupied with trying to provide an epistemological justification of Critical Theory. His reflections centered on the question of what methodological place a theory can occupy whose statements should be suitable at once as explanations of societal processes of development and as initiations of emancipatory action. His answer moves along what was outlined by Habermas, according to whom a critical theory must be understood as a mode of reflection of the universal claim to maturity inherent in the structures of the human practice of reaching understanding.

Among the collaborators Habermas gathered around himself, Albrecht Wellmer was at the time certainly the one who made the greatest contribution to the communication theoretical reconstruction of Critical Theory. His growing knowledge of analytic philosophy, above all his familiarity with the new theory of science, enabled him to collaborate on equal footing with teachers and colleagues on the thesis that intersubjective action, thanks to its linguistic character, possesses an emancipatory power for overcoming domination and heteronomy. When in 1971 Wellmer presented his habilitation thesis, tracing back the mode of explanation of the recent natural sciences epistemologically to its pragmatic roots in the circulation of instrumental measurements,[10] his further philosophical future appeared as good as settled: everything, the origin in the natural sciences, the knowledge of analytic philosophy, the confirmation in the epistemological works—all of it seemed to predispose him to become a theorist of science of a second generation of Critical Theory, led by Habermas.

That it did not turn out that way, that Wellmer took quite a different road, may be connected with a predisposition toward reserved thoughtfulness, toward caution and circumspection, that was characteristic of his intellectual physiognomy as a whole.[11] At any rate, after the habilitation, Wellmer took up an offer from Toronto, changing with his location the emphasis of his intellectual work considerably. He set about trying, in teaching as well as research, to relate the changes in Critical Theory's self-understanding brought about by Habermas and himself to the beginning of their own tradition. Already in 1969, two years before his habilitation, Wellmer had published a slim volume where, taking Marx as his point of departure and traversing through the contemporary theory of science, he had sketched all the consequences that would result for Critical Theory from the dislocation of its normative point of reference from social production to social interaction.[12] The contradictions of capitalist modernity ought no longer be analyzed primarily in the form of a critique of political economy but by way of a critique of modern science, because its positivistic self-understanding very clearly mirrored the whole extent of repression and denial to which, in the course of accelerating technologization and economization, the rational potential of communicative conduct of life was sacrificed.

For me, who at that time had just started my studies, Wellmer's reflections in his slim volume were not just immediately the most suitable means to come to grips with the social and political significance of all the fuss made of epistemology and the theory of science at Frankfurt in those years but, even more, offered a young student the first and only chance to fit the communicative theory energetically advanced by Habermas within the greater context of the tradition of a critical social theory, extending from Marx through Horkheimer to Adorno.

It must have been such a hermeneutic contextualization, even an exoteric presentation, of what first was achieved with and under Habermas, that Wellmer, on the other side of the Atlantic, made his aim. At first as associate professor at Toronto, then spending nearly four years at the renowned New School for Social Research in New York City, he limited himself to elaborating the political and philosophical consequences for Critical Theory of the paradigm shift from production to communication, from the philosophy of consciousness to the philosophy of language. In publications and seminars, Wellmer attempted to counter the generally prevalent Marxist orthodoxy by demonstrating, with the help of linguistic analysis, that it is not in the processes of societal work but in structures of linguistic intersubjectivity that the potential for liberating reason, on which we can place our emancipatory hopes, rests. Of enduring effect on an entire generation is the essay, written at the time in English, "Communication and Emancipation," which for the first time succeeded in conceptualizing Critical Theory's linguistic turn.[13] Legendary, too, are the seminars at the New School, in which he gathered around himself, as a gifted and highly engaged teacher, a rapidly growing group of students in order to familiarize them with the intellectual roots of the new approach—and in this way he almost involuntarily came to contribute to the formation of the highly vital circle in which political scientists and philosophers today, like

Andrew Arato, Jean Cohen, and Joel Whitebook, are working on a North American variation of the continuation of Critical Theory.

Altogether, however, this period still intellectually harbored something peculiarly curbed back, something restrained, standing in marked contrast to the previously evident energy and creativity of Albrecht Wellmer's mind. Too soon to satisfy himself with what he already accomplished, he seemed to hesitate over which direction to turn his philosophical interests, toward what horizons he should direct the new approach. Apparently nothing in this was changed by the return to the Federal Republic, where in 1974 he assumed a professorship at the University of Konstanz. Here, too, he rapidly developed a rousing and far-reaching pedagogy, was politically and intellectually highly engaged, joined a great number of aesthetic and philosophical debates—it is only which direction his own development should take that was not quite apparent to those who viewed him from outside. Only in hindsight, from today, can we see that this long phase, though rich indeed in discussions and pedagogical successes, was also curiously undecided, a kind of intellectual incubation. The unwieldy ideas that in this period were confined to Wellmer's intellectual interior, and with which he evidently grappled conceptually over the years, were theoretical barbed hooks and tensions in that very conception of communicative reason that he had until then so firmly represented.

The gateway for the objections that Wellmer only gradually and hesitantly brought forward against the communication theoretic approach of Critical Theory was above all aesthetics. Although aesthetic and musicological interests had originally brought him to Frankfurt, Adorno's place of activity, he had thus far scarcely pursued art as topic in his philosophical development. It is first from his chair in Konstanz that he started to make his capabilities in the philosophy of language fruitful for the field of aesthetics as well, and quite soon the success of this new effort made itself felt in that his students entered the philosophical stage with significant works in aesthetics.[14] By reinterpreting Adorno's *Aesthetic Theory* in terms of the theory of rationality, Wellmer attempted to examine the relation of communicative understanding to aesthetic experience.[15] He thereby hit on a phenomenon whose implications would, at first only gradually, unfold a subversive force in his thinking: the truth that a work of art conveys does not easily align itself with the differentiations in everyday language that may be undertaken by way of the pragmatics of language among the three validity dimensions of empirical truth, normative rightness, and subjective truthfulness.[16]

Rather, aesthetic truth seems to cause a kind of interference between these three aspects in that it effects an examination or revision of individual views, in which interpretations, feelings, and valuations mingle in peculiar ways. The cognitive effect of a work of art—one could also say its capacity for truth—cannot be adequately apprehended within the differentiated frames of rational understanding, for it relates to subjective attitudes or worldviews that in some measure preexist rational opinion formation in discursive speech because they form syntheses of all three aspects of validity. With this, the weight is shifted between intersubjective speech and art, between communicative understanding and aesthetic experience. Instead of simply subsuming art as one of its aspects of validity, discourse stands in need of it from the outside because it is indebted to it for the precondition of sufficiently articulated and unbounded worldviews. Cautiously, Wellmer claims that reason depends on the illuminating power of art: "without aesthetic experience and the subversive potential it contains, our moral discourse would necessarily become blind and our interpretations of the world empty."[17]

What here still sounds like only a minimal dislocation within the architectonics of a Habermasian communication theory, however, soon compels Wellmer to far-reaching and increasingly radicalizing consequences. In relation to Adorno, the analysis undertaken primarily results in the idea that the truth potential of art, which was disclosed with his help, cannot be associated with just one aesthetic current of modernity. If the insight provided by a work of art has the effect of which it is capable, of opening our relations to ourselves and the world, then a development of the arts is imaginable far and above that on which Adorno, in his unacknowledged traditionalism, was firmly set. The rigorous condemnation of jazz to which Adorno adhered his entire life suffers for Wellmer from the fact that here, in aesthetic analysis, culturally determined prejudices unintentionally creep in. If these are bracketed or abandoned, it immediately becomes apparent that more popular art forms, even the aesthetic inclusion of the audience, can effect that expansion of our relation to ourselves and the world that Adorno considered the cognitive achievement of successful works of art. Reflections of this kind are made from his first studies of Adorno's aesthetics through Wellmer's entire work. They issue today in the surprising attempt to retroactively again bring into play, against Adorno, Benjamin's incomparably more sanguine aesthetics, which, from the new, unbounded art form of film, or of radio, hoped for a chance for more flexible and intellectual world-relations.[18]

More important, however, for the development of his work than the corrections to Adorno that Wellmer undertakes via Benjamin are the objections that he begins to develop over the years with recourse to Adorno, against the integrating force of communicative reason. The transition to a professorate at the Free University in Berlin, which followed in 1990, evidently situated our prize recipient in an intellectual environment that enabled him to take the step of completing such a release from his own theoretical past. Like New York, the only place of activity to which he has regularly been drawn to return, Berlin possesses a cultural vitality and energy that might have helped advance the depersonalization of his thinking of which I spoke in the beginning. What Wellmer had commenced in Konstanz—the limiting of communicative rationality through the dimension of aesthetic experience that elides it—he continued in Berlin with increasing radicalism. In rapid succession, there appeared a series of articles, essays, and lectures that belong to the best of what the history of Critical Theory has brought forth.[19] The theoretical horizon within which Wellmer continued to develop his own position was not only determined by the German tradition of critical thought and Anglo-Saxon analysis of language; rather, he now increasingly draws on French deconstruction in his argument, giving additional boost to the already sown skepticism.[20]

There are two opposing directions in which Wellmer advances this questioning of communicative reason. On the one hand, he undertakes an attempt, in continuation of his aesthetic studies, to make the outlined interpretation of modern art fruitful for a determination of individual freedom.[21] The considerations prompting him to take this unusual step result from his clarification of the cognitive content of aesthetic experience. If, in confronting works of modern art, subjects are going to be able to attain release from their bounded relations to themselves and the world, then it must be asked what social preconditions for freedom they are due in order to have such experiences at all. The determination of individual freedom thereby develops no longer through the guidance of moral subjectivity but from the point of view of aesthetic subjectivity. The question now is how the extent of rights and freedoms of individual subjects must be determined in order for them to be thought of meaningfully as addressees of modern art. It is this aesthetic radicalization of the idea of modern freedom that permits Wellmer to arrive at the conclusion of letting individual autonomy begin before the threshold of participation in intersubjective discourse. Each subject must, under the terms of liberal democratic societies, have disposal over a "space of negative freedom," giving him or her the right "not to be fully rational."[22] For without such an established right of freedom to unreason, we could add, the subject would not have the chance to hold himself or herself open to the experiences of eccentric, even selfish, unaccountable self-examination that modern art provides.

With this train of thought, however, Wellmer does not just relocate individual rights to freedom as, to a certain degree, existing before the conditions of communicative understanding. Communicative understanding itself thereby enters into an insoluble, interminable tension with aesthetic subjectivity, to whose unbounding, transgressive experience it at the same time owes its continual renewal. Hence, communicative reason hits, on the one hand, the limit of an inaccessible, aesthetically electrified subject and, on the other hand, the limit of political power. Most recently, Wellmer has investigated the limits of discursive understanding not only in the direction of aesthetics but also in the sphere of the political.[23] Stimulated by Derrida yet at the greatest possible distance from Carl

Schmitt, at this other end of the spectrum of modernity, he encounters a second stubborn instance where the rationalizing force of intersubjective reason comes up short. In every process of discursive will-formation, uncoerced and free of domination though it may be, there is a moment in which the communicatively reasoned and justified convictions of the participants must be transferred into binding decisions. At such points of transformation from justifications into juridical or political action, Wellmer holds, there asserts itself in all discourse an unavoidable moment of decision, which inheres in the performative character of a determination by power:

> Whatever fixed point one may attempt to have recourse to, at every such point—and be it the constituting act of a constituent assembly—the moment of a law-*creating* decision always surfaces, which could not have awaited the consensus that would legitimize it and which nonetheless includes the possibility of a justification of coercive sanctions.[24]

As in the sphere of aesthetics vis-à-vis Adorno, Wellmer appears here vis-à-vis Habermas to retroactively want to mobilize an insight of Walter Benjamin. In every hope for the reconciling power of discussion, so this free-spirited representative of the Frankfurt School was already convinced, we may not deceive ourselves about the fact that in all interpersonal relations of recognition there intrudes an element of unjustified power; every democratic will-formation always comes up against the point of a lawmaking decision.[25] The power of communicative reason, Wellmer would also say, is limited even in modern, democratic constitutional states through a necessary moment of decision beyond justification. But our prize recipient will still not let himself be carried away with the messianic expectations Benjamin had connected to his not entirely risk-free reflections. With all his sense for the possible limits of intersubjective understanding, he unflinchingly maintains that all elements that are alien, inaccessible to it, must flow back into the stream of the communicative formation of reason.

So as indeed to be able to think such a backflow—in order, that is, to be able to refer the two discourse-limiting powers of aesthetic subjectivity and political decision back to the single reason in discursive will-formation—Wellmer must take a further, third step, which in some measure runs counter to the previously mentioned train of thought. He must be able to envisage the process of democratic discourse that constitutes the motor of the project of modernity, not only as constitutionally guaranteed procedures but also as the embodiment of a whole form of life. Once democratic procedures were incorporated into the everyday attitudes and practices of all of its citizens (that is, as soon as communicative reason became an interpersonal mode of interaction), the aesthetically unchained subject and the political decision-maker would also know as a matter of course that they are bound to the democratic consensus. Wellmer wants at this decisive point to compensate retroactively for the inadequately integrative force of discursive rationality to which he previously had attested through the idea of a habituation, a routinization of rational procedures. What communicative reason could not penetrate by its own powers—namely, the aesthetic conduct of life and the always unavoidable decisions in politics and law—should in the end still be fostered through a transformation of this reason's potential into the mores and customs of society's members.

Wellmer borrows from Hegel's *Philosophy of Right* the theoretical apparatus necessary to devise such an ethical conception of a democratic, reflexive way of life. Likely as one of the first, he undertook the attempt to make fruitful the latter's dusty concept of ethical life [*Sittlichkeit*] for relations within ultramodern societies.[26] A "democratic ethical life" would thus be a way of life in which citizens orient themselves to democratic principles from habit and with heart, where they would not be convinced solely through rational arguments. Their aesthetic conduct of life and their political decisions (both of these poles that Wellmer had represented as limits of communicative reason) possess an orientation that would come to benefit the democratic project of modernity.[27]

With these considerations, the last word has certainly not been said in the continuing discourse conducted today about the opportunities and limits of a further rationalization of our lifeworld. The question arises, for example, of whether the dissemination of reflexive attitudes of solidarity could not be a creation of reason itself, as, for example, Kant imagined in many of his historical-philosophical essays. The supplement of a democratic ethical life would then come to the aid of communicative rationality not as if from the outside but out of its own tendency to realization. But as far as I know, Albrecht Wellmer—and according to what I have said about him growing carefree in relation to public attributions and determinations—he is not at all interested in such a final word. I know hardly any other philosopher who would more openly and dauntlessly, at the same time free from prejudices yet highly committed, discuss the possibilities at our disposal today for a rational justification of our emancipatory hopes and yearnings. The more strongly these discordant features could assert themselves in Albrecht Wellmer's thought, I hope to have shown, the more attentive it became to the nonidentical in communicative reason, to that which is conceptually inaccessible to it. It is not the smallest merit of this impressive, constantly radicalizing movement of thought to have shown us that the subterranean conversation between Adorno, Benjamin, and Habermas has yet to fully play out, that the history of Critical Theory remains open ended as well.

Translated by Reidar K. Maliks

APPENDIX

IDIOSYNCRASY AS A TOOL OF KNOWLEDGE

Social Criticism in the Age of the Normalized Intellectual

In an article with the suggestive title "Courage, Sympathy, and a Good Eye," Michael Walzer energetically sets the debate about social criticism on the track of virtue ethics.[1] The argument with which he grounds this reorientation initially sounds as plausible as it is timely. Since social theory can provide neither necessary nor sufficient grounds for successful social criticism, its quality cannot be measured primarily by the merits of its theoretical content but, rather, more urgently by the qualities of the critic. According to Walzer, he or she must have developed a capacity for sympathy and finally a sense of proportion when applying it.

What sounds plausible in this conclusion is the fact that the forcefulness and practical effect of social criticism seldom results from the measure of the theory in which it is invested but, rather, from the perspicuity of its central concern. And today this results in a turn to the virtues of the critic, since it feeds the devaluation of sociological knowledge and meets up with the tendency to personalize intellectual contexts. All the same, the self-evidence with which Walzer still regards even the intellectuals of our day as born governors of social criticism is surprising. He does not speak of bold Enlighteners—we might think of figures on the model of Émile Zola—but of the ubiquitous sort of author who participates with generalizing arguments in the debates of a democratic public sphere. Is this normalized intellectual, a spiritual agent in the fora of public opinion formation, really the natural representative today of what was once called "social criticism"? Here I first trace an epochal transformation in the form of the intellectual before outlining a completely different physiognomy of the social critic than that found in Walzer's work.

$$\text{\small ◁(I)▷}$$

Of the two broad prognoses contained in Joseph Schumpeter's excursus on the "Sociology of Intellectuals," one has meanwhile been mostly fulfilled, the other largely refuted.[2] Schumpeter clairvoyantly assumed that, with the expansion of education and the spread of media, the number of intellectuals would rise dramatically in the coming decades. This trend has been completely confirmed by ensuing developments, so that even in Germany, despite the setback produced by National Socialism, we can speak of a normalization of the role of the intellectual. The successful establishment of a political public sphere in which people can argue over questions of general interest has led to a pluralization of the type of authors involved in this use of his or her specific expertise in the reflexive interrogation and consideration of public issues. In newspapers and radio, on television and the internet, today an ever-greater number of intellectuals take part in enlightened opinion formation about an ever-greater number of specialized problems. Thus, the talk of the disappearance of the intellectual that pops up in the culture and opinion pages with dumb regularity is anything but justified. Never has the discussion conducted on all sides with more or less expertise about public issues been brisker or livelier.

There are at least four professional milieus from which personnel are recruited to take positions on the key problems of the day with the self-evident attitude of generalists. In the first rank is the media industry itself, into which public demand has drawn more and more authors and pundits with broad competence in matters of moral and political relevance. The growing establishment of issue-specific commissions and expert committees in which specialized academic knowledge is sought has undone traditional reservations about the media within the professoriate, so that today the universities are also increasing as a recruiting ground for media intellectuals. Another milieu that feeds the intellectual contributions to the formation of public opinion is the academic apparatuses of the parties, churches, and unions, which have undergone a hefty expansion in the last decades. Finally, we must consider the army of unemployed university graduates, who, by means of insecure contracts, perform regular supply work for the big media companies and outlets, and thereby also participate in the production of public positions. Individual writers or artists whose intellectual engagement occasionally attracts attention, in contrast, do not constitute a unified milieu, since they lack the precondition of group-specific professional socialization.

This social expansion has naturally produced a normalization of the role of the intellectual not only in a quantitative but also in a qualitative sense. The intellectual position-taking that today fills the op-ed pages, television talk shows, and computer screens emanates from the whole breadth of the political spectrum. Now even conservative thinkers and authors, who once saw in the intellectual the danger of a politicization of the mind or a "disintegration" of civic loyalty, have adapted to the rules of the democratic public sphere to the extent that they inject their opinions and convictions as arguments into the established channels of the print and visual media. However, the second prognosis that Schumpeter advanced in his "Sociology of the Intellectual" remains entirely unfulfilled. For he had predicted not only an expansion of the intellectual class but also its social radicalization, since their insecure, precarious professional situations would cumulatively strengthen the critique of capitalism.[3] Today we can probably say without fear of exaggeration that the opposite has occurred. The specific function of the public sphere, which by means of internal conduits provides only a few transfers of attention that can be managed by the media, has contributed to a constantly growing number of intellectuals who by and large deal only with questions of day-to-day politics. A social reservoir for a form of criticism that inquires behind the premises of publicly accepted problem descriptions and tries to see through their construction is no longer found in the class of intellectuals.

At the same time, it would be negligent to see in this only something to be regretted or bemoaned. Rather, this seems to the cultural byproduct of what can be described as the successful establishment of a democratic public sphere. Its vitality grows with the influx of objectively generalizable convictions in which citizens can recognize their own untutored opinions so that, with the help of the additional information and perspectives, they can to come to decentered and carefully weighed judgments. The publicly available arguments and convictions that take on this enlightening function must therefore be universalizable not only in their structure but, taken together, must be able when possible to represent the whole spectrum of private opinions. To this extent, the normalization of the intellectual that we see everywhere today is nothing other than the cultural manifestation of an intensification of the democratic public sphere. Personal convictions crystallize on politically relevant issues—be it abortion, military intervention, or pension reform—that can further develop under the influence of intellectual positions and enter into the process of democratic opinion formation. But with this development, the tight interlocking that once existed between "intellectuality" and social criticism is definitively broken. To the extent that an interrogation of what can be said in public is no longer to be expected from the intellectuals, social criticism no longer finds its home in the field of intellectual exchange. Walzer's mistake consists in transferring virtues that are only useful for describing normalized intellectuals to the business of social criticism.

Walzer clearly takes the personal characteristics or virtues for his sketch of the conditions for successful social criticism from key intellectual figures from the first half of the twentieth century.[4] For the most part, these intellectuals had to act in a political public sphere that was far from the liberal conditions that prevail in Western democratic societies when it comes to legal guarantees of freedom of speech and opinion. Whereas then it was necessary to risk life and limb, these kinds of demands are completely inapplicable to the Western intellectuals of our day. To this extent, as Ralf Dahrendorf says in his reply, at least in our latitudes today "courage" no longer represents a quality that can meaningfully be ranked among the intellectual virtues.[5] The position of an Ignazio Silone, who as an oppositional writer in totalitarian Italy had to win Mussolini's ear, is in no way comparable with the personal situation of someone who today, for example, speaks out against the death penalty in the United States.

In contrast, the two other virtues that Walzer names in his catalogue can be understood as thoroughly helpful dispositions—not for social critics, however, but for present-day intellectuals. The latter require both the ability to identify with the social suffering of oppressed groups and a sense of the politically achievable, so that publicly neglected interests and convictions can be lastingly asserted in the processes of democratic will-formation. Indeed, it may be just these two properties that today distinguish widely visible intellectuals from the innumerable gaggle of those whose skillful generalization of issues and demands connected to their expertise goes with practiced routine and without rhetorical imagination. But all that has very little to do with the conditions for illuminating, let alone successful, social criticism, since not even the cultural or social mechanisms that establish the conditions of acceptance for positions in public debate are put into question.

While today intellectuals have to abide not just by procedural rules but also by the conceptual guidelines of the political public sphere in order to win a public hearing, social criticism confronts a completely different task. What Siegfried Kracauer described seventy years ago as a central concern of intellectual activity still applies: it has to involve the attempted "destruction of all mythical powers around and within us."[6] Along with such myths, which he elsewhere calls "natural powers," Kracauer means all conceptual presuppositions that establish behind our backs what publicly counts as sayable and unsayable. To this extent, it might be even better to speak of a conceptual picture or an apparatus that holds us captive in the sense that, owing to our fixed descriptions, certain procedures seem to us like parts of nature from which we can no longer detach ourselves. If the intellectual of the present depends on moving within a conceptual framework of this kind because he wants to win quick public agreement for his positions, social criticism must conversely devote itself entirely to skillfully drilling holes in these tried and tested frameworks and tentatively suspending them.

The interest by which this is led is of a fundamentally different kind than that which inheres in the activity of intellectuals today. For intellectuals, it is a matter of correcting the perspective of public issues within the descriptive system accepted by the democratic public sphere, whereas for social critics, it is a matter of interrogating that descriptive system itself. The normalization of the role of the intellectual has in a certain sense completed the change of position that made them agents in the fora of political will-formation as long as the task of social criticism could no longer even be perceived. For that would require stepping out of the horizon of the publicly apportioned self-understanding that is today the ultimate reference point for their own activity. Walzer's diagnosis collapses on the results of this internal displacement, since it is in no way suited to determining the behavioral dispositions that are constitutive of social criticism after its final separation from the intellectuals.

An element of outsiderness has always been a spiritual source of social criticism. Be it through political persecution leading to exile or cultural isolation on the periphery of their own country, the most important critics of society often take a position that gives them a certain distance from socially rehearsed interpretive models— Rousseau disgustedly turned his back on the vanity fair of Paris; Marx lived out the uprooted existence of a political exile; Kracauer is said to have had a physically based inferiority complex; as a Jew, Marcuse like many others belonged to a cultural minority. In none of the cases can their marginal position be located in a simple topography, within which the contemporary discussion often distinguishes only between "inside" and "outside."

These social critics were neither so alienated from their cultures of origin that they had to take a simply external perspective nor did they have enough trust and loyalty with regard to them to be able to enjoy a simply internal critical perspective. If a topographical picture can be helpful here at all, it would be that of an "internal abroad": from the side, from an internal perspective that has been displaced to the outside, they observe the whole of practices and convictions that have spread in their own culture of origin with a growing distance as a second nature. It was such a marginal position that put them in a position to see a unified mechanism in the immense multiplicity of public statements and events. But only their remaining connected to this culture enabled them to put the verve, care, and energy into their work that is necessary for a successful critique of social self-understandings. Two peculiarities of social criticism result from the fact that it is written from a perspective of connection with a social lifeworld that as a whole has become alien.

Unlike the activity of contemporary intellectuals, which despite all its appeals to generalizable norms nevertheless constantly raises publicly relevant issues, social criticism always has a holistic character. It does not interrogate the dominant interpretation of a particular specialized problem, public ignorance about dissenting opinions, or the selective perception of the material available for a decision; rather, it questions the social and cultural network of conditions under which these processes of will-formation arise. Rousseau's critique of the self-referentiality of modern subjectivity is as good an example of what I am calling "holism" here as Adorno and Horkheimer's culture-industry thesis. What these writings criticize is not individual events, particular mistakes, or relative injustices but the structural properties of the constitution of a social sphere as a whole. What drives social criticism is the impression that the institutional mechanisms and need interpretations that underlie public will-formation like a quasi-natural precondition are themselves highly dubious. It must therefore put everything into producing a picture of these apparently self-evident presuppositions that problematizes them. The second peculiarity of social criticism also results from the attempt to get a distance from a whole network of conditions: unlike the interventions of intellectuals, it structurally depends on using a theory that in one or another way possesses an explanatory character.

What Walzer wrongly claims about the task of social criticism may apply to the activity of intellectuals today. Intervention in the political public sphere that aims at correcting dominant interpretations or propagating new perspectives not only depends on theoretical explanations; it can also be easily influenced by them. For the greater the investment in sociological or historical explanation, the greater the danger of losing sight of the practical political demands of the addressees. If contemporary intellectuals must therefore practice a certain abstinence with regard to explanatory theories, social criticism, to the contrary, now as ever is fundamentally reliant on them. To be able to justify why accustomed practices or convictions are questionable as a whole, social criticism must offer a theoretical explanation that allows the development of an apparatus to be understood as the unintended consequence of a chain of intended circumstances or actions. As much as the theoretical contents may be distinguished from one another, as manifold as the explanations may be, their task within social criticism is the same in all cases: they help show that we cannot endorse the institutional totality or form of life we practice everyday because it is the merely causal result of a developmental process that can be understood in its individual components.

This common function also explains a generic characteristic of all theories that can be used in social criticism. Despite their methodological differences, they must provide an explanation for the mechanisms through which it was historically or socially possible for a practical model, needs schema, or attitudinal syndrome that contradicts our most deep-seated desires or intentions to penetrate into our institutional practices. According to the temperament of the critic and the epistemic culture, Rousseau's theory of civilization delivers as appropriate an instrument as Nietzsche's genealogy, Marx's political economy as tested a tool as Weber's concept of rationalization. But sociological action theories, as developed in different ways by Bourdieu and Giddens, can fulfill this function within the framework of critique of society. Essentially, there are hardly any limits to the explanatory possibilities as long as the demand is met of explaining how a chain of intended circumstances leads to the unintended consequence of a form of life that is questionable as a whole.

Of course, just like intellectual interventions, the political line of attack of social criticism can spread across the whole spectrum of contemporary positions. The difference between the two enterprises does not lie in the fact that pluralism prevails today in the intellectual field whereas there is an underlying consensus in the field of social criticism. It is the kind of pluralism that allows two types of reflexive positions to be distinguished in the present. If the normalized intellectual is bound to a political consensus that is the expression of all the moral convictions cutting across the plurality of worldviews,[7] social critical is free from limitations of this kind, since it seeks to put precisely the background convictions of this consensus in question. Although they can afford ethical exaggerations and one-sidedness, intellectuals today are largely compelled to neutralize their worldviews, since when possible they must seek agreement in the political public sphere. The limits on social criticism thus arise from what a public composed of highly mixed worldviews is prepared to understand; those the intellectual comes up against, however, are established by the liberal principles of a public sphere that reasons democratically. The intellectual must promote his opinion with artful arguments while respecting these principles, whereas the social critic can try to convince us that accustomed modes of practice are questionable by using an ethically laden theory. This difference also establishes the difference between the cognitive virtues of the two enterprises.

Probably the virtue that is least useful for social criticism is a "good eye." Even if Walzer is not entirely clear whether by this he means a sense for real political pressures or social context, the immediate advantages of this ability for contemporary intellectuals are undisputed. To be able to make their argumentative interventions in public discourse convincing, they must not only possess a correct view of what can be achieved politically but also appropriately judge the chances of arguments prevailing socially. Nothing would be more detrimental to social criticism than making its revelation of questionable social practices depend on their prospects of political implementation. Social criticism does not aim at rapid success in the democratic exchange of opinions but at the distant effect of gradually growing doubt about whether given models of practice or schemas of needs are in fact appropriate (for us). It is paid in the coin not of momentary argumentative convincingness but in justified reorientation in future processes.

For this task, the sense of proportion that Walzer demands from criticism proves to be a hindrance rather than a benefit. Those who look to favorable political circumstances and the intellectual climate will hardly be able to achieve the change of perspective necessary to burst habitual forms of life like a soap bubble. The disposition social criticism requires is the hypertrophic, the idiosyncratic view of those who see in the beloved everyday of the institutional order the abyss of failed sociality, in routinized differences of opinion the outlines of collective delusion. It is this easily displaced perspective that looks in from the margins that also allows us to understand why social criticism, unlike intellectual activity, requires the application of theory. For its task is to explain the distance between perceived reality and the public self-understanding of social practices.

Empathy, too, is a virtue whose characteristics can prove to be highly ambivalent for the practice of the social critic. Of course, the ultimate emotional basis of his or her critical initiative is nothing other than identification with the pain and suffering that the mechanism of social action he or she takes to be questionable causes in individuals. How else could the energy he or she puts into formulating a theoretical account with dubious prospects of political implementation be explained? But this identification is not with an articulated suffering that is already subjectively perceived but with a pain that is only suspected, in a certain sense attributed, beyond what can be socially articulated. The social critic takes the generalizable interests of all members of society to be injured when he or she speaks of the questionability of a socially practiced form of life. "Empathy" is surely not the word for the affective situation at play here. Instead, it is a matter of a kind of higher-level though no less intense identification with a suffering that under given conditions cannot even find linguistic expression. This abstract, broken sympathy also explains why a tone of bitterness and even coldness creeps into the language of social criticism. It is not pure arrogance that diffuses an atmosphere of distance but bitterness and resentment that the hypertrophically perceived suffering still has not found resonance in the public space of articulation. These ingredients of social criticism can certainly not be called virtues, personal dispositions worthy of imitation, or model elements of texts. But in this case, there is a bit of necessity even within the sin that results from spiritual isolation which, in contrast to intellectual position-taking, compels the interrogation of a form of life.

The virtues that really distinguish social criticism are not properties of its representatives, however, but of the texts themselves. While personal abilities may be of particular importance among the intellectuals of our day since they help make their arguments convincing to the public, in this second case they largely recede behind the linguistic form of their interpretations. This is also why it seems to be so much easier to speak evaluatively of the figure of the intellectual, whereas regarding social criticism it is difficult to reach judgments about the personality of the author. The success of their activity is not measured, this would mean, by quickly convincing a quarrelsome, divided public but, rather, through the long-term reorientation of a public confident in prevailing ideas. What among intellectuals is a sense of proportion, a convincing argument, or recognizable engagement for a minority must be almost completely replaced for the social critic by the creative ability to give texts a disintegrating effect on social myths. The task of rhetorically equipping dry explanations with suggestive power therefore represents the real challenge of social criticism, and as many authors as have mastered it may have dramatically failed.

Of the many tools available to social criticism, two rhetorical figures in particular stand out for their widespread use. A creative element that is used again and again is the skillful application of exaggerations, with which the theoretically deduced condition is cast in such a garish, bizarre light that its questionability will appear as the scales fall from the readers' eyes. Rousseau's *Second Discourse* is as good an example of this kind of art of exaggeration as the *Dialectic of Enlightenment*.[8] Here, of course, the rhetorically exaggerated result must not be confused with the process by which theoretical explanations are brought to bear in these forms of social criticism. Only the questionable condition of the present itself is outfitted with the stylistic elements of the art of exaggeration, whereas its historical genesis is soberly explained as the unintended consequence of intentional processes.

The tool that no doubt most often finds application in social criticism is the coining of catchy formulas in which a complex explanation of social processes is compressed and given expression in a single denominator. If Foucault speaks of the "disciplinary society" or "biopolitics," if the "colonization of the lifeworld" runs like a leitmotif through Habermas's work, or if Marcuse uses the expression "repressive tolerance," hidden behind these expressions are demanding theories in which a questionable condition of our social form of life is explained as the result of a developmental process that has not yet been completed. Here again, the rhetorical emphasis applies only to the result, not to the historical event that is to have caused it. The formula clearly and effectively captures the features especially worthy of criticism in this condition that has emerged "behind our backs" through a historical chain of intentional processes. In this respect, there are hardly any limits to the application of rhetorical tools, as long as the theoretical demand of making comprehensible the genesis of a problematic social order by means of causal explanation is vouchsafed.[9]

Unlike the interventions of intellectuals, however, social criticism that is suggestively charged in this way possesses only a highly indirect, long-distance effect that can hardly be empirically measured. In general, it does not precipitate dramatic ruptures in public opinion or the statements of public officials. That social criticism is nonetheless not without prospects of success, that in the long run it can contribute to a change of orientation, is impressively shown by a social-theoretical formula whose catchiness seems not to have suffered from rising doubts about its theoretical explanatory content. When Horkheimer and Adorno coined the concept of the "culture industry" to criticize various processes of commercialization in the cultural sector, they could not have suspected that they had set in motion a cultural learning process that led to demands for higher quality in radio and television in Germany than in almost any other country.

The way this efficacy hesitantly came about can stand paradigmatically for how social criticism can contribute to the transformation of social conditions. First of all, with the rhetorical means of the chiasmus, a formula was made whose content was much too cumbersome or even incomprehensible to change the perceptions and convictions of the reading public. Moreover, understanding it assumed a familiarity with social-theoretical arguments—the conventional opposition of the concepts of "culture" and "industry," the particular point that the fusion of the two concepts had to insist on—in order to have direct influence on scattered opinion formation in the public sphere. There the idea of a "culture industry" initially influenced only a small circle of intellectuals, students, and culture producers by giving them a heightened sense of the dangers connected to the infiltration of commercial imperatives and profitability perspectives into the cultural sphere. Only from here did this leitmotiv-like formula find a larger public by way of the complex tracks of cultural communication, where, without clear awareness of its theoretical origins, it reinforced reservations against economic tendencies that seriously threatened the cultural standards of radio, television, and book production.

At the end of a process rich with detours there were finally political and legal measures whereby price limits on books, public self-supervision, and the guarantee of so-called culture quotas were to ensure that the production of the cultural media was not completely subjected to the pressure of commercialization. The history of this public learning process in Germany has not yet been written, but the few insights we have into the subterranean effects of Horkheimer and Adorno's idea make the influence their social criticism had on the sensibilities and perceptions of the German public sphere clear enough.[10] And if today the price limits on books and the diverse pro-gramming on television are threatened, the resistance that is stirring is probably fallout from the indirect effect that the social-critical formula of the culture industry left in the political consciousness of the educated public. Compared with the productive flow of normal-ized intellectuals, the rare products of social criticism need a long time before their effects can unfold in the form of a transformation of social perceptions. But the change of orientation it subcutane-ously promoted is of much greater persistence and durability than any intellectual position taking could bring about today.

NOTES

1. THE IRREDUCIBILITY OF PROGRESS

1. Immanuel Kant, "The Contest of the Faculties," in *Kant: Political Writings*, ed. H. Reiss, trans. H. B. Nisbet (Cambridge: Cambridge University Press, 1970), 177 ff.
2. Walter Benjamin, "Theses on the Philosophy of History," in *Illuminations*, ed. H. Arendt, trans. H. Zohn (London: Fontana, 1992), 249.
3. Kant, "Contest of the Faculties," 178.
4. Immanuel Kant, "An Answer to the Question: 'What Is Enlightenment?'" in *Kant: Political Writings*, 57.
5. Kant, "Contest of the Faculties," 190.
6. Immanuel Kant, *Anthropology from a Pragmatic Point of View*, trans. M. G. McGregor (The Hague: Martinus Nijhoff, 1974), 185.
7. An instructive comparison of Benjamin's philosophy of history with that of Kant is provided by Rudolf Langthaler, "Benjamin und Kant oder: Über den Versuch, Geschichte philosophisch zu denken," *Deutsche Zeitschrift für Philosophie* 50, no. 2 (2002): 203–25. I do not believe, however, that the convergences between the two approaches extend as far as Langthaler tries to show.
8. Axel Honneth, "A Communicative Disclosure of the Past: On the Relation Between Anthropology and Philosophy of History in Walter Benjamin," *New Formations* 20 (1993): 83–94.
9. Kant, "Contest of the Faculties," 179.
10. Pauline Kleingeld has presented a fine overview of the different and, to an extent, competing approaches of the Kantian philosophy of history (Kleingeld, *Fortschritt und Vernunft: Zur Geschichtsphilosophie Kants* [Würzburg: Konigshausen und Neumann, 1995]; see also Kleingeld, "Kant, History, and

the Idea of Moral Development," *History of Philosophy Quarterly* 16, no. 1 [1999]: 59–80). My own proposal to identify a system-bursting approach in the Kantian philosophy of history, however, deviates from Kleingeld's interpretative approach. In contrast to her, I am convinced that in this "hermeneutic-explicative" model, as I will call it, Kant had in fact already undertaken a step toward the de-transcendentalization of reason.

11. Kleingeld, *Fortschritt und Vernunft*, chs. 1, 2, and 6.
12. Immanuel Kant, *Critique of Judgment*, trans. W. S. Pluhar (Indianapolis: Hackett, 1987), 18–19.
13. Immanuel Kant, "Idea for a Universal History with a Cosmopolitan Purpose," in *Kant: Political Writings*, 42.
14. Kant, *Critique of Judgment*, 319.
15. Ibid.
16. Kant, "Idea for a Universal History," 50 ff.
17. Ibid., 43–45.
18. Immanuel Kant, *Critique of Practical Reason*, trans. M. Gregor (Cambridge: Cambridge University Press, 1997), 118–19.
19. Immanuel Kant, "On the Common Saying: 'This May Be True in Theory, but It Does Not Apply in Practice,'" in *Kant: Political Writings*, 88.
20. Immanuel Kant, "Perpetual Peace," in *Kant: Political Writings*, 108; Kant, "What Is Enlightenment," 59–60.
21. Kant, "On the Common Saying," 89.
22. Ibid.
23. Until now, Yimiyahu Yovel, *Kant and the Philosophy of History* (Princeton, N.J.: Princeton University Press, 1980), has defended most decisively the thesis that in his philosophy of history Kant moved toward Hegel via a historicization of reason. In contrast to Yovel, however, I do not wish to assert that Kant was compelled by the premises of his own system to de-transcendentalize moral reason and to comprehend it as something of historically increasing significance (ch. 7). I am convinced, rather, along with a host of other authors, that such a step remains incompatible with the presuppositions of the Kantian moral philosophy (e.g., Paul Stern, "The Problem of History and Temporality in Kantian Ethics," *Review of Metaphysics* 39 [1986]: 505–45). For this reason, I describe the "hermeneutic-explicative" model as having the tendency to be "system-bursting." Incidentally, an elaboration of this third approach in the Kantian philosophy of history would, in fact, lead to a historicization of reason in Hegel's sense, but it certainly would not lead to the basic assumptions of his philosophy of history. For, on the contrary, as Rolf-Peter Horstmann (*Die Grenzen der Vernunft* [Frankfurt: Anton Hain, 1991], 221–44) has convincingly shown, Hegel is indebted to Kant for an objectification of this heuristic idea of a natural teleology, which

Kant placed at the foundation of his official, system-conforming philosophy of history.

24. Kant, "Idea for a Universal History," 44.

25. For an excellent reconstruction, see Allen Wood, "Unsociable Sociability: The Anthropological Basis of Kantian Ethics," *Philosophical Topics* 19, no. 1 (1991): 325–51.

26. Kant, "Idea for a Universal History," 45.

27. The idea of interpreting Kant's model of conflict according to the (Hegelian) model of a "struggle for recognition" derives from Yovel, *Kant and the Philosophy of History*, 148 ff.

28. Immanuel Kant, "Conjectures on the Beginnings of Human History," in *Kant: Political Writings*, 230–32; Kant, "Perpetual Peace," 111–12.

29. Kant, "Conjectures on the Beginnings of Human History," 230–31.

30. Kant, "What Is Enlightenment?," 59.

31. Discussed further in Kleingeld, *Fortschritt und Vernunft*, 171 ff.

32. Kant, "What Is Enlightenment?," 54.

33. On this problem complex, see the impressive investigation by Andrea Marlen, *"Eine Ethik für Endliche": Kants Tugendlehre in der Gegenwart* (Stuttgart: Frommann-Holzboog, 2004).

34. Kant, "What Is Enlightenment?," 54.

35. Kant, "Contest of the Faculties," 185.

36. Ibid.

2. A SOCIAL PATHOLOGY OF REASON

1. Jürgen Habermas, "Nach Dreißig Jahren: Bemerkungen zu *Erkenntnis und Interesse*," in *Das Interesse der Vernunft*, ed. Stefan Müller-Doohm (Frankfurt: Suhrkamp, 2000), 12.

2. For an exemplary work of social criticism in Foucault's sense, see James Tully, "Political Philosophy as Critical Activity," *Political Theory* 30 (2002): 533–55. In further pursuing such motives, Martin Saar has meanwhile produced a highly convincing monograph, *Genealogie als Kritik: Geschichte und Theorie des Subjekts nach Nietzsche und Foucault* (Frankfurt: Campus, 2007). See also Michael Walzer, *Interpretation and Social Criticism* (Cambridge: Harvard University Press, 1987). I attempt to develop a criticism of this model of social criticism in the appendix to this volume.

3. On the concept of "negativity," and above all on the distinction between content-centered and methodological negativism, see Michael Theunissen, *Das Selbst auf dem Grund der Verzweiflung: Kierkegaards negativistische Methode* (Berlin: Hain, 1999); Theunissen, "Negativität bei Adorno," in *Adorno-*

Konferenz 1983, ed. Ludwig von Friedeburg and Jürgen Habermas (Frankfurt: Suhrkamp, 1983), 41–65. On *Negative Dialectics*, see chapter 5 of this volume.

4. On the distinction between the center and the periphery of Critical Theory, see Axel Honneth, "Critical Theory," trans. John Farrell, in *The Fragmented World of the Social: Essays in Social and Political Philosophy*, ed. Charles W. Wright (Albany: State University of New York Press, 1995).

5. On this distinction, see Axel Honneth, "Pathologies of the Social: The Past and Present of Social Philosophy," in *Disrespect: The Normative Foundations of Critical Theory* (Cambridge: Polity, 2007).

6. Max Horkheimer, "Traditional and Critical Theory," in *Critical Theory: Selected Essays*, trans. Matthew O'Connell (New York: Continuum, 1975), 188–243; Theodor W. Adorno, "Cultural Criticism and Society," in *Prisms*, trans. Samuel Weber and Shierry Weber (Cambridge, Mass.: MIT Press, 1983), 17–34; Herbert Marcuse, *One-Dimensional Man* (Boston: Beacon, 1964); Marcuse, "Repressive Tolerance," in *A Critique of Pure Tolerance*, by Robert Paul Wolff, Barrington Moore Jr., and Marcuse(Boston: Beacon, 1969), 95–137; and Jürgen Habermas, *Theory of Communicative Action*, 2 vols., trans. Thomas McCarthy (Boston: Beacon, 1987), vol. 2, ch. 8.

7. For further discussion, see Axel Honneth, *Leiden an Unbestimmtheit: Eine Reaktualisierung der Hegelschen Rechtsphilosophie* (Stuttgart: Reclam, 2001); Michael Theunissen, *Selbstverwirklichung und Allgemeinheit: Zur Kritik des gegenwärtigen Bewusstseins* (Berlin: de Gruyter, 1982).

8. Horkheimer, "Traditional and Critical Theory," 213 ff.

9. Herbert Marcuse, *An Essay on Liberation* (Boston: Beacon, 1969); Marcuse, *Eros and Civilization: A Philosophical Inquiry into Freud* (Boston: Beacon, 1955), esp. ch. 2.

10. Habermas, *Theory of Communicative Action*, vol. 2, ch. 6. See also Maeve Cooke, *Language and Reason: A Study of Habermas's Pragmatics* (Cambridge, Mass.: MIT Press, 1994), esp. ch. 5.

11. Horkheimer, "Traditional and Critical Theory," 217.

12. This aim of proceduralizing the Hegelian idea of a rational universal is especially clear in Jürgen Habermas, "Können komplexe Gesellschaften eine vernünftige Identität ausbilden?" in *Zwei Reden: Aus Anlass der Verleihung des Hegel-Preises der Stadt Stuttgart*, by Jürgen Habermas and Dieter Henrich (Frankfurt: Suhrkamp, 1974), 23–84.

13. It is this ethical perspective that I think presents a certain point of contact between Critical Theory and American pragmatism. It is all the more astonishing that it is only with Habermas that a productive reception of pragmatism sets in, while the first generation's reactions to pragmatism essentially range from skepticism to outright disapproval. On the history of its reception, see Hans Joas, "An Underestimated Alternative: America and the Lim-

its of 'Critical Theory,'" in *Pragmatism and Social Theory* (Chicago: University of Chicago Press, 1993).

14. Theodor W. Adorno, *Minima Moralia*, trans. E. F. N. Jephcott (London: Verso, 1974), nos. 11, 16.

15. Ibid., esp. nos. 11, 15, 21, 110. On this motif, see Martin Seel, "Adornos kontemplative Ethik: Philosophie—Eine Kolumne," *Merkur* 638 (2002): 512–18.

16. Horkheimer, "Traditional and Critical Theory," 217.

17. On "communitarianism," see Axel Honneth, ed., *Kommunitarianismus: Eine Debatte über die moralischen Grundlagen moderner Gesellschaften* (Frankfurt: Campus, 1993).

18. Karl Marx, *Capital: A Critique of Political Economy*, trans. Ben Fowkes (New York: Penguin, 1992), 163–77. For an excellent analysis, see Georg Lohmann, *Indifferenz und Gesellschaft: Eine kritische Auseinandersetzung mit Marx* (Frankfurt: Campus, 1991), esp. ch. 5.

19. See generally Max Horkheimer and Theodor W. Adorno, *Dialectic of Enlightenment: Philosophical Fragments*, trans. Edmund Jephcott (Stanford: Stanford University Press, 2002); Marcuse, *One-Dimensional Man*; Theodor W. Adorno, introduction to *The Positivist Dispute in German Sociology*, trans. Glyn Adey and David Frisby (New York: Harper and Row, 1976); Jürgen Habermas, *Towards a Rational Society*, trans. Jeremy Shapiro (Boston: Beacon, 1971).

20. Adorno, "Cultural Criticism and Society," 24.

21. Georg Lukács, "Reification and the Consciousness of the Proletariat," in *History and Class Consciousness: Studies in Marxist Dialectics*, trans. Rodney Livingstone (Cambridge, Mass.: MIT Press, 1971), 83–221. On the significance of the Lukácsian analysis of reification for early Critical Theory, see Jürgen Habermas, *Theory of Communicative Action*, trans. Thomas McCarthy (Boston: Beacon, 1984), vol. 1, ch. 6.

22. Horkheimer, "Traditional and Critical Theory." On the problematic, see Axel Honneth, *The Critique of Power: Reflective Stages in a Critical Social Theory*, trans. Kenneth Baynes (Cambridge, Mass.: MIT Press, 1991), ch. 1.

23. Theodor W. Adorno, "Some Ideas on the Sociology of Music," in *Sounds Figures*, trans. Rodney Livingstone (Stanford: Stanford University Press, 1999), 1–14.

24. Marcuse, *Eros and Civilization*, esp. ch. 6.

25. Habermas, *Toward a Rational Society*, 81–121; Habermas, *Theory of Communicative Action*, vol. 2, ch. 6.

26. Pierre Bourdieu and Jean-Claude Passeron, *Reproduction in Education, Society and Culture*, 2nd ed., trans. Richard Nice (London: Sage, 1990).

27. Lukács, *History and Class Consciousness*, 90–91.

28. For more discussion, see Axel Honneth, "'Invisibility: On the Epistemology of Recognition," *Proceedings of the Aristotelian Society* 75 suppl. (2001): 111–26.

29. Horkheimer, "Traditional and Critical Theory," 213.
30. Max Horkheimer, "Authority and the Family," in *Critical Theory*, 47–128. Horkheimer develops the same motif with unmistakable religious undertones in "Die verwaltete Welt kennt keine Liebe: Gespräch mit Janko Muselin," in *Gesammelte Schriften*, ed. Gunzelin Schmid-Noerr and A. Schmidt, 19 vols. (Frankfurt: Fischer, 1987–), vol. 7, 358–67.
31. Adorno, *Minima Moralia*, nos. 10, 11, 107, 110.
32. Marcuse, *Eros and Civilization*, ch. 4. See also Johànn P. Arnason, *Von Marcuse zu Marx* (Neuwied: Luchterhand, 1971), esp. ch. 5.
33. Habermas, *Theory of Communicative Action*, vol. 2, ch. 8.
34. For example, Anthony Giddens, *Modernity and Self-Identity: Self and Society in the Late Modern Age* (Cambridge: Polity, 1991), esp. 196 ff.
35. Of significance in this connection are Wilhelm Hennis, *Max Webers Fragestellung* (Tübingen: Mohr, 1987), and Cornelius Castoriadis, *The Imaginary Institution of Society*, trans. Kathleen Blamey (Cambridge, Mass.: MIT Press, 1987). For a more recent study, see Luc Boltanski and Eve Chiapello, *The New Spirit of Capitalism*, trans. Gregory Elliott (London: Verso, 2007).
36. Exemplary in this connection is Judith Butler, *The Psychic Life of Power: Theories in Subjection* (Stanford: Stanford University Press, 1997), chs. 2–4.
37. For example, Karl Löwith, *From Hegel to Nietzsche: The Revolution in Nineteenth-Century Thought*, trans. David Green (New York: Columbia University Press, 1964), ch. 2; Jürgen Habermas, *The Philosophical Discourse of Modernity*, trans. Frederick Lawrence (Cambridge, Mass.: MIT Press, 1990), ch. 3.
38. For example, Theodor W. Adorno, "Resignation," in *Critical Models: Interventions and Catchwords*, trans. Henry W. Pickford (New York: Columbia University Press, 1998), 289–94.
39. Erich Fromm, *The Working Class in Weimar Germany: A Psychological and Sociological Study*, trans. B. Weinberger (Cambridge: Harvard University Press, 1984).
40. Helmut Dubiel, *Theory and Politics: Studies in the Development of Critical Theory*, trans. Benjamin Gregg (Cambridge, Mass.: MIT Press, 1985), ch. 5.
41. See chapter 7 of this volume.
42. Jürgen Habermas, *Knowledge and Human Interests*, trans. Jeremy Shapiro (Boston: Beacon, 1971), ch. 12.
43. Max Horkeimer, "History and Psychology," in *Between Philosophy and Social Science*, trans. Frederick Hunter, Matthew S. Kramer, and John Torpey (Cambridge, Mass.: MIT Press, 1995), 111–28.
44. Theodor W. Adorno, *Negative Dialectics*, trans. E. B. Ashton (London: Routledge, 1973), 203.
45. For an exception to this generalization, see Josef Früchtl, *Mimesis: Konstella-

tion eines Zentralbegriffs bei Adorno (Würzburg: Königshausen und Neumann, 1986), ch. 3.

46. Theodor W. Adorno, "Bemerkungen über Politik und Neurose," in *Gesammelte Schriften*, 20 vols., ed. Rolf Tiedemann (Frankfurt: Suhrkamp, 1972), 8: 437.

47. For the reflections on Marx, see Habermas, *Theory of Communicative Action*, vol. 2, ch. 8. Habermas wavers here, however, between a lifeworld use and a merely functional use of the idea of a social pathology. On these difficulties, see Robin Celikates and Arnd Pollmann, "Baustellen der Vernunft: 25 Jahre Theorie des kommunikativen Handelns—Zur Gegenwart eines Paradigmenwechsels," *Westend* 3, no. 2 (2006): 97–113.

48. Früchtl, *Mimesis*, ch. 5.

49. Marcuse, *Eros and Civilization*, 204.

50. Herbert Marcuse, Jürgen Habermas, Silvia Bovenschen, Tilman Spengler, Marianne Schuller, Berthold Rothschild, et al., *Gespräche mit Herbert Marcuse* (Frankfurt: Suhrkamp, 1978).

51. Habermas, *Knowledge and Human Interests*, ch. 3.

52. Jürgen Habermas, "The Relationship Between Theory and Practice Revisited," in *Truth and Justification*, trans. Barbara Fultner (Cambridge, Mass.: MIT Press, 2003), 277–92.

3. RECONSTRUCTIVE SOCIAL CRITICISM WITH A GENEALOGICAL PROVISO

1. Michael Walzer, *Interpretation and Social Criticism* (Cambridge: Harvard University Press, 1987). See also Walzer, *The Company of Critics: Social Criticism and Political Commitment in the Twentieth Century*, 2nd ed. (New York: Basic Books, 2002).

2. John Rawls, *A Theory of Justice* (Cambridge: Harvard University Press, 1971).

3. For example, Michel Foucault, *Discipline and Punish: The Birth of the Prison*, trans. Alan Sheridan (New York: Vintage, 1977).

4. For discussion of this kind of critical model, see Samantha Ashenden and David Owen, eds., *Foucault Contra Habermas: Recasting the Dialogue Between Genealogy and Critical Theory* (London: Sage, 1999); Axel Honneth and Martin Saar, eds., *Michel Foucault: Zwischenbilanz einer Rezeption* (Frankfurt: Suhrkamp, 2003), esp. pt. 3; Martin Saar, *Genealogie als Kritik: Geschichte und Theorie des Subjekts nach Nietzsche und Foucault* (Frankfurt: Campus, 2007).

5. Max Horkheimer, "Traditional and Critical Theory," in *Critical Theory: Selected Essays*, trans. Matthew O'Connell (New York: Continuum, 1975). See also Herbert Marcuse, "Philosophy and Critical Theory," in *Critical Theory:*

The Essential Readings, ed. David Ingram and Julia Simon-Ingram (St. Paul, Minn.: Paragon House, 1991).

6. Walzer, *Interpretation and Social Criticism.*

7. Axel Honneth, *The Critique of Power: Reflective Stages in a Critical Social Theory*, trans. Kenneth Baynes (Cambridge, Mass.: MIT Press, 1991).

8. I develop reflections in the direction of such a conception of progress in chapter 1 of this volume.

9. For example, Ludwig Marcuse, Theodor W. Adorno, Günther Anders, Max Horkheimer, Herbert Marcuse, and Friedrich Nürnberg, "Need and Culture in Nietzsche," *Constellations* 8, no. 1 (2001): 130–35.

4. A PHYSIOGNOMY OF THE CAPITALIST FORM OF LIFE

1. Theodor W. Adorno, "Late Capitalism or Industrial Society?" and "Reflections on Class Theory," in *Can One Live After Auschwitz? A Philosophical Reader*, ed. Rolf Tiedemann (Stanford: Stanford University Press, 2003).

2. I have developed a critique of this kind in Axel Honneth, *The Critique of Power: Reflective Stages in a Critical Social Theory*, trans. Kenneth Baynes (Cambridge, Mass.: MIT Press, 1991), ch. 3. Although I am convinced that this original criticism, based on a particular perspective which was then for me decisive, can be maintained on all points, here I undertake an alternative interpretation by considering Adorno's social as no longer an explanatory endeavor but a hermeneutic project. This new perspective deprives the old objections of their bases, since elements now have to be understood not as attempts at sociological explanation but as parts of an ideal-typical interpretation of the capitalist form of life.

3. Ludwig von Friedeburg and Jürgen Habermas, eds., *Adorno-Konferenz 1983* (Frankfurt: Suhrkamp, 1983). The colloquium on Adorno's sociological writings has contributions by Hauke Brunkhorst, Christoph Deutschmann, Helmut Dubiel, and Alfons Söllner, 293–350.

4. Theodor W. Adorno, "The Actuality of Philosophy," trans. Benjamin Snow, in *The Adorno Reader*, ed. Brian O'Connor (Oxford: Blackwell, 2000).

5. Ibid., 34.

6. For example, Walter Benjamin, "On the Program of the Coming Philosophy," in *Selected Writings*, Vol. 1: *1913–1926*, ed. Marcus Bullock and Michael W. Jennings (Cambridge: Harvard University Press, 1996).

7. On the differences, see, for example, Jürgen Habermas, "Walter Benjamin: Consciousness-Raising or Saving Critique," in *Philosophical-Political Profiles*, trans. Frederick G. Lawrence (Cambridge, Mass.: MIT Press, 1983).

8. Georg Lukács, "Reification and the Consciousness of the Proletariat," in

History and Class Consciousness: Studies in Marxist Dialectics, trans. Rodney Livingstone (Cambridge, Mass.: MIT Press, 1971).

9. For example, Martin Jay, "Georg Lukács and the Origins of the Western Marxist Paradigm," in *Marxism and Totality: The Adventures of a Concept from Lukács to Habermas* (Berkeley: University of California Press, 1986), 81–127.

10. Adorno, "Actuality of Philosophy," 25.

11. For example, Walter Benjamin, *Charles Baudelaire: A Lyric Poet of the Era of High Capitalism*, trans. Harry Zohn (London: Verso, 1983); see also Axel Honneth, "A Communicative Disclosure of the Past: On the Relation Between Anthropology and Philosophy of History in Walter Benjamin," *New Formations* 20 (1993): 83–94.

12. Adorno, "Actuality of Philosophy," 36.

13. Ibid., 32, 31, 35.

14. Max Weber, "Objectivity in Social Science and Social Policy," in *Max Weber on the Methodology of the Social Sciences*, ed. and trans. Edward A. Shils and Henry A. Finch (Glencoe, Ill.: Free Press, 1949), 90.

15. Adorno, "Actuality of Philosophy," 32.

16. Ibid., 37 (trans. modified).

17. Weber, "Objectivity in Social Science and Social Policy," 90.

18. Ibid.; Adorno, "Actuality of Philosophy," 36.

19. Dieter Henrich, *Die Einheit der Wissenschaftslehre Max Webers* (Tübingen: J. C. B. Mohr, 1952); Michael Schmid, "Idealisierung und Idealtypus: Zur Logik der Typenbildung bei Max Weber," in *Max Webers Wissenschaftslehre*, ed. Gerhard Wagner and Heinz Zipprian (Frankfurt: Suhrkamp, 1994), 415–44.

20. Weber, "Objectivity in Social Science and Social Policy," 91.

21. Theodor W. Adorno, *Minima Moralia*, trans. E. F. N. Jephcott (London: Verso, 1974), no. 99.

22. For example, Michael Tomasello, *The Cultural Origins of Human Cognition* (Cambridge: Harvard University Press, 1999), esp. chs. 2 and 3; Peter Hobson, *The Cradle of Thought* (London: Macmillan, 2002), esp. chs. 3 and 4. On these "mimetic" or emotional-intersubjective presupposition of human thinking as a whole, see Martin Dornes, "Die intersubjektiven Ursprünge des Denkens," *WestEnd: Neue Zeitschrift für Sozialforschung* 1 (2005): 3–48.

23. Theodor W. Adorno, *Minima Moralia*, in *Gesammelte Schriften*, ed. Rolf Tiedemann (Frankfurt: Suhrkamp, 1977), 8: 292 and no. 127 ("Wishful Thinking"). [Appendix not in English translation—trans.]

24. See chapter 2 of this volume.

25. For example, Bert van den Brink, "Gesellschaftstheorie und Übertreibungskunst: Für eine alternative Lesart der 'Dialektik der Aufklärung,'" *Neue Rundschau* 1 (1997): 37–59.

26. For example, Theodor W. Adorno, "Notes on Kafka," in *Prisms*, trans. Samuel Weber and Shierry Weber (Cambridge, Mass.: MIT Press, 1981); Adorno, *Mahler: A Musical Physiognomy*, trans. Edmund Jephcott (Chicago: University of Chicago Press, 1992); Adorno, "Karl Korn: Sprache in der verwalteten Welt" and "Anmerkung zum sozialen Konflikt heute," in *Gesammelte Schriften*, 20: 517 and 8: 194.

27. Numbers 18 ("Refuge for the Homeless") and 19 ("Do Not Knock") in *Minima Moralia* are exemplary here.

28. Theodor W. Adorno, "Individuum und Organisation," in *Gesammelte Schriften*, 8: 440, 443, 441, 442.

29. Ibid., 442.

30. The following is based on Adorno's short 1954 "Bemerkungen über Politik und Neurose," in *Gesammelte Schriften*, 8: 434–39.

31. Adorno, "Individuen und Organisation," 8: 446.

32. Adorno, "Bemerkungen über Politik und Neurose," 8: 437.

33. Ibid., 436.

34. Theodor W. Adorno, "Résümé über Kulturindustrie," and "Theorie der Halbbildung," both in *Gesammelte Schriften*, 10: 337–45 and 8: 93–121.

35. Theodor W. Adorno, "Marginalia to Theory and Practice," in *Critical Models: Interventions and Catchwords*, trans. Henry W. Pickford (New York: Columbia University Press, 1998).

36. See chapter 2 in this volume.

37. For example, Sigmund Freud, "On Beginning the Treatment (Techniques of Psycho-analysis, I)," in *The Standard Edition of the Complete Works of Sigmund Freud*, 24 vols., ed. James Strachey, with Anna Freud (London: Hogarth Press and the Institute of Psycho-Analysis, 1953–1974), 12: 123–44.

38. Theodor W. Adorno, *Negative Dialectics*, trans. E. B. Ashton (London: Routledge, 1973), 203.

39. Sigmund Freud, *Outline of Psychoanalysis*, trans. Helena Ragg-Kirkby (New York: Penguin, 2003).

40. For example, *Minima Moralia*, nos. 2, 72, 79, and 146.

5. PERFORMING JUSTICE

1. Theodor W. Adorno, *Negative Dialectics*, trans. E. B. Ashton. London: Routledge, 1973.

   In view of the well-known shortcomings of the existing English translation, I have frequently relied on Dennis Redmond's version, available online at http://www.efn.org/~dredmond/ndtrans.html. Page numbers are given parenthetically in the text first to Redmond's translation, then to Adorno,

"Negative Dialektik," in *Gesammelte Schriften* (Frankfurt: Suhrkamp, 1979), 6: 7–412.—Trans.

2. Theodor W. Adorno, "The Actuality of Philosophy," trans. Benjamin Snow, in *The Adorno Reader*, ed. Brian O'Connor (Oxford: Blackwell, 2000), 22–39.

3. For example, Richard J. Bernstein, *Praxis and Action: Contemporary Philosophies of Human Action* (Philadelphia: University of Pennsylvania Press, 1971); Sami Philström, *Naturalizing the Transcendental: A Pragmatic View* (Amherst, N.Y.: Prometheus/Humanity, 2003).

4. For example, Herbert Schnädelbach, ed., *Rationalität: Philosophische Beiträge* (Frankfurt: Suhrkamp, 1984); Jürgen Habermas, *Postmetaphysical Thinking: Philosophical Essays*, trans. William Mark Hohengarten (Cambridge, Mass.: MIT Press, 1992).

5. For example, Adorno, "Actuality of Philosophy," 24 ff.

6. Theodor W. Adorno, *Hegel: Three Studies*, trans. Shierry Weber Nicholson (Cambridge, Mass.: MIT Press, 1993).

7. Max Horkheimer and Theodor W. Adorno, *Dialectic of Enlightenment: Philosophical Fragments*, trans. Edmund Jephcott (Stanford: Stanford University Press, 2002), 137 ff.

8. On such a genealogical counterprogram to Hegelian dialectics, see Christoph Menke, "Geist und Leben: Zu einer genealogischen Kritik der Phänomenologie," in *Von der Logik zur Sprache: Stuttgarter Hegel-Kongreß 2005*, ed. Rüdiger Bubner and Gunnar Hindrichs (Stuttgart: Klett-Cotta, 2007), 321–48.

9. On this problematic, see John McDowell, *Mind and World* (Cambridge: Harvard University Press, 1994).

10. Theodor W. Adorno, *Minima Moralia*, trans. E. F. N. Jephcott (London: Verso, 1974), no. 79.

11. For more, see Axel Honneth, "Decentered Autonomy: The Subject After the Fall," in *Disrespect* (Cambridge: Polity, 2007), 181–94.

12. For more, see Axel Honneth, *The Critique of Power: Reflective Stages in a Critical Social Theory*, trans. Kenneth Baynes (Cambridge, Mass.: MIT Press, 1991), ch. 3.

6. SAVING THE SACRED WITH A PHILOSOPHY OF HISTORY

1. On the developmental history of Benjamin's work, see Walter Benjamin, *Gesammelte Schriften*, 7 vols. (Frankfurt: Suhrkamp, 1977), 2: 943–45.

2. Walter Benjamin, *Gesammelte Briefe*, Vol. 2: *1919–1924*, ed. Christoph Gödde and Heinz Lonitz (Frankfurt: Suhrkamp, 1996), 44, 46–47, 57, 62, 72–73, 74–75.

3. Walter Benjamin, "Critique of Violence," in *Selected Writings*, Vol. 1: *1913–*

1926, ed. Marcus Bullock and Michael W. Jennings (Cambridge: Harvard University Press, 2004), hereafter cited parenthetically.

4. Walter Benjamin, "Fate and Character," in ibid.
5. Benjamin, *Gesammelte Briefe*, 2: 182 ff.
6. Ibid., 109, 119, 127.
7. Ibid., 943.
8. Margarete Kohlenbach, *Walter Benjamin: Self-Reference and Religiosity* (Basingstoke: Palgrave-Macmillan, 2002).
9. Ibid.
10. Benjamin, *Gesammelte Briefe*, 2: 45, 94–95, 101.
11. Ibid., 101, 104.
12. Ibid., 127.
13. A. E. Pilkington, *Bergson and His Influence* (Cambridge: Cambridge University Press, 1976), 27–90.
14. Marjorie Villiers, *Charles Péguy: A Study in Integrity* (New York: Harper and Row, 1965), ch. 10.
15. Georges Sorel, *Reflections on Violence*, trans. T. E. Hulme and J. Roth (Glencoe, Ill.: Free Press, 1950), ch. 4.
16. Villiers, *Charles Péguy*.
17. Isaiah Berlin, *Against the Current: Essays in the History of Ideas* (Princeton, N.J.: Princeton University Press, 2001), 296–323.
18. Walter Benjamin, "On the Program of the Coming Philosophy," in *Selected Writings*, vol. 1.
19. Erich Unger, *Politik und Metaphysik*, ed. Manfred Voigts (Würzburg: Konigshausen und Neumann, 1989 [1921]), 38. See also Margarete Kohlenbach and Raymond Geuss, eds., *The Early Frankfurt School and Religion* (Basingstoke: Palgrave-Macmillan, 2005), 64–84.
20. Ernst Bloch, *The Spirit of Utopia*, trans. Anthony A. Nassar (Stanford: Stanford University Press, 2006 [1918]), 246–74.
21. For more, see Uwe Steiner, "Kritik," in *Benjamins Begriffe*, ed. Michael Opitz and Erdmut Wizisla (Frankfurt: Suhrkamp, 2002), 479–523.
22. Benjamin, "On the Program of the Coming Philosophy"; Steiner, "Kritik," 480–89; Axel Honneth, "A Communicative Disclosure of the Past: On the Relation Between Anthropology and Philosophy of History in Walter Benjamin," *New Formations* 20 (1993): 83–94.
23. Benjamin, "On the Program of the Coming Philosophy."
24. Georg Lukács, *The Theory of the Novel*, trans. Anna Bostock (Cambridge, Mass.: MIT Press, 1974), 18.
25. On this tradition, see Jürgen Habermas, "Ernst Bloch: A Marxist Schelling," in *Philosophical-Political Profiles*, trans. Frederick G. Lawrence (Cambridge, Mass.: MIT Press, 1983), 61–77.

26. Georg Lukács, "Reification and the Consciousness of the Proletariat," in *History and Class Consciousness: Studies in Marxist Dialectics*, trans. Rodney Livingstone (Cambridge, Mass.: MIT Press, 1971), 83–222.

27. Ibid., 108.

28. Ibid., 109.

29. Sorel, *Reflections on Violence*, 285.

30. For more, see Axel Honneth, *The Struggle for Recognition: The Moral Grammar of Social Conflicts*, trans. Joel Anderson (Cambridge, Mass.: MIT Press, 1996), 151 ff.

31. For more, see Michael Freund, *Georges Sorel: Der revolutionäre Konservatismus* (Frankfurt: Klostermann, 1972).

32. Rudolf von Jhering, *Der Zweck im Recht*, 2 vols. (Leipzig: Breitkopf und Härtel, 1884 [1877]), 1: 439, 451–52.

33. Ibid., 452 ff.

34. Ibid., 457 ff.

35. Ibid., vol. 2.

36. Jacques Derrida, "Force of Law: The 'Mystical Foundation of Authority,'" in *Acts of Religion*, ed. Gil Anidjar (New York: Routledge, 2002).

37. Karl Heinz Ilting, *Naturrecht und Sittlichkeit: Begriffsgeschichtliche Studien* (Stuttgart: Klett-Cotta, 1983)

38. Carl Schmitt, *Crisis of Parliamentary Democracy*, trans. Ellen Kennedy (Cambridge, Mass.: MIT Press, 1988).

39. Sorel, *Reflections on Violence*, ch. 7.

40. Ibid., 261 ff.

41. Discussed further in Kohlenbach, *Walter Benjamin*.

42. Herbert Marcuse, "Revolution und Kritik der Gewalt," in *Materialien zu Benjamins "Über den Begriff der Geschichte*," ed. Peter Bulthaup (Frankfurt: Suhrkamp, 1965), 23–27.

43. Derrida, "Force of Law."

44. Giorgio Agamben, *Homo Sacer: Sovereign Power and Bare Life*, trans. Daniel Heller-Roazen (Stanford: Stanford University Press, 1998).

7. APPROPRIATING FREEDOM

I am grateful to Martin Dornes and Christine Pries-Honneth for valuable advice and tips.

1. Martin Dornes, *Die Seele des Kindes: Entstehung und Entwicklung* (Frankfurt: Fischer, 2006), chs. 2 and 6.

2. Morris N. Eagle, *Recent Developments in Psychoanalysis: A Critical Evaluation* (New York: McGraw-Hill, 1984).

3. Jonathan Lear, "The Shrink Is In," *Psyche* 50, no. 7 (1996): 599–616.

4. In this chapter, I quote Freud's writings from *The Standard Edition of the Complete Psychological Works of Sigmund Freud* (SE), 24 vols., gen. ed. James Strachey, with Anna Freud (London: Hogarth Press and the Institute of Psycho-Analysis, 1953–1974), 6: 278.

5. Freud, "Mourning and Melancholia," in *SE* 14: 239–60.

6. Ibid., 244.

7. Ibid., 430.

8. A magnificent portrayal of such pathological fantasies for processing the loss of a loved one is provided by Joan Didion, *The Year of Magical Thinking* (New York: Knopf, 2005).

9. Freud says: "That no sharp line can be drawn between 'neurotic' and 'normal' people—whether children or adults—that our conception of 'disease' is a purely practical one and a question of summation, that predisposition and the eventualities of life must combine before the threshold of this summation is overstepped, and that consequently a number of individuals are constantly passing from the class of healthy people into that of neurotic patients, while a far smaller number also make the journey in the opposite direction,—all of these are things which have been said so often and have met with so much agreement that I am certainly not alone in maintaining their truth." Freud, "Analysis of a Phobia in a Five-Year-Old Boy" (1909), in *SE* 10: 145–46.

10. Freud, "A Metapsychological Supplement to the Theory of Dreams," in *SE* 14: 219–35.

11. Ibid., 222.

12. Ibid., 230.

13. A good account of these theoretical shifts is found in Richard Wollheim, *Freud* (London: Fontana, 1971).

14. Freud, "Inhibitions, Symptoms and Anxiety," in *SE* 20: 77–175.

15. Ibid., 129.

16. Ibid., 93.

17. Ibid.

18. Otto Rank, *The Trauma of Birth* (New York: Robert Brunner, 1952).

19. Freud, "Inhibitions, Symptoms and Anxiety," 138.

20. Arnold Gehlen, *Man: His Nature and Place in the World*, trans. Clare McMillan and Karl Pillemer (New York: Columbia University Press, 1987).

21. Ibid., pt. 1.

22. Freud, "Inhibitions, Symptoms and Anxiety," 154–55.

23. Ibid., 137.

24. Ibid., 98.

25. Ibid.

26. Ibid., 90.

27. Ibid., 88.

28. On this ethical core of Freud's endeavor, see John Cottingham, *Philosophy and the Good Life* (Cambridge: Cambridge University Press, 1998); Jonathan Lear, *Freud* (New York: Routledge, 2005).

29. "Aristotelian" because it is asserted as an objective claim that what contributes to the prosperity of its natural functionality (that is, of its ego, of its deliberative faculty) is "good" for humans. On the structure of such an ethics, see Philippa Foot, *Natural Goodness* (Oxford: Oxford University Press, 2003).

30. Lutz Wingert, "Grenzen der naturalistischen Selbstobjektivierung," in *Philosophie und Neurowissenschaften*, ed. Dieter Sturma (Frankfurt: Suhrkamp, 2006), 240–60.

31. Particularly striking in this regard is Ludwig Binswanger, "Freuds Auffassung des Menschen im Lichte der Anthropologie," in *Ausgewählte Vorträge und Aufsätze*, Vol.1: *Zur phänomenologischen Anthropologie* (Bern: Francke, 1947), 159–89.

32. Thomas Mann, "Die Stellung Freuds in der modernen Geistesgeschichte," in *Leiden und Größe der Meister: Gesammelte Werke in Einzelbänden* (Frankfurt edition), ed. Peter de Mendelssohn (Frankfurt: Fischer, 1982), 879–903.

33. For more, see Axel Honneth, *Verdinglichung: Eine anerkennungstheoretische Studie* (Frankfurt: Suhrkamp, 2005), ch. 5; Richard Moran, *Autonomy and Estrangement: An Essay on Self-Knowledge* (Princeton, N.J.: Princeton University Press, 2001), ch. 1.

34. On the use of political metaphors in Freud's works, see the fine study by José Brunner, *Freud and the Politics of Psychoanalysis* (Oxford: Blackwell, 1995). The question of how Freud's idea of an inner-psychic, mental exchange, or dialogue should be appropriately understood is so far largely unclarified. An energetic attempt is made by David J. Velleman, "The Voice of Conscience," in *Self to Self: Selected Essays* (Cambridge: Cambridge University Press, 2006), 110–28.

35. Freud, "Inhibitions, Symptoms and Anxiety,", 114

36. I see three attempts to found such a deep-lying interest in one's own rational freedom with recourse to Freud's writings. First, Jürgen Habermas's classic attempt to impute to reason, also with Freud, an interest in eliminating all its restrictions and distortions through itself (*Knowledge and Human Interests*, trans. Jeremy Shapiro [Boston: Beacon, 1972], ch. 12). Second, the recent attempt by Jonathan Lear to discern such a drive to produce a transparent and free whole in Freud's "eros" (*Freud*, chs. 2 and 6). Third, David Vellemann's attempt to understand the "ego ideal" in Freud's sense as a bio-

graphically acquired instance that incessantly presses for orientation according to the norms of practical rationality and hence also demands the freedom of one's own will ("A Rational Superego," in *Self to Self*, 129–55).

37. For different, yet largely convergent accounts of these processes of intuitive self-assurance, see Peter Bieri, *Das Handwerk der Freiheit: Über die Entdeckung des eigenen Willens* (Munich: Hanser, 2001), ch. 10; Richard Wollheim, *The Thread of Life* (Cambridge: Cambridge University Press, 1984), ch. 6.

38. Freud, "Negation," in *SE* 19: 234–39.

39. I am here guided by Bieri's use of the concept of "appropriation" in *Das Handwerk der Freiheit*, ch. 10. See also the penetrating account in Rahel Jaeggi, *Entfremdung: Zur Aktualität eines sozialphilosophischen Problems* (Frankfurt: Campus, 2005), ch. 3.

40. Freud, "Negation," 235–36.

41. On these two different forms of acceptance or recognition in Freud, see the pioneering essay by Andreas Wildt, " 'Anerkennung' in der Psychoanalyse," *Deutsche Zeitschrift für Philosophie* 53, no. 2 (2005): 461–78.

42. Tilo Wesche, *Kierkegaard: Eine philosophische Einführung* (Stuttgart: Reclam, 2003), 82 ff., 206 ff.

43. For example, Freud, "On the History of the Psycho-analytic Movement," in *SE* 14: 123.

8. "ANXIETY AND POLITICS"

1. Franz Neumann, "Anxiety and Politics," in *The Democratic and the Authoritarian State: Essays in Political and Legal Theory*, ed. Herbert Marcuse (Glencoe, Ill.: Free Press, 1957), 270–300.

2. Ken Hirschkop, *Mikhail Bakhtin: An Aesthetic for Democracy* (Oxford: Oxford University Press, 1999), 272–98.

3. Martin Dornes, *Die frühe Kindheit: Entwicklungspsychologie der ersten Lebensjahre* (Frankfurt: Fischer, 1997), ch. 6.

4. Michael Balint, *Thrills and Regressions* (New York: International Universities Press, 1959).

5. Neumann, "Anxiety and Politics," 277 ff.

6. Ibid., 279.

7. Otto Kernberg, *Internal World and External Reality: Object Relations Theory Applied* (New York: Scribner, 1985); Kernberg, *Ideologie, Konflikt und Führung: Psychoanalyse von Gruppenprozessen und Persönlichkeitsstruktur* (Stuttgart: Klett-Cotta, 2000).

8. Axel Honneth, "Postmodern Identity and Object-Relations Theory: On the

Seeming Obsolescence of Psychoanalysis," *Philosophical Explorations* 2, no. 3 (1999): 225–42.

9. Neumann, "Anxiety and Politics," 290.

10. Erich Fromm, Escape from Freedom (New York: Farrar and Rinehart, 1942).

11. Neumann, "Anxiety and Politics," 279 ff.

12. Theodor W. Adorno, *The Psychological Technique of Martin Luther Thomas' Radio Addresses* (Stanford: Stanford University Press, 2000).

13. Neumann, "Anxiety and Politics," 293–94.

14. Axel Honneth, "Critical Theory," trans. John Farrell, in *The Fragmented World of the Social: Essays in Social and Political Philosophy*, ed. Charles W. Wright (Albany: State University of New York Press, 1995).

15. On this, see Bernard Yack, ed., *Liberalism Without Illusions: Essays on Liberal Theory and the Political Vision of Judith Shklar* (Chicago: University of Chicago Press, 1996).

9. DEMOCRACY AND INNER FREEDOM

1. For example, Arnold Gehlen, *Man in the Age of Technology*, trans. Patricia Lipscomb (New York: Columbia University Press, 1980).

2. Alexander Mitscherlich, "Die Unwirtlichkeit unserer Städte," in *Gesammelte Schriften*, 10 vols. (Frankfurt: Suhrkamp, 1983), 7: 515–624; Mitscherlich, *Society Without the Father: A Contribution to Social Psychology*, trans. Eric Mosbacher (New York: Harcourt Brace and World, 1969).

3. Franz Neumann, "Anxiety and Politics," in *The Democratic and the Authoritarian State: Essays in Political and Legal Theory*, ed. Herbert Marcuse (Glencoe, Ill.: Free Press, 1957), 270–300.

4. Alexander Mitscherlich, "Freiheit und Unfreiheit in der Krankheit," in *Gesammelte Schriften*, 1: 13–135.

5. Ibid., 79.

6. Ibid., 73.

7. Ibid., 80–81.

8. Alexander Mitscherlich and Fred Mielke, eds., *Das Diktat der Menschenverachtung* (Heidelberg: Lambert Schneider, 1947).

9. Alexander Mitscherlich, " 'Wie ich mir—so ich dir': Zur Psychologie der Toleranz," and "Toleranz: Überprüfung eines Begriffs," both in *Gesammelte Schriften*, 5: 410–44.

10. Mitscherlich, "Toleranz," 440.

11. Andreas Wildt, " 'Anerkennung' in der Psychanalyse," *Deutsche Zeitschrift für Philosophie* 53, no. 2 (2005): 461–78.

12. Donald W. Winnicott, *Playing and Reality* (London: Routledge, 1982).

13. Mitscherlich, "'Wie ich mir—so ich dir,'" 419.

14. Here I take my bearings from Peter Bieri, *Das Handwerk der Freiheit: Über die Entdeckung des eigenen Willens* (Munich: Hanser, 2001), ch. 10.

15. Mitscherlich, "'Wie ich mir—so ich dir,'" 414.

10. DISSONANCES OF COMMUNICATIVE REASON

The following text is the written version of the laudatio I gave for Albrecht Wellmer on the occasion of the award of the 2006 Adorno Prize in St. Paul's Church in Frankfurt.

1. Theodor W. Adorno, *Beethoven: The Philosophy of Music*, ed. Rolf Tiedemann, trans. Edmond Jephcott (Stanford: Stanford University Press, 1997), chs. 9–11.

2. Ibid., 157.

3. Ibid., 180.

4. Ibid., 125.

5. Ibid., 157.

6. These early works in the theory of science were later collected in Jürgen Habermas, *On the Logic of the Social Sciences*, trans. Shierry Weber Nicholsen and Jerry A. Stark (Cambridge, Mass.: MIT Press, 1988 [1970]).

7. Albrecht Wellmer, *Methodologie als Erkenntnistheorie: Zur Wissenschaftslehre Karl R. Poppers* (Frankfurt: Suhrkamp, 1967).

8. Jürgen Habermas, *Knowledge and Human Interests*, trans. Jeremy Shapiro (Boston: Beacon, 1971).

9. Albrecht Wellmer, "Terrorismus und Gesellschaftskritik" [1971], in *Endspiele: Die unversöhnliche Moderne* (Frankfurt: Suhrkamp, 1993), 279–305 [not included in the English translation of this book].

10. Albrecht Wellmer, "Erklärung und Kausalität: Zur Kritik des Hempel-Oppenheim-Modells der Erklärung," habilitation thesis, Johann Wolfgang Goethe University–Frankfurt, 1971.

11. With regard to Wellmer's "deportment of hesitation," see the preface to *Zur Verteidigung der Vernunft gegen ihre Liebhaber und Verächter*, ed. Christoph Menke and Martin Seel (Frankfurt: Suhrkamp, 1993), 9 ff.

12. Albrecht Wellmer, *Critical Theory of Society*, trans. John Cumming (New York: Herder and Herder, 1971).

13. Albrecht Wellmer, "Communication and Emancipation: Reflections on the Linguistic Turn in Critical Theory," in *On Critical Theory*, ed. John O'Neill (Lanham, Md.: University Press of America, 1989), 231–63.

14. For more, see Martin Seel, *Die Kunst der Entzweiung: Zum Begriff der ästhetischen Rationalität* (Frankfurt: Suhrkamp, 1985); Christoph Menke, *The Sovereignty of Art: Aesthetic Negativity in Adorno and Derrida*, trans. Neil Solomon (Cambridge, Mass.: MIT Press, 1999).

15. Albrecht Wellmer, "Truth, Semblance, Reconciliation: Adorno's Aesthetic Redemption of Modernity," in *The Persistence of Modernity: Essays on Aesthetics, Ethics, and Postmodernism*, trans. David Midgley (Cambridge, Mass.: MIT Press, 1991), 1–35.

16. On the distinctions between the three validity claims, see Jürgen Habermas, "What Is Universal Pragmatics?" in *On the Pragmatics of Communication*, ed. Maeve Cooke (Cambridge, Mass.: MIT Press, 1998), 21–103.

17. Wellmer, "Truth, Semblance, Reconciliation," 34.

18. For example, Albrecht Wellmer, "Über Negativität und Autonomie der Kunst: Die Aktualität von Adornos Ästhetik und blinde Flecken seiner Musikphilosophie," in *Dialektik der Freiheit: Frankfurter Adorno-Konferenz 2003*, ed. Axel Honneth (Frankfurt: Suhrkamp, 2005), 237–78. See also Walter Benjamin, "The Work of Art in the Age of Its Technological Reproducibility: Third Version," in *Walter Benjamin: Selected Writings*, Vol. 4: *1938–1940*, ed. Howard Eiland and Michael W. Jennings; trans. Edmund Jephcott, Howard Eiland, et al. (Cambridge: Harvard University Press, 2006).

19. Albrecht Wellmer, *Endgames: The Irreconcilable Nature of Modernity—Essays and Lectures*, trans. David Midgley (Cambridge, Mass.: MIT Press, 1998).

20. For example, Albrecht Wellmer, "Hermeneutische Reflexion und 'dekonstruktive' Radikalisierung: Kommentar zu Emil Angehrn," in *Philosophie der Dekonstruktion*, ed. Andrea Kern and Christoph Menke (Frankfurt: Suhrkamp, 2002), 200–215.

21. Albrecht Wellmer, "Models of Freedom in the Modern World," in *Endgames*, 3–37.

22. Ibid., 24.

23. Albrecht Wellmer, *Revolution und Interpretation: Demokratie ohne Letztbegründung* (Spinoza Lectures) (Assen: Van Gorcum, 1998).

24. Ibid., 25–26.

25. Walter Benjamin, "Critique of Violence," in Walter Benjamin: Selected Writings, Vol. 1: 1913–1926, ed. Marcus Bullock and Michael W. Jennings (Cambridge: Harvard University Press, 2004).

26. Albrecht Wellmer, "Conditions of a Democratic Culture: Remarks on the Liberal-Communitarian Debate," in *Endgames*, 39–61.

27. Ibid. The following texts also contain references to the conditions for a democratic ethical life: Albrecht Wellmer, "Does the End of the Eastern Block

Also Mean the End of Marxist Humanism? Twelve Theses," in *Endgames*, 63–76; Wellmer, "Art and Industrial Production: The Dialectics of Modernism and Postmodernism," in *Persistence of Modernity*, 95–112.

APPENDIX

1. Michael Walzer, "Mut, Mitleid und ein gutes Augen: Tugenden der Sozialkritik und der Nutzen von Gesellschaftstheorie," *Deutsche Zeitschrift für Philosophie* 48 (2000): 709–18; published in English in *The Company of Critics: Social Criticism and Political Commitment in the Twentieth Century*, 2nd ed. (New York: Basic Books, 2002), xi–xviii.
2. Joseph Schumpeter, *Capitalism, Socialism and Democracy*, 3rd ed. (New York: Harper and Row, 1950), 145–55.
3. Ibid., 143.
4. Walzer, *In the Company of Critics*.
5. Ralf Dahrendorf, "Theorie ist wichtiger als Tugend," *Neue Zürcher Zeitung*, 12 December 2000.
6. Siegfried Kracauer, "Minimalforderung an die Intellektuellen," in *Schriften* (Frankfurt: Suhrkamp, 1990), 5: 353.
7. On the idea of an "overlapping consensus," see John Rawls, *Political Liberalism*, new ed. (New York: Columbia University Press, 1995).
8. For more, see Bert van den Brink, "Gesellschaftstheorie als Übertreibungskunst: Für eine alternative Lesart der 'Dialektik der Aufklärung,'" *Neue Rundschau* 1 (1997): 37–59.
9. I have discussed rhetorical tools of social criticism in more depth in Axel Honneth, "The Possibility of a Disclosing Critique of Society: The *Dialectic of Enlightenment* in Light of Current Debates in Social Criticism," in *Disrespect: The Normative Foundations of Critical Theory* (Cambridge: Polity, 2007).
10. Alex Demirovic, *Der nonkonformistische Intellektuelle: Die Entwicklung der Kritische Theorie zur Frankfurter Schule* (Frankfurt: Suhrkamp, 1999).

BIBLIOGRAPHY

Adorno, Theodor W. *The Adorno Reader*. Ed. Brian O'Connor. Oxford: Blackwell, 2000.

———. *Beethoven: The Philosophy of Music*. Ed. Rolf Tiedemann. Trans. Edmond Jephcott. Stanford: Stanford University Press, 1997.

—— *Can One Live After Auschwitz? A Philosophical Reader*. Ed. Rolf Tiedemann. Stanford: Stanford University Press, 2003.

———. *Critical Models: Interventions and Catchwords*. Trans. Henry W. Pickford. New York: Columbia University Press, 1998.

———. *Gesammelte Schriften*. 20 vols. Ed. Rolf Tiedemann. Frankfurt: Suhrkamp, 1972–1979.

———. *Hegel: Three Studies*. Trans. Shierry Weber Nicholson. Cambridge, Mass.: MIT Press, 1993.

———. *Mahler: A Musical Physiognomy*. Trans. Edmund Jephcott. Chicago: University of Chicago Press, 1992.

———. *Minima Moralia*. Trans. E. F. N. Jephcott. London: Verso, 1974.

———. *Negative Dialectics*. Trans. E. B. Ashton. London: Routledge, 1973.

———. *The Positivist Dispute in German Sociology*. Trans. Glyn Adey and David Frisby. New York: Harper and Row, 1976.

———. *Prisms*. Trans. Samuel Weber and Shierry Weber. Cambridge, Mass.: MIT Press, 1983.

———. *The Psychological Technique of Martin Luther Thomas' Radio Addresses*. Stanford: Stanford University Press, 2000.

———. *Sounds Figures*. Trans. Rodney Livingstone. Stanford: Stanford University Press, 1999.

Adorno, Theodor W., Günther Anders, Max Horkheimer, Herbert Marcuse, and Friedrich Nürnberg. "Need and Culture in Nietzsche." *Constellations* 8, no. 1 (2001): 130–35.

Agamben, Giorgio. *Homo Sacer: Sovereign Power and Bare Life*. Trans. Daniel Heller-Roazen. Stanford: Stanford University Press, 1998.

Arnason, Johànn P. *Von Marcuse zu Marx*. Neuwied: Luchterhand, 1971.

Ashenden, Samantha, and David Owen (eds.). *Foucault Contra Habermas: Recasting the Dialogue Between Genealogy and Critical Theory*. London: Sage, 1999.

Balint, Michael. *Thrills and Regressions*. New York: International Universities Press, 1959.

Benjamin, Walter. *Charles Baudelaire: A Lyric Poet of the Era of High Capitalism*. Trans. Harry Zohn. London: Verso, 1983.

——. *Gesammelte Briefe*, Vol. 2: *1919–1924*. Ed. Christoph Gödde and Heinz Lonitz. Frankfurt: Suhrkamp, 1996.

——. *Gesammelte Schriften*. 7 vols. Frankfurt: Suhrkamp, 1977.

——. *Selected Writings*, Vol. 1: *1913–1926*. Ed. Marcus Bullock and Michael W. Jennings. Cambridge: Harvard University Press, 2004.

——. *Selected Writings*, Vol. 4: *1938–1940*. Ed. Howard Eiland and Michael W. Jennings. Trans. Edmund Jephcott, Howard Eiland, et al. Cambridge: Harvard University Press, 2006.

——. "Theses on the Philosophy of History." In *Illuminations*. Ed. H. Arendt. Trans. H. Zohn. London: Fontana, 1992.

Berlin, Isaiah. *Against the Current: Essays in the History of Ideas*. Princeton, N.J.: Princeton University Press, 2001.

Bernstein, Richard J. *Praxis and Action: Contemporary Philosophies of Human Action*. Philadelphia: University of Pennsylvania Press, 1971.

Bieri, Peter. *Das Handwerk der Freiheit: Über die Entdeckung des eigenen Willens*. Munich: Hanser, 2001.

Binswanger, Ludwig. "Freuds Auffassung des Menschen im Lichte der Anthropologie." In *Ausgewählte Vorträge und Aufsätze*, Vol. 1: *Zur phänomenologischen Anthropologie*. Bern: Francke, 1947.

Bloch, Ernst. *The Spirit of Utopia*. Trans. Anthony A. Nassar. Stanford: Stanford University Press, 2006 [1918].

Boltanski, Luc, and Eve Chiapello. *The New Spirit of Capitalism*. Trans. Gregory Elliott. London: Verso, 2007.

Bourdieu, Pierre, and Jean-Claude Passeron. *Reproduction in Education, Society and Culture*. 2nd ed. Trans. Richard Nice. London: Sage, 1990.

Brunner, José. *Freud and the Politics of Psychoanalysis*. Oxford: Blackwell, 1995.

Butler, Judith. *The Psychic Life of Power: Theories in Subjection*. Stanford: Stanford University Press, 1997.

Castoriadis, Cornelius. *The Imaginary Institution of Society*. Trans. Kathleen Blamey. Cambridge, Mass.: MIT Press, 1987.

Celikates, Robin, and Arnd Pollmann. "Baustellen der Vernunft: 25 Jahre Theorie des kommunikativen Handelns—Zur Gegenwart eines Paradigmenwechsels." *Westend* 3, no. 2 (2006): 97–113.

Cooke, Maeve. *Language and Reason: A Study of Habermas's Pragmatics*. Cambridge, Mass.: MIT Press, 1994.

Cottingham, John. *Philosophy and the Good Life*. Cambridge: Cambridge University Press, 1998.

Dahrendorf, Ralf. "Theorie ist wichtiger als Tugend." *Neue Zürcher Zeitung*, 12 December 2000.

Demirovic, Alex. *Der nonkonformistische Intellektuelle: Die Entwicklung der Kritische Theorie zur Frankfurter Schule*. Frankfurt: Suhrkamp, 1999.

Derrida, Jacques. "Force of Law: The 'Mystical Foundation of Authority.'" In *Acts of Religion*, ed. Gil Anidjar. New York: Routledge, 2002.

Didion, Joan. *The Year of Magical Thinking*. New York: Knopf, 2005.

Dornes, Martin. *Die frühe Kindheit: Entwicklungspsychologie der ersten Lebensjahre*. Frankfurt: Fischer, 1997.

——. "Die intersubjektiven Ursprünge des Denkens." *WestEnd: Neue Zeitschrift für Sozialforschung* 1 (2005): 3–48.

——. *Die Seele des Kindes: Entstehung und Entwicklung*. Frankfurt: Fischer, 2006.

Dubiel, Helmut. *Theory and Politics: Studies in the Development of Critical Theory*. Trans. Benjamin Gregg. Cambridge, Mass.: MIT Press, 1985.

Eagle, Morris N. *Recent Developments in Psychoanalysis: A Critical Evaluation*. New York: McGraw-Hill, 1984.

Foot, Philippa. *Natural Goodness*. Oxford: Oxford University Press, 2003.

Foucault, Michel. *Discipline and Punish: The Birth of the Prison*. Trans. Alan Sheridan. New York: Vintage, 1977.

Freud, Sigmund. *Outline of Psychoanalysis*. Trans. Helena Ragg-Kirkby. New York: Penguin, 2003.

——. *The Standard Edition of the Complete Psychological Works of Sigmund Freud*, 24 vols., gen. ed. James Strachey, with Anna Freud. London: Hogarth Press and the Institute of Psycho-Analysis, 1953–1974.

Freund, Michael. *Georges Sorel: Der revolutionäre Konservatismus*. Frankfurt: Klostermann, 1972.

Fromm, Erich. *Escape from Freedom*. New York: Farrar and Rinehart, 1942.

——. *The Working Class in Weimar Germany: A Psychological and Sociological Study*. Trans. B. Weinberger. Cambridge: Harvard University Press, 1984.

Früchtl, Josef. *Mimesis: Konstellation eines Zentralbegriffs bei Adorno*. Würzburg: Königshausen und Neumann, 1986.

Gehlen, Arnold. *Man: His Nature and Place in the World*. Trans. Clare McMillan and Karl Pillemer. New York: Columbia University Press, 1987.

——. *Man in the Age of Technology*. Trans. Patricia Lipscomb. New York: Columbia University Press, 1980.

Giddens, Anthony. *Modernity and Self-Identity: Self and Society in the Late Modern Age*. Cambridge: Polity, 1991.

Habermas, Jürgen. *Knowledge and Human Interests*. Trans. Jeremy Shapiro. Boston: Beacon, 1971.

——. "Können komplexe Gesellschaften eine vernünftige Identität ausbilden?" In *Zwei Reden: Aus Anlass der Verleihung des Hegel-Preises der Stadt Stuttgart*, by Jürgen Habermas and Dieter Henrich. Frankfurt: Suhrkamp, 1974.

——. "Nach dreißig Jahren: Bemerkungen zu *Erkenntnis und Interesse*." In *Das Interesse der Vernunft*. Ed. Stefan Müller-Doohm. Frankfurt: Suhrkamp, 2000

——. *On the Logic of the Social Sciences*. Trans. Shierry Weber Nicholsen and Jerry A. Stark. Cambridge, Mass.: MIT Press, 1988 [1970].

——. *On the Pragmatics of Communication*. Ed. Maeve Cooke. Cambridge, Mass.: MIT Press, 1998.

——. *The Philosophical Discourse of Modernity*. Trans. Frederick Lawrence. Cambridge, Mass.: MIT Press, 1990.

——. *Philosophical-Political Profiles*. Trans. Frederick G. Lawrence. Cambridge, Mass.: MIT Press, 1983.

——. *Postmetaphysical Thinking: Philosophical Essays*. Trans. William Mark Hohengarten. Cambridge, Mass.: MIT Press, 1992.

——. "The Relationship Between Theory and Practice Revisited." In *Truth and Justification*. Trans. Barbara Fultner. Cambridge, Mass.: MIT Press, 2003.

——. *Theory of Communicative Action*, 2 vols.. Trans. Thomas McCarthy. Boston: Beacon, 1984, 1987.

——. *Towards a Rational Society*. Trans. Jeremy Shapiro. Boston: Beacon, 1971.

Habermas, Jürgen, Silvia Bovenschen, Tilman Spengler, Marianne Schuller, Berthold Rothschild, et al. *Gespräche mit Herbert Marcuse*. Frankfurt: Suhrkamp, 1978.

Hennis, Wilhelm. *Max Webers Fragestellung*. Tübingen: Mohr, 1987.

Henrich, Dieter. *Die Einheit der Wissenschaftslehre Max Webers*. Tübingen: J. C. B. Mohr, 1952.

Hirschkop, Ken. *Mikhail Bakhtin: An Aesthetic for Democracy*. Oxford: Oxford University Press, 1999.

Hobson, Peter. *The Cradle of Thought*. London: Macmillan, 2002.

Honneth, Axel. "A Communicative Disclosure of the Past: On the Relation Between Anthropology and Philosophy of History in Walter Benjamin." *New Formations* 20 (1993): 83–94.

——. *The Critique of Power: Reflective Stages in a Critical Social Theory.* Trans. Kenneth Baynes. Cambridge, Mass.: MIT Press, 1991.

——. *Disrespect: The Normative Foundations of Critical Theory.* Cambridge: Polity, 2007.

——. *The Fragmented World of the Social: Essays in Social and Political Philosophy.* Ed. Charles W. Wright. Albany: State University of New York Press, 1995.

——. "'Invisibility—On the Epistemology of Recognition." *Proceedings of the Aristotelian Society* 75 suppl. (2001): 111–26.

——. *Leiden an Unbestimmtheit: Eine Reaktualisierung der Hegelschen Rechtsphilosophie.* Stuttgart: Reclam, 2001.

——. "Postmodern Identity and Object-Relations Theory: On the Seeming Obsolescence of Psychoanalysis." *Philosophical Explorations* 2, no. 3 (1999): 225–42.

——. *The Struggle for Recognition: The Moral Grammar of Social Conflicts.* Trans. Joel Anderson. Cambridge, Mass.: MIT Press, 1996.

——. *Verdinglichung: Eine anerkennungstheoretische Studie.* Frankfurt: Suhrkamp, 2005.

—— (ed.). *Kommunitarianismus: Eine Debatte über die moralischen Grundlagen moderner Gesellschaften.* Frankfurt: Campus, 1993.

Honneth, Axel, and Martin Saar (eds.). *Michel Foucault: Zwischenbilanz einer Rezeption.* Frankfurt: Suhrkamp, 2003.

Horkheimer, Max. *Critical Theory: Selected Essays.* Trans. Matthew O'Connell. New York: Continuum, 1975.

——. *Gesammelte Schriften.* Ed. Gunzelin Schmid-Noerr and A. Schmidt. 19 vols. Frankfurt: Fischer, 1987– .

——. "History and Psychology." In *Between Philosophy and Social Science.* Trans. Frederick Hunter, Matthew S. Kramer, and John Torpey. Cambridge, Mass.: MIT Press, 1995.

Horkheimer, Max, and Theodor W. Adorno. *Dialectic of Enlightenment: Philosophical Fragments.* Trans. Edmund Jephcott. Stanford: Stanford University Press, 2002.

Horstmann, Rolf-Peter. *Die Grenzen der Vernunft.* Frankfurt: Anton Hain, 1991.

Ilting, Karl Heinz. *Naturrecht und Sittlichkeit: Begriffsgeschichtliche Studien.* Stuttgart: Klett-Cotta, 1983.

Jaeggi, Rahel. *Entfremdung: Zur Aktualität eines sozialphilosophischen Problems.* Frankfurt: Campus, 2005.

Jay, Martin. "Georg Lukács and the Origins of the Western Marxist Paradigm." In *Marxism and Totality: The Adventures of a Concept from Lukács to Habermas.* Berkeley: University of California Press, 1986.

Joas, Hans. "An Underestimated Alternative: America and the Limits of 'Critical Theory.'" In *Pragmatism and Social Theory.* Chicago: University of Chicago Press, 1993.

Kant, Immanuel. *Anthropology from a Pragmatic Point of View*. Trans. M. G. Mc-
Gregor. The Hague: Martinus Nijhoff, 1974.

——. *Critique of Judgment*. Trans. W. S. Pluhar. Indianapolis: Hackett, 1987.

——. *Critique of Practical Reason*. Trans. M. Gregor. Cambridge: Cambridge University Press, 1997.

——. *Kant: Political Writings*. Ed. H. Reiss. Trans. H. B. Nisbet. Cambridge: Cambridge University Press, 1970.

Kernberg, Otto. *Ideologie, Konflikt und Führung: Psychoanalyse von Gruppenprozessen und Persönlichkeitsstruktur*. Stuttgart: Klett-Cotta, 2000.

——. *Internal World and External Reality: Object Relations Theory Applied*. New York:
Scribner, 1985.

Kleingeld, Pauline. *Fortschritt und Vernunft: Zur Geschichtsphilosophie Kants*. Würzburg: Konigshausen und Neumann, 1995.

——. "Kant, History, and the Idea of Moral Development." *History of Philosophy
Quarterly* 16, no. 1 (1999): 59–80.

Kohlenbach, Margarete. *Walter Benjamin: Self-Reference and Religiosity*. Basingstoke: Palgrave-Macmillan, 2002.

Kohlenbach, Margarete, and Raymond Geuss (eds.). *The Early Frankfurt School and
Religion*. Basingstoke: Palgrave-Macmillan, 2005.

Kracauer, Siegfried. "Minimalforderung an die Intellektuellen." In *Schriften*, Vol. 5.
Frankfurt: Suhrkamp, 1990.

Langthaler, Rudolf. "Benjamin und Kant oder: Über den Versuch, Geschichte
philosophisch zu denken." *Deutsche Zeitschrift für Philosophie* 50, no. 2 (2002):
203–25.

Lear, Jonathan. *Freud*. New York: Routledge, 2005.

——. "The Shrink Is In." *Psyche* 50, no. 7 (1996): 599–616.

Lohmann, Georg. *Indifferenz und Gesellschaft: Eine kritische Auseinandersetzung mit
Marx*. Frankfurt: Campus, 1991.

Löwith, Karl. *From Hegel to Nietzsche: The Revolution in Nineteenth-Century Thought*.
Trans. David Green. New York: Columbia University Press, 1964.

Lukács, Georg. *History and Class Consciousness: Studies in Marxist Dialectics*. Trans.
Rodney Livingstone. Cambridge, Mass.: MIT Press, 1971.

——. *The Theory of the Novel*. Trans. Anna Bostock. Cambridge, Mass.: MIT Press,
1974.

Mann, Thomas. "Die Stellung Freuds in der modernen Geistesgeschichte." In
Leiden und Größe der Meister: Gesammelte Werke in Einzelbänden. Frankfurt edition. Ed. Peter de Mendelssohn. Frankfurt: Fischer, 1982.

Marcuse, Herbert. *Eros and Civilization: A Philosophical Inquiry into Freud*. Boston:
Beacon, 1955.

——. *An Essay on Liberation*. Boston: Beacon, 1969.

——. *One-Dimensional Man*. Boston: Beacon, 1964.

———. "Philosophy and Critical Theory." In *Critical Theory: The Essential Readings*, ed. David Ingram and Julia Simon-Ingram. St. Paul, Minn.: Paragon House, 1991.

———. "Repressive Tolerance." In *A Critique of Pure Tolerance*, by Robert Paul Wolff, Barrington Moore Jr., and Marcuse, Boston: Beacon, 1969.

———. "Revolution und Kritik der Gewalt." In *Materialien zu Benjamins "Über den Begriff der Geschichte*," ed. Peter Bulthaup. Frankfurt: Suhrkamp, 1965.

Marlen, Andrea. *"Eine Ethik für Endliche": Kants Tugendlehre in der Gegenwart.* Stuttgart: Frommann-Holzboog, 2004.

Marx, Karl. *Capital: A Critique of Political Economy.* Trans. Ben Fowkes. New York: Penguin, 1992.

McDowell, John. *Mind and World.* Cambridge: Harvard University Press, 1994.

Menke, Christoph. "Geist und Leben: Zu einer genealogischen Kritik der Phänomenologie." In *Von der Logik zur Sprache: Stuttgarter Hegel-Kongreß 2005*, ed. Rüdiger Bubner and Gunnar Hindrichs. Stuttgart: Klett-Cotta, 2007.

———. *The Sovereignty of Art: Aesthetic Negativity in Adorno and Derrida.* Trans. Neil Solomon. Cambridge, Mass.: MIT Press, 1999.

Menke, Christoph, and Martin Seel (eds.). *Zur Verteidigung der Vernunft gegen ihre Liebhaber und Verächter.* Frankfurt: Suhrkamp, 1993.

Mitscherlich, Alexander. *Gesammelte Schriften.* 10 vols. Frankfurt: Suhrkamp, 1983.

———. *Society Without the Father: A Contribution to Social Psychology.* Trans. Eric Mosbacher. New York: Harcourt Brace and World, 1969.

Mitscherlich, Alexander, and Fred Mielke (eds.). *Das Diktat der Menschenverachtung.* Heidelberg: Lambert Schneider, 1947.

Moran, Richard. *Autonomy and Estrangement: An Essay on Self-Knowledge.* Princeton, N.J.: Princeton University Press, 2001.

Neumann, Franz. "Anxiety and Politics." In *The Democratic and the Authoritarian State: Essays in Political and Legal Theory*, ed. Herbert Marcuse. Glencoe, Ill.: Free Press, 1957.

Philström, Sami. *Naturalizing the Transcendental: A Pragmatic View.* Amherst, N.Y.: Prometheus/Humanity, 2003.

Pilkington, A. E. *Bergson and His Influence.* Cambridge: Cambridge University Press, 1976.

Rank, Otto. *The Trauma of Birth.* New York: Robert Brunner, 1952.

Rawls, John. *Political Liberalism.* New ed. New York: Columbia University Press, 1995.

———. *A Theory of Justice.* Cambridge: Harvard University Press, 1971.

Saar, Martin. *Genealogie als Kritik: Geschichte und Theorie des Subjekts nach Nietzsche und Foucault.* Frankfurt: Campus, 2007.

Schmid, Michael. "Idealisierung und Idealtypus: Zur Logik der Typenbildung bei

Max Weber." In *Max Webers Wissenschaftslehre*, ed. Gerhard Wagner and Heinz Zipprian. Frankfurtn: Suhrkamp, 1994.

Schmitt, Carl. *Crisis of Parliamentary Democracy*. Trans. Ellen Kennedy. Cambridge, Mass.: MIT Press, 1988.

Schnädelbach, Herbert (ed.). *Rationalität: Philosophische Beiträge*. Frankfurt: Suhrkamp, 1984.

Schumpeter, Joseph. *Capitalism, Socialism and Democracy*. 3rd ed. New York: Harper and Row, 1950.

Seel, Martin. "Adornos kontemplative Ethik: Philosophie—Eine Kolumne." *Merkur* 638 (2002): 512–18.

——. *Die Kunst der Entzweiung: Zum Begriff der äesthetischen Rationalität*. Frankfurt: Suhrkamp, 1985.

Sorel, Georges. *Reflections on Violence*. Trans. T. E. Hulme and J. Roth. Glencoe, Ill.: Free Press, 1950.

Steiner, Uwe. "Kritik." In *Benjamins Begriffe*, ed. Michael Opitz and Erdmut Wizisla. Frankfurt: Suhrkamp, 2002.

Stern, Paul. "The Problem of History and Temporality in Kantian Ethics." *Review of Metaphysics* 39 (1986): 505–45.

Theunissen, Michael. *Das Selbst auf dem Grund der Verzweiflung: Kierkegaards negativistische Methode*. Berlin: Hain, 1999.

——. "Negativität bei Adorno." In *Adorno-Konferenz 1983*. Ed. Ludwig von Friedeburg and Jürgen Habermas. Frankfurt: Suhrkamp, 1983.

——. *Selbstverwirklichung und Allgemeinheit: Zur Kritik des gegenwärtigen Bewusstseins*. Berlin: de Gruyter, 1982.

Tomasello, Michael. *The Cultural Origins of Human Cognition*. Cambridge: Harvard University Press, 1999.

Tully, James. "Political Philosophy as Critical Activity." *Political Theory* 30 (2002): 533–55.

Unger, Erich. *Politik und Metaphysik*. Ed. Manfred Voigts. Würzburg: Konigshausen und Neumann, 1989 [1921].

van den Brink, Bert. "Gesellschaftstheorie als Übertreibungskunst: Für eine alternative Lesart der 'Dialektik der Aufklärung.'" *Neue Rundschau* 1 (1997): 37–59.

Velleman, David J. *Self to Self: Selected Essays*. Cambridge: Cambridge University Press, 2006.

Villiers, Marjorie. *Charles Péguy: A Study in Integrity*. New York: Harper and Row, 1965.

von Friedeburg, Ludwig, and Jürgen Habermas (eds.). *Adorno-Konferenz 1983*. Frankfurt: Suhrkamp, 1983.

von Jhering, Rudolf. *Der Zweck im Recht*. 2 vols. Leipzig: Breitkopf und Härtel, 1884 [1877].

Walzer, Michael. *The Company of Critics: Social Criticism and Political Commitment in the Twentieth Century*. 2nd ed. New York: Basic Books, 2002.
——. *Interpretation and Social Criticism*. Cambridge: Harvard University Press, 1987.
——. "Mut, Mitleid und ein gutes Augen: Tugenden der Sozialkritik und der Nutzen von Gesellschaftstheorie." *Deutsche Zeitschrift für Philosophie* 48 (2000): 709–18.
Weber, Max. "Objectivity in Social Science and Social Policy." In *Max Weber on the Methodology of the Social Sciences*. Ed. and trans. Edward A. Shils and Henry A. Finch. Glencoe, Ill.: Free Press, 1949.
Wellmer, Albrecht. "Communication and Emancipation: Reflections on the Linguistic Turn in Critical Theory." In *On Critical Theory*, ed. John O'Neill. Lanham, Md.: University Press of America, 1989.
——. *Critical Theory of Society*. Trans. John Cumming. New York: Herder and Herder, 1971 [1969].
——. *Endgames: The Irreconcilable Nature of Modernity—Essays and Lectures*. Trans. David Midgley. Cambridge, Mass.: MIT Press, 1998.
——. "Erklärung und Kausalität: Zur Kritik des Hempel-Oppenheim-Modells der Erklärung." Habilitation thesis. Johann Wolfgang Goethe University–Frankfurt, 1971.
——. "Hermeneutische Reflexion und 'dekonstruktive' Radikalisierung. Kommentar zu Emil Angehrn." In *Philosophie der Dekonstruktion*, ed. Andrea Kern and Christoph Menke. Frankfurt: Suhrkamp, 2002.
——. *Methodologie als Erkenntnistheorie: Zur Wissenschaftslehre Karl R. Poppers*. Frankfurt: Suhrkamp, 1967.
——. *The Persistence of Modernity: Essays on Aesthetics, Ethics, and Postmodernism*. Trans. David Midgley. Cambridge, Mass.: MIT Press, 1991.
——. *Revolution und Interpretation: Demokratie ohne Letztbegründung*. Spinoza Lectures. Assen: Van Gorcum, 1998.
——. "Terrorismus und Gesellschaftskritik." In *Endspiele: Die unversöhnliche Moderne*. Frankfurt: Suhrkamp, 1993.
——. "Über Negativität und Autonomie der Kunst: Die Aktualität von Adornos Ästhetik und blinde Flecken seiner Musikphilosophie." In *Dialektik der Freiheit: Frankfurter Adorno-Konferenz 2003*, ed. Axel Honneth. Frankfurt: Suhrkamp, 2005.
Wesche, Tilo. *Kierkegaard: Eine philosophische Einführung*. Stuttgart: Reclam, 2003.
Wildt, Andreas. "'Anerkennung' in der Psychoanalyse." *Deutsche Zeitschrift für Philosophie* 53, no. 2 (2005): 461–78.
Wingert, Lutz. "Grenzen der naturalistischen Selbstobjektivierung." In *Philosophie und Neurowissenschaften*, ed. Dieter Sturma. Frankfurt: Suhrkamp, 2006.

Winnicott, Donald W. *Playing and Reality*. London: Routledge, 1982.

Wollheim, Richard. *Freud*. London: Fontana, 1971.

——. *The Thread of Life*. Cambridge: Cambridge University Press, 1984.

Wood, Allen. "Unsociable Sociability: The Anthropological Basis of Kantian Ethics." *Philosophical Topics* 19, no. 1 (1991): 325–51.

Yack, Bernard (ed.). *Liberalism Without Illusion: Essays on Liberal Theory and the Political Vision of Judith Shklar*. Chicago: University of Chicago Press, 1996.

Yovel, Yimiyahu. *Kant and the Philosophy of History*. Princeton, N.J.: Princeton University Press, 1980.